VARIATIONS IN C

VARIATIONS IN C

Steve Schustack

Programming techniques

for developing efficient

professional applications.

MICROSOFT PRESS

PUBLISHED BY
Microsoft Press
A Division of Microsoft Corporation
10700 Northup Way, Box 97200, Bellevue, Washington 98009

Library of Congress Cataloging in Publication Data
Schustack, Steve, 1952–
Variations in C.
Includes index.
1. C (Computer program language)   2. Business—Data processing. I. Title.
HF5548.5.C12S38   1985   650'.028'5425   85-5033
ISBN 0-914845-48-9

Printed and bound in the United States of America.

   5 6 7 8 9 FGFG 8 9 0 9 8 7

Distributed to the book trade in the United States by Harper & Row.

Distributed to the book trade in Canada by General Publishing Co., Ltd.

Distributed to the book trade outside the United States of America
and Canada by Penguin Books Ltd.

Penguin Books Ltd., Harmondsworth, Middlesex, England
Penguin Books Australia Ltd., Ringwood, Victoria, Australia
Penguin Books N.Z. Ltd., 182-190 Wairau Road, Auckland 10,
New Zealand

British Cataloging in Publication Data available

To my mother and father

Contents

SECTION V

SECTION VI

SECTION VII

Foreword

C is a computer programming language whose name has no more exciting origin than the fact that C is a successor to an earlier language named B. But I like to think that C stands for craftsman—a competent artisan in control of the computer and the tools of programming, confident of his skill at his craft.

Steve Schustack is such a craftsman. He "speaks" C as if it were his native tongue, and he uses the language with the style and precision its originators intended. Not only that, Steve can communicate these qualities to other programmers. His list of successful corporate training programs attests to that.

I was among the many who encouraged Steve to make his knowledge and experience with real-world C available to a wider audience, so I was delighted when I received a draft of the manuscript that was to become *Variations in C*. The book is everything I'd expect from Steve—thorough, lucid, and utterly professional. Also down-to-earth and just plain practical.

But *Variations in C* is not for every programmer. It's definitely not for beginners, and it's really not for amateurs with little interest in machine-level functions. It's for serious programmers who want to produce business applications that will work so efficiently and so transparently that people will be willing to pay for them.

Steve really hasn't written about variations in C at all, but about variations in the way people *use* C. Even a variation as simple as using C on different hardware or with a different compiler has a great deal to do with the programmer. The portability of C programs is as much a property of the way each programmer uses C as of the C language itself. C makes portability *possible*, but the programmer must bring that possibility to realization. In *Variations in C*, Steve simply teaches the programmer how.

In a very real sense, *Variations in C* is about style. C is known as a "powerful" language, but that power is undifferentiated. It can produce good or bad results. You can write a good program in any language, but it's easier in C than in most. You can write a bad program in any language, too, but it's *a lot* easier in C than in most. Steve Schustack teaches you how to write good programs. More than that, he teaches you how to stay out of trouble!

I've said that *Variations in C* is not a beginner's book, but I'd like to see beginners have it by their sides as they learn, so they can develop elegance and precision in programming style right from the start. It's not an easy book, because applications programming isn't easy, but unlike some difficult books, it rewards those who devote themselves to its subject. If you're willing to take the time to understand each of Steve's carefully chosen examples, your style, and therefore your power in C, will grow steadily.

Programming is complicated, and because each program is a bit different from the previous one, magic formulas aren't possible. So Steve has written a guidebook, not a book of formulas. Many good programming books teach you *how* to do things in a specific language—only a few of the best teach you *why* you do them (or shouldn't do them). *Variations in C* is one of the best.

— Gerald Weinberg

Preface

Because of its efficiency and portability, C has become the language of choice for professional software developers. It is being implemented in new environments almost daily, to meet the need for compact, efficient code that requires little or no modification to run on a large variety of systems. I've written this book to enable you, the experienced programmer, to take advantage of this powerful development tool.

I've said that *Variations in C* is for the experienced programmer. However, it does not require knowledge of the C language. I'll teach you that as we go along. And you'll see the programming techniques you're learning used to develop a large, high-quality, interactive order-entry application that can be used as part of a business system.

The chapters in Section I will give you the skills you need to write useful programs with a powerful subset of C. Section II will then help you to extend your knowledge of C data structures and the program constructs used to implement them. All the examples used in these chapters, and indeed throughout the book, are oriented toward the development and maintenance of serious, real-world C applications.

In Section III, you'll meet the application that is central to this book: The Software Vendor Order-Entry Application, with over 1500 lines of source code. Rather than mystify you by including untaught features in the code, I use a few "stub" functions at this stage. These are replaced later in the book, as the relevant new topics are covered. The completed application is a fully functional order-entry program that you can use in your own systems.

Section IV presents the essentials of two of C's most powerful tools: pointers and structures. Enough practical detail is presented here to enable you to replace some of the stub functions in Section III with functional code. The "acrobatics" are saved for later.

The chapters in Section V show you how to call library functions to access and manage files and to communicate with peripheral devices.

These chapters cover both the capabilities and the limitations of the stream-file type of data organization as implemented by the standard-library file functions.

Section VI discusses jobs formerly done primarily in assembler—jobs that can be done more quickly in C, and with more maintainable results. The linked-list data structure, dynamic allocation of memory, and the bit-level operators are all included here, in one place, where they may easily be turned to or skipped, depending upon your needs. And finally, the last chapter presents performance-tuning techniques for optimizing the efficiency of your C programs.

The example programs used throughout the book are practical ones, and will be useful to you in coding your own applications. The style rules for writing readable C code have been followed rigorously, so you will have little trouble maintaining or modifying the programs to suit your needs.

I have used an IBM PC with two floppy-disk drives and 512K RAM, MS-DOS, version 2.00, and the Microsoft C Compiler, version 3.00, to develop and test all the code in this book. I chose Microsoft's C for teaching because it implements most of the recommendations from the ANSI *Proposed C Standard*. However, if you use a different vendor's C compiler, you will still benefit from the knowledge of standard C taught here, because you will learn to write C programs that port easily to other environments.

I hope you will enjoy this book, and feel the same thrill I did when I discovered the infinite *Variations in C*.

Acknowledgments

Many good people have contributed to the creation of this book and I am delighted to have this opportunity to extend my appreciation to all of them. Thanks!

Jerry Weinberg, my teacher and good friend of many years, has been, and continues to be, an inspiration in my writing, learning, and teaching. His philosophy and methods have contributed much, both to my career and to this book.

The people at Microsoft Press showed their care for quality with the many hours of hard work they contributed, far beyond the call of duty. Their deep dedication to their work and the quality of their final products have been a delight. Nahum Stiskin started the Press rolling and took a special interest in me and in this book. Salley Oberlin, editorial director, and Dorothy Shattuck, editor, both deserve a special thank-you for their superior editorial support, as does Barry Preppernau, senior technical reviewer, for his careful review of the manuscript. Tracy Smith, Karen-Lynne de Robinson, Ken Sánchez, Greg Hickman, Marianne Moon, Lee Thomas, Paul Doremus, Lesley Link-Moore, Debbie Kem, Stephanie Ideta, David Rygmyr, Lia Matteson, Ralph Ryan, Tandy Trower, Brian Williamson, and Rob Bowman are all dedicated Microsoft professionals for whose help I am grateful.

John Socha, author and assembler authority, generously provided the assembler code in the last chapter. Brook Jarret helped with suggestions for the appendices.

My friends Bill and Cynthia Gladstone of Waterside Productions are agents par excellence of books and software, and their efforts laid the groundwork for this book.

My close friends Greg Gilbert and Barbara Lang have earned my gratitude for their ideas, patience, and support during my writing efforts.

Thanks, too, to *Nacho's* in Mission Beach, who often fueled me with their delicious carne asada burritos.

Section I explores C as a programming language. Chapter 1 introduces C: how it arrived on the scene, its advantages and special features, and the importance of an ANSI C standard. Chapters 2 through 5 provide a fast-paced introduction to the C language, at a level suitable for experienced programmers: Chapter 2 deals with data types and the declaration and manipulation of variables; Chapter 3 discusses C's operators and their use with data in constants and variables; Chapter 4 presents the control-flow statements used to direct conditional execution and repetition; and finally, Chapter 5 analyzes the basic unit of all C programs, the function.

SECTION I

About C 1

When you first heard of a new programming language called C, I suspect that you, like many others, may have asked, "Why do we need yet another programming language?" Well, there are actually several answers to that question.

The Need for C

Systems programmers have long been forced to labor with assembler in order to produce fast, compact code that doesn't waste the resources of the computer. But assembler code is cumbersome to work with, time-consuming to develop, and specific to the hardware and operating system for which it is written.

C was developed as an alternative to assembler for system-level coding. C's operators and statements are close to the computer's own machine instructions, yet C's data-handling and program-control constructs make it a high-level language. At last, system programmers have high-level benefits in a language that generates programs compact and fast enough for stringent operating-system efficiency requirements—benefits like more readable and modifiable code, to name but two.

Dennis Ritchie, working at Bell Telephone Laboratories, is credited with creating C around 1972, for use in developing the UNIX operating system. C evolved from a language called B, and B came from a language called BCPL. (C was briefly called NB, short for New B.) Use of C, except at Bell and a few universities, remained minimal until about 1981, when commercial interest in the language began to develop as a result of the promotion of UNIX as a "standard" operating system.

But the popularity of C has far outstripped that of UNIX. In fact, C has opened up a whole new software industry. C compilers have been created for most current operating-system and hardware environments, and new C productivity tools reach the marketplace every month.

The Philosophy of C

As I've already mentioned, C has been called both a high-level and a low-level language. Its high-level aspects include support for a modular programming style, numerous data types, and a good set of control-flow statements. Its low-level side consists of powerful bit-level and memory-addressing data structures and operators closely tied to the capabilities of the underlying hardware.

C is so versatile and general-purpose that it can be used to control complex machinery, crunch numbers, play video games, or perform business accounting and inventory control. And C is not tied to any particular hardware configuration. In fact, C programs are executing right now in environments with no terminals, no printers, no disks, even no operating system. Can you picture such a system? Well, consider a C program controlling an elevator. The program controls the movement of the elevator and "listens" for inputs from the elevator's control buttons and other sensors. But that's all. Such a C program has little use for library functions that interact with a terminal or access data files!

C provides maximum support for modular programming, which speeds program development and simplifies maintenance, since each module can be designed and tested independently. A modular program is one that is constructed from a set of small, independent functions, each of which does a single clearly defined job. High-level functions outline or manage the overall processing in a general way, and call low-level functions to perform detailed data manipulations. The high-level functions don't care how the low-level functions do their jobs, just as long as the jobs get done.

Clearly, C's flexibility goes far beyond the norm. Many ways exist for doing almost any job in C. The right tools are there; we just need to learn how to get the most from them.

C Source Code and Portability

Picture yourself for a moment as the owner of a successful software company. Nice? Well, yes and no. Since most programs are restricted to the machine or operating system (or both) for which they were compiled, you could be faced with a very difficult maintenance task. You will probably have to sell and maintain different versions of your programs for different operating systems and for each specific hardware configuration. Every time a new computer or operating system becomes popular, which happens surprisingly often, your programs will have to be modified if they are to continue to ride the wave of popularity. And when an established client upgrades to a more powerful computer installation, you may face costly software rewrites if you want the customer to continue using your programs.

Not only that, you'll want to continue to improve your programs and increase their capabilities, and the probability of programmer error when adding an enhancement to all those versions of all your programs is high. The cost of fixing problems *after* a sale is also high, both monetarily and professionally.

Well, if your programs are written in C, you've already solved most of these problems. Much of the rewriting of software to accommodate new and changing computer environments has been eliminated by C. (By environment here, I mean a specific combination of operating system, computer hardware, and C compiler.) Many (but not all) C programs can be compiled and executed in one environment and later recompiled and executed in a different environment, with exactly the same behavior in both. The principal factor in defining your program's portability is simply the amount of work it will take to port your source code from environment A to environment B. (The term *source code* refers to uncompiled C programs, in human-readable text form. C programs in compiled form are much more limited in their range of portability.)

How did C achieve such a high degree of source-code portability among different environments? Well, for one thing, many features included as part of other languages are not found in C itself. These features are instead supplied by the standard library that comes with your C compiler.

This standard library permits you to deal with many variations in environment without any modification to the C language or your source code. You choose the proper compiler for a given environment, and the compiler takes care of the specifics.

Function Libraries

The standard library supplied with your compiler contains useful functions in object form, ready to be linked with and called by functions that you write yourself. These library functions extend, but are not part of, the C language. Standard library functions are available to interact with a user, to access file data, to manipulate strings of text, to perform mathematical calculations, and to handle many other routine tasks.

You can also write your own libraries of functions, or you can purchase specialized libraries containing business-oriented file-access methods, programmer-productivity tools, or graphics and screen-control routines, to name just a few. All of these additions extend and customize your C programming tools.

File Handling and Device Independence

File handling is also accomplished by library functions, rather than by C statements, which means that C programs are not limited to machines that support a specific type of file input and output. C programs can be *device independent:* That is, they can, without modification, accept input from a terminal, a modem, a disk file, or some other special device. The source of input is said to be *transparent* to the program, because the program doesn't care where its data come from.

Device independence also applies to program output, which can be redirected to a disk file, printer, terminal, modem, or some other device, again without program modification. (The conversion of *PRINT* statements to *LPRINT* statements to divert a BASIC program's screen output to a printer is an example of the device dependence of BASIC programs.)

Input- and output-device information for C programs is usually given with the operating-system command that causes a program to execute. We'll discuss this in detail later on.

Of course, C programs are not *totally* device independent. For example, it would make no sense to try to clear the screen of a disk, or to *input* data from a standard printer. Some device dependence is inevitable.

How C Programs Are Created

As we've already seen, a C program is simply a set of independent functions (known as subroutines in some other languages) that call each other to perform some task. Each function may be written separately and saved in its own file.

But there's more to the story. Development of a C program isn't a one-step process. Like assembler code, C source code must be compiled and modules must be linked before a C program can be executed. Let's look at the sequence a little more closely.

▶ You use a text-editing utility like the MS-DOS *EDLIN* program to build or modify C programs in source form.

▶ Then you use a C compiler to translate C source code to *object code*. C object code consists of binary machine instructions, so you can't edit or list object files.

▶ Finally, you use an operating-system utility called a linker (supplied with your compiler) to link your object modules with one another and with the library functions called by your code. You invoke the linker only after all compilations have been completed. Its output is the executable program, saved in a file, ready for use on computers that use your operating system or one compatible with it.

Standards for C

At this time, not all C compilers behave in exactly the same way. However, efforts are under way to develop a document that describes a standard implementation of the C programming language. The goal of the standard is to eliminate ambiguities and extend the capabilities of the C language. It will describe, in great detail, how a generic C compiler should behave, including details of syntax, operators, expressions, statements, data structures, and eventually, library functions.

Is there a C standard as this book goes to press? Well, almost. In April 1984, the X3J11 Language Subcommittee of ANSI (the American National Standards Institute) prepared a *Proposed C Standard* in draft form. The draft has yet to be approved by ANSI, but the suggested improvements have been incorporated into the Microsoft C compiler, which is the one I use for the examples in this book. (The ANSI standard does not discuss the implementation or behavior of library functions.) Copies of the draft proposal are available from the American National Standards Institute, X3 Secretariat, 311 First Street NW, Suite 500, Washington, DC 20001.

Peeking Ahead

C programs look strange at first. They are terse, not wordy. They use symbols extensively: for example, { and } in place of the words *BEGIN* and *END* found in some other languages. Nor are C statements very English-like, which means fewer keystrokes for programmers and less valuable disk space devoted to storage on the computer, but less familiar-looking code. And C is a lowercase language. Where uppercase *is* used, the characters are distinct from lowercase characters in C source code, so that the names *num, Num,* and *NUM* all represent different variables.

C supports many different data types, and the data type of a variable must be declared before the variable can be used. But C also permits many data conversions, making it a "weakly typed" language. This means that C expressions can "legally" combine different data types for such special operations as arithmetic on characters (as in the expression *'a'+1,* whose value is *'b'*).

Another C characteristic that may take some getting used to, depending upon which programming language you have used in the past, is the fact that the index of the first element in any C array is always zero, not one. So expect to be "off by one" array element from time to time during your initiation into C.

More about all that later. For now, I hope I've given you enough information about this exciting and powerful programming language to make you want to read more. If you've already written a few C programs, you'll probably just want to skim the next few chapters. For the rest of you, let's get down to business and learn how to "speak" C.

Data Output and Input

This chapter will take you from the most basic C program possible to compiled programs that input and output various types of data. We have a lot to cover in between, so let's jump right in.

```
/* The most portable C program. It does nothing everywhere! It is an empty */
/* shell, a bread sandwich with nothing inside.                            */
/* Note: The function name main() must always be in lowercase.             */

main()
   {
   }
```

You may think that was a joke, but it wasn't. Every C program *must* have a *main()* function. In this case *main()* does absolutely nothing and immediately terminates, returning control to the operating system, but it still constitutes a legitimate C program.

The first three lines of the program are comments. Comments always begin with /* and must end with */. They can legally continue for many lines, but if you forget to close the last line with */, the rest of your program will become just one long comment!

The next line begins the function named *main()* (although all C programs are simply collections of functions that you write yourself or call from a library, only *main()* is a *required* function). The last two lines hold an opening curly brace ({) and a closing curly brace (}), each indented three spaces. The curly-brace symbols act like the keywords *BEGIN* and *END* in other languages.

The style you'll learn in this book is to indent braces alone on a line, so that you can easily locate them and the blocks of code they surround. Program format is of special importance with a language as terse as C. The compiler actually ignores most white space (indenting spaces, tabs, and skipped lines), so we're free to use spacing and indenting in any way we wish to help improve readability (use the tab key to ensure consistent indentation). To see why a structured format is so important in C, look at the following two programs. Both of them are equivalent to the bread-sandwich program.

```
main(
      )   {

}
```

```
main(){}
```

The first program is nearly incomprehensible. The second would work only in this bread-sandwich situation. Clearly, structure is going to be very important in helping us keep track of what's going on.

The example listings in this book will be indented in increments of three, for reasons of page width. A five- or eight-space tab is perfectly acceptable if your viewing screen and printer output are at least 80 characters wide.

Now that we've dealt with the basics, let's see how to write and compile useful programs—programs that produce some output.

Programs That Output Text

First we'll write a C program that outputs the text that makes up the bread-sandwich program. We'll store the code in a source file named *testmain.c,* and then we'll look at the simple series of commands used to compile, link, and execute it.

```
/* Output a 4-line program using printf(). */

main()
   {
   printf("/* bread sandwich */\n\n");
   printf("main()\n");
   printf("\t{\n");
   printf("\t}\n");
   }
```

Here's how the output from our progam will look:

```
/* bread sandwich */

main()
        {
        }
```

The term *printf()* is the name of a library function used for formatted printing. The character pair \n (read as "backslash n") is the abbreviation for a *newline* character. You may know this character as *line feed*. They are the same: The \n you output with *printf()* moves the cursor to the beginning of a new line. The symbol \t is the abbreviation for a horizontal tab character, which is expanded to eight spaces before it is displayed.

This source code provides another good example of the importance of a structured program format. The body of the *main()* function, which has four statements, could be replaced with the single statement

```
printf("/* bread sandwich */\n\nmain()\n\t{\n\t}\n");
```

but the sacrifice in readability is tremendous and would make the program difficult to debug and maintain.

Producing Executable Code

We'll use the *EDLIN* text editor to create the *testmain.c* source file that holds the statements from the first version of our sample program. (Most other text editors and word-processing programs are equally suitable for editing C source code.) Just press the tab key or ^I to indent lines 4 through 9. Your *EDLIN* screen will look like this:

```
B>EDLIN TESTMAIN.C
New File
*i
        1:*/* Output a 4-line program using printf(). */
        2:*
        3:*main()
        4:*          {
        5:*              printf("/* bread sandwich */\n\n");
        6:*              printf("main()\n");
        7:*              printf("\t{\n");
        8:*              printf("\t}\n");
        9:*          }
       10:*^C    (control-break typed)
*e

B>
```

After you've finished editing, load your compiler and use either the *MSC* or the *CL* command to compile your C source file into relocatable object code (the *MSC* and *CL* commands and file names may be entered in either upper- or lowercase):

```
B>MSC TESTMAIN.C;
```

If you use the *MSC* command, you must invoke the linker after *MSC* has been executed, in order to link the object files with the library functions they call:

```
B>LINK TESTMAIN;
```

Following a successful link, the executable program is saved in a file with the extension *.exe* (in our example, *testmain.exe*) and may then be executed by simply typing the file name (without the extension):

```
B>TESTMAIN
/* bread sandwich */

main()
   {
   }
B>
```

If you use *CL*, you can compile and link with just one command. (*CL* can also compile more than one source file with a single command.) The *CL* command resembles the UNIX and XENIX *CC* commands, but the options (switches) are different. To compile and link *testmain.c* using *CL*, enter this command:

```
B>CL TESTMAIN.C
```

Then, to execute the program, use the same command that was used in the *MSC* example:

```
B>TESTMAIN
```

Capturing Diagnostics and Output

The operating system, in conjunction with the compiler, provides two output-redirection commands, *>* and *>>*, that permit program output to be diverted from the screen to the file or device named after the redirection symbol. These output-redirection commands come from UNIX and XENIX, and are implemented under most other operating systems as part of the compiler package. We'll discuss them further in Chapter 8, along with two additional redirection commands: < for redirecting input and | for piping the output of one command as input into the next. For now, let's look at some simple examples of output redirection that can help us in developing and debugging C programs:

```
B>CL TESTMAIN.C > TESTMAIN.LST
B>TESTMAIN > TESTMAIN.OUT
B>TESTMAIN > LPT1:
```

The first command compiles and links the source code in *testmain.c* and stores the compiler output in *testmain.lst*. The second command executes the compiled program *testmain* and sends the output to the disk file *testmain.out*. The last command executes *testmain* and sends the output to the printer.

   If you use redirection to save the compiler's diagnostic output in a file, as in the preceding example, you can view the diagnostics as you correct the mistakes that caused the output. The easiest way to do this is to use your editor to read the saved output (in this case, *testmain.lst*) into your source file and then surround the copy of the diagnostics with /* and */, making it one big comment that you can use to remind you of the changes needed.

   A couple of words of warning about output redirection. The > command creates an empty file into which output is directed. If a file by the name specified after the > symbol already exists, its old data are *erased*, so *be very careful* with >. The >> command appends output to the *end* of the file named after the symbol, creating an empty file only if the named file does not already exist. Therefore, >> is both safe and handy for collecting the output of a series of programs into a single file.

Special Characters in String Constants

   A series of zero or more characters surrounded by double quotes (" ") is called a *string constant*. You know from our *testmain* example that messages you want printed can be surrounded by double quotes and passed as a string expression to the library function *printf()*. But what if you want to print a message that *contains* a backslash and some double quotes? Well, the backslash itself can take care of the problem by combining with the character following it to create a special abbreviation. You've already seen the backslash behave in a special way in the \n and \t abbreviations for newline and tab. In this next example, you'll see how two backslashes(\\) can be used to print a single backslash, \" to print a quotation mark, and \\n to print the symbol \n rather than newline. In order to print the program statement

```
printf("C no evil!\n");
```

as output, you could just use the *printf()* function like this:

```
printf("printf(\"C no evil!\\n\");\n");
```

Here's a list of the backslash abbreviations that are permitted in string constants:

SYMBOL	OUTPUT	SYMBOL	OUTPUT
\\	Backslash	\t	Horizontal tab
\b	Backspace	\n	Newline (line feed)
\r	Carriage return	\'	Single quote
\"	Double quote	\v	Vertical tab
\f	Form feed		

In order to output a character that cannot be represented as a printable ASCII character and has no abbreviation, you would need to specify that character's value in octal (base 8) or hexadecimal (base 16) notation, using the appropriate backslash code. In octal notation, the backslash is followed by one to three octal digits (0 through 7), as in these examples:

C   A   U   T   I   O   N

Be careful not to confuse the slash (/) and backslash (\). The slash is the division operator; the backslash is used before other characters to give them a different meaning, or to continue a line of C source code (see Chapter 6).

OCTAL NOTATION	ASCII NONPRINTABLE EQUIVALENT
\0	Null character
\33	ESC (escape) character
\7	
\07	} BEL (bell) character
\007	

Most programmers do seem to prefer hexadecimal notation over octal (if you have no preference, I recommend you use hex). In hexadecimal notation, the backslash is followed by an *x* and one or two hex digits (0 through 9 and A through F or a through f). Here are the same ASCII characters in hex notation:

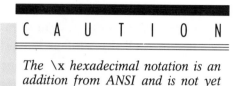

The \x *hexadecimal notation is an addition from ANSI and is not yet supported by many compilers.*

HEXADECIMAL NOTATION	ASCII NONPRINTABLE EQUIVALENT
\x0	Null character
\x1b	ESC (escape) character
\x07	BEL (bell) character

Identifiers and Data Types

By far the most important step a programmer can take to make C programs more readable and easier to modify is to use *meaningful* identifier names. Use of meaningful names for variables and constants helps shorten coding and debugging time by reducing confusion. It helps eliminate the kind of bug you really kick yourself for missing, after you've wasted 12 hours hunting for it. One-letter identifier names were forced on us by toy languages; they make programs difficult to understand and therefore should always be avoided. C is a serious working language that allows you room for clarity, so take advantage of it!

Misleading identifier names also confuse program readers and writers alike. Misleading names, perhaps more than meaningless names, can lead to bugs that take hours to locate. Resist the temptation to reuse an existing variable for something other than what its name implies. Instead, declare a new variable with its own meaningful and honest name. You'll be glad later that you took the time.

Identifier names must begin with a letter or an underscore (_), and can include numbers, as well as additional letters and underscores. Two identifier names must differ within the first eight characters to be recognized as different by most C compilers, although Microsoft C allows 31 significant characters in identifiers. C treats upper- and lowercase letters in identifier names as distinct (that is, *b* and *B* are not equivalent).

C   A   U   T   I   O   N

Even though it's legal, don't use the underscore as the first character of a name. You risk conflict with a compiler- or linker-generated symbol.

Reserved words must not be used as identifier names, but they may be part of a longer name. Most C compilers reserve the following 30 lowercase keywords:

auto	*default*	*float*	*register*	*switch*
break	*do*	*for*	*return*	*typedef*
case	*double*	*goto*	*short*	*union*
char	*else*	*if*	*sizeof*	*unsigned*
const	*enum*	*int*	*static*	*void*
continue	*extern*	*long*	*struct*	*while*

and Microsoft C reserves these six additional keywords as well:

asm	*huge*
fortran	*far*
pascal	*near*

It is good C programming style to use lowercase letters for variable names and uppercase letters for the names of constants (see Chapters 9 and 11), to make it easy to distinguish between them.

Data Types

The appropriate data type for a variable depends upon the range of values the variable must hold. Data types that can hold a wider range of values take up more memory than narrower-range data types, but provide greater flexibility for data manipulation. Figure 2-1 shows C's standard simple data types. The ranges of permissible values may vary among compilers: These are for Microsoft C.

DATA TYPE	BYTES REQUIRED	MINIMUM VALUE	MAXIMUM VALUE
char	1	-128	127
unsigned char	1	0	255
short or *int*	2	$-32,768$	32,767
unsigned short	2	0	65,535
long	4	$-2,147,483,648$	2,147,483,647
unsigned long	4	0	4,294,967,295
float	4	$\pm 1.701411E - 38$	$\pm 1.701411E38$
double	8	$\pm 1.0E - 307$	$\pm 1.0E307$

FIGURE 2-1 | *C's standard data types and their ranges on 16-bit CPUs*

The *unsigned* modifier means that no value is considered negative. The floating-point type *double* allows approximately 15 significant digits, whereas type *float* allows only seven.

If not handled carefully, C's *int* data type can limit source-code portability. On 16-bit CPUs, type *int* is equivalent to *short,* as shown in Figure 2-1, but on 32-bit machines *int* is equivalent to type *long.* Similarly, *unsigned int* is equivalent to either *unsigned short* or *unsigned long.* Therefore, it is good style to use *short* or *long,* explicitly, with C data.

Numeric constants.   But which data type does C assign to numeric expressions whose values never change? Let's turn from variables for a moment and see how we represent constant expressions in C.

A series of digits 0 through 9, possibly preceded by a minus sign, is called an *integer constant.* Neither commas nor leading plus signs may be included in integer constants. Here are some typical examples:

$$
\begin{array}{rr}
24 & -17 \\
-4587 & 7 \\
10596 & -30545
\end{array}
$$

The range of values an integer constant may take on and the amount of memory consumed to hold that value are the same as for an *int*-type variable: that is, 2 or 4 bytes, depending upon the CPU being used. Integer constants too large to store in an *int* variable automatically become type *long.* The letter *L,* when used as the last digit of an integer constant, makes the constant type *long* even if its present value would fit the *int* type. Here are some examples of *long* constants:

```
546767
    0L
  −35L
```

Not all constants in our programs are whole numbers, however; sometimes we need to use fractions. C has provided a special data type called the *floating-point constant* to handle fractional values. Although C has two sizes of floating-point variables (*float* and *double*), it has only one size of floating-point constant: type *double*, 8 bytes wide.

You can choose between two floating-point notations: decimal and scientific. Here are some examples of the familiar decimal notation:

```
  24.387551
      −1.0
  −1763.73
```

The less familiar scientific notation (*E notation*) uses powers of base 10 to express very large numbers. An E value consists of a decimal constant multiplied by an integral power of 10 (positive or negative), like this:

E NOTATION	INTERPRETATION	VALUE
1E5	1.0×10^5	100,000.0
−1.3495E3	$−1.3495 \times 10^3$	−1,349.5
4E−2	4.0×10^{-2}	0.04

Declaring Variables

C requires that all variables be *declared* before they are used. A declaration is simply a statement of the data type, followed by one or more variable names separated by commas, and ending with a semicolon.

Here are some examples of variable declarations and the sorts of descriptive comments you should get into the habit of including in your programs:

DECLARATION	COMMENT
`char prod_code;`	`/* 1-digit product code */`
`long salary;`	`/* long type necessary for higher salaries */`
`double tax_rate;`	`/* double-precision sales tax (use .06 for 6%) */`

Declarations with initializers. The value of a variable is not predictable unless it has been *initialized*, or assigned a starting value. Fortunately, C gives you the option of assigning an initial value to a scalar (non-array) variable right in the declaration.

The syntax is simply *variable = initializing_expression*. Each initializer applies only to the variable it follows and not to any others in the same declaration. The following example initializes all variables declared except *not_init*:

> **C A U T I O N**
>
> *Be sure the initializing expression is of the same data type as its variable; otherwise the compiler will send you an error message.*

```
short not_init, number_of_accounts = 50;
short account_months = number_of_accounts * 12;
long total_salary = 0L;
double sales_tax = .06;
```

Formatted Input and Output

Values that remain locked within the computer do us little good. We need to find ways to send data to our programs and get information back. Let's take a look at how C handles these activities.

The library functions *scanf()* and *printf()* control formatted input and output, respectively. You've already seen how to call *printf()* to display characters and strings of characters. The values listed in parentheses after the name of the function to be called are the *arguments* to the called function. Basically, arguments are the vehicle by which a function sends values to a subfunction it calls.

The first argument to both *printf()* and *scanf()* is the format string that allows you some control over the size and appearance of output and input data. The format string is made up of one or more format specifiers, literal text, or both. (So far all the arguments we've passed to *printf()* have been only literal text.)

The format specifiers that dictate the types of data to be input by *scanf()* or output by *printf()* consist of a percent sign and a character code for the data type (for example, %*d* for integer). The format specifier may

DATA	FORMAT SPECIFIER	OUTPUT	FORMAT DESCRIPTION
234	%d	234	Decimal (base 10) integer
191543L	%ld	191543	*long* decimal integer
−1	%u	65535	*unsigned* decimal integer; unexpected output
7	%4d	7	4-digit decimal integer, right-justified
1985	%2d	1985	2-digit decimal integer; value too wide, but is output completely
8	%03d	008	3-digit decimal integer, zero-filled
2	%−03d	200	3-digit decimal integer, left-justified, zero-filled
2.735	%f	2.735000	Floating-point decimal, zero-filled to default precision (6)
3.18	%5.1f	3.1	5-digit, floating-point decimal, 1 decimal place
10000.0	%e	1.000000e + 004	Scientific notation

FIGURE 2-2 | *Format specifiers for numeric output*

also dictate field width (%3d for a 3-digit integer), precision (%12.5f for 5-decimal accuracy), and justification (% − 4d for a 4-digit integer, left-justified). Figures 2-2 and 2-3 show some of the more common C numeric format specifiers and their meanings (see Appendix F for complete listings). Notice the effect of the %u specifier on a negative value, and the different behavior of the %2d specifier with output and input values too wide for the format.

Don't let all this overwhelm you. You'll see plenty of examples as we go along. We'll start with some simple ones, to make things a bit clearer.

DATA	FORMAT SPECIFIER	INPUT	FORMAT DESCRIPTION
234	*%d*	*234*	Decimal (base 10) integer
191543L	*%D*	*191543*	*long* decimal integer
−1	*%u*	*65535*	*unsigned* decimal integer; unexpected input
7	*%4d*	*7*	4-digit decimal integer
1985	*%2d*	*19*	2-digit decimal integer; value too wide and is truncated
2.735	*%f*	*2.735*	Floating-point decimal
3.18	*%5f*	*3.18*	5-digit floating-point decimal
10000.0	*%e*	*1.0e4*	Scientific notation

FIGURE 2-3 | *Equivalent format specifiers for numeric input*

The following program declares a *short* variable named *number*, assigns the value 7 to it, and prints *number*'s value and then its value multiplied by 2:

```
/* Assign value to short int variable and display it using formatted output. */
main()
    {
    short number;               /* Declare name and type of number to display. */

    number = 7;                                 /* Assign integer 7 to number. */
    printf("Number is now %d.\n", number);   /* Display messages and values. */
    printf("%d * 2 = %d\n", number, number * 2);
    }
```

A format string with more than one format specifier will cause the input or output of more than one piece of data. In the preceding example, the first call to *printf()* uses one *%d* format specifier to output *number*'s value. The second call to *printf()* must output two values, so the format string has two *%d* format specifiers. In the output, each of the specifiers is replaced by a number, like this:

```
Number is now 7.
7 * 2 = 14
```

In this next program you see the input and output of both *long* integer and *double* floating-point data. (The scalar arguments *lng* and *dbl* in *scanf()* require the & *address-of* prefix to let *scanf()* know where in memory to store the converted input. We'll discuss this in detail in Chapter 14.)

```
/* This program will input and output long and double data. */

#include <stdio.h>                              /* We'll learn about this later. */

main()
  {
  long lng;                              /* Declare variables and their types. */
  double dbl;

  printf("Enter long int and double: ");              /* Prompt for numbers. */
  scanf("%D %F", &lng, &dbl);                            /* Input numbers. */
  printf("You entered %ld %f.\n", lng, dbl);           /* Display results. */
  }
```

Here, input and output require different format specifiers: *%D* and *%ld*, respectively, for *long* data, and *%F* and *%f*, respectively, for *double* data. It is very important that the specifiers in the format string match the data types of the arguments that follow, or results may become meaningless, at best.

COMMENT

Since 32-bit systems distinguish between short *and* int *data, you can ensure portability of your code by using* %hd *to input* short *integer values.*

Portability of Variables

We've already noted that not all C data types are implemented identically in all environments, which can lead to unpredictability in program behavior (otherwise known as portability concerns). Let's look at some examples.

Programs that declare *int* and *unsigned int* variables can have portability problems because the range of values these variables may hold differs among environments. Compare the behavior of the following program on 16- and 32-bit systems:

```
main()
  {
  int count;                    /* Variable count is either 2 or 4 bytes wide. */

  count = 32766;                     /* Assign (maximum value of a short) - 1. */
  printf("%d, %d, %d\n", count + 1, count + 2, count + 3);
  }
```

On a 16-bit CPU computer, the *int* data type is 2 bytes wide, the same size as a *short,* so the output is:

```
32767, -32768, -32767
```

(Notice that the commas in the format string are treated as literal text and are printed between the numbers listed.)

On a 32-bit computer, the *int* data type is 4 bytes wide, the same size as a *long.* The additional width of *int* on the 32-bit system prevents the integer overflow that we got on the 16-bit system, so the 32-bit output is:

```
32767, 32768, 32769
```

The integer overflow on 16-bit systems, caused in this case by the expressions *count + 2* and *count + 3,* is not considered an error and therefore goes unreported during program execution. (C unfortunately provides minimal run-time protection. This is a good example of the kinds of problems that can result.)

What would the behavior of this program be on 16- and 32-bit systems if *count* were declared as type *long*? The output would be the same on both machines, so the program becomes portable.

The *char* data type can also create portability problems, since some C compilers treat it as *signed,* giving it a range of −128 through +127, while other C compilers treat it as *unsigned,* yielding a range of 0 through 255. The easiest solution to this potential problem is to make it a rule to store only ASCII characters or numbers in the range 0 through 127 in a *char* variable.

C A U T I O N

To avoid portability problems, do not use int *type for counter variables. Use* short *or* long *instead.*

The types *unsigned char, unsigned short,* and *unsigned long* are described in the ANSI X3 *Proposed C Standard* and are supported by Microsoft C. However, these types are not supported by *all* C compilers, making them somewhat of a portability problem until compilers become more standardized. (The type *unsigned* is equivalent to *unsigned int,* and is supported on all compilers.) It is good style to use the *signed* types over the *unsigned* types, except where *unsigned* offers some special advantage (for example, when no negative values are needed and you want to count to a higher positive value than the signed type would permit).

So far, we've limited our discussion of the input and output of numeric data to single values. However, much of our programming will involve *numeric expressions* containing more than one value. Since the techniques for managing these expressions are quite detailed, we'll cover them separately, in the next chapter.

The Value of Expressions

3

In the previous chapter you learned how to input and display values. Now you'll learn how to operate on C data to produce useful results. C provides an unusually rich set of operations for you to use in managing your data, but we'll examine just two of them here: arithmetic on numbers and accessing array elements.

Operators, Operands, and Expressions

Operators are the symbols you use to specify the actions to be performed on data. They are the verbs of C. The values acted on by the operator, or used by the operator to calculate a result, are called *operands*. Depending upon the exact operator and the context in which it is used, C operators take from one to three operands. Unary operators take only one operand, binary (or dyadic) operators need two, and C has one ternary conditional operator (?:) that takes three operands.

A variable or constant alone is called an *expression*. We use operators to combine these simple expressions into new and larger

C O M M E N T

It is good programming style to break up overly complex expressions that might be difficult to understand into smaller, more obvious ones by using intermediate variables.

expressions. Any legal combination of constants, variables, and expressions joined by operators is also considered an expression. Here are some examples:

EXPRESSION	TYPE
9	Constant
quantity_ordered	Variable
*(12 * dozens) + units*	Compound expression

Precedence and Grouping

Precedence and *grouping* are terms we use to explain the way expressions involving two or more operators are evaluated. Precedence rules define the priority of an operator in relation to other operators in the same expression. The higher-precedence operation takes place first. The use of parentheses ensures that operations that would otherwise violate the rules of precedence take place in the order we desire. For example, the expressions *2 * 15 + 10 / 5* and *(2 * 15) + (10 / 5)* are equivalent, since the higher precedence of both multiplication and division over addition would make addition the last operation in either case. But the expressions *2 * 15 + 10 / 5* and *2 * (15 + 10) / 5* are not equivalent, since the parentheses cause the addition to be executed first in the latter example, yielding 10 rather than 32.

Figure 3-1 lists the C operators and their actions in descending order of precedence. We'll look at specific examples as we go along.

Notice that the precedence and meaning of the minus (−) operator depend upon how many operands it has in the expression where it is used. With only one operand (−*num*), we have a unary minus with very high precedence; with two operands (*high − low*), the minus means subtraction and has lower precedence.

The grouping (sometimes called *associativity*) of operators controls the order of operations in an expression with two or more of the same operator or with operators of equal precedence. Most operators automatically group left to right. The exceptions are the unary operators (the last

PRECEDENCE LEVEL	OPERATOR	ACTION
15	() [] -> .	Precedence, array subscript, structure pointer, structure member
14	! ~ ++ -- - *(type)* * & *sizeof*	Logical not, one's complement, increment, decrement, unary minus, data type, indirection, address-of, size of an object
13	* / %	Multiplication, division, modulo
12	+ -	Addition, subtraction
11	<< >>	Shift left, shift right
10	< <= > >=	Less than, less than or equal, greater than, greater than or equal
9	== !=	Relational equal, not equal
8	&	Bitwise AND
7	^	Bitwise XOR
6	|	Bitwise OR
5	&&	Logical AND
4	||	Logical OR
3	?:	Conditional expression
2	= += -= etc.	Assignment
1	,	Comma

FIGURE 3-1 | *C operators in descending order of precedence*

expression in the following example), the assignment operators, and the conditional operator, all of which group right to left.

EXPRESSION	PARENTHESIZED EQUIVALENT
balance − principal − interest	*((balance − principal) − interest)*
*tax_pcnt / 100.0 * balance*	*((tax_pcnt / 100.0) * balance*
first = last = 0	*(first = (last = 0))*

All this seems clear enough, but what happens if your C operators have operands of two different data types? We'll discuss this addition of apples and oranges next.

Data Type Conversions

How is an expression with an operator and two operands of different data types evaluated? Well, it's not as mysterious as you might have expected. C simply converts a copy of one (or both) of the operands to a common data type before the operation takes place. *Conversion* is automatic in these cases, and the new values are as equivalent as possible to the original ones. The operation you specified with the operator then takes place with the new data types, rather than the originals.

C performs any necessary data-type conversions *before* evaluation of an expression or assignment of a value to a variable. There are some rules that control conversions, but before we discuss them, let's look at how type conversion happens.

How C Converts Data Types

The combination of data of types *long* and *double* causes two conversions to take place in the assignment statement at the end of this code segment:

```
double rate;
long total, price;

    /* ... */
total = rate * price;  /* Two conversions needed: one for * and one for =.   */
```

Before the multiplication is performed, C converts a copy of *price*'s value to type *double*. It then multiplies *rate* by the converted *price*; the result is, of course, type *double*. But in order to assign the result to *total*, C must convert that result to the same type as *total*, a *long*. Any fractional portion of the *double* result is simply truncated (discarded without rounding) during the conversion to *long*. Two different kinds of conversion occurred in this example: one to evaluate an expression *(rate * price)* and one to assign the result to a variable *(total)*.

The evaluation of expressions containing a mixture of operand data types can be more complex than assignment conversion. For example, let's look at conversions among the integral data types *char, short, int, long,* and their *unsigned* counterparts.

Conversions among the signed and unsigned integral types *char, short, int,* and *long* may involve either widening or truncation. A change of value may or may not occur during widening, but truncation always causes one or more of the *most significant bytes* of data to be discarded, which can mean a large change in value if the discarded bytes are non-zero.

C　O　M　M　E　N　T

Careful planning of data types to be used in arithmetic operations is very important for the success and efficiency of your program.

Here is a list of the integral widening and truncation conversions. (The term *sign bit extended* in the widening conversion refers to the internal bit manipulation performed by the CPU to maintain the positive or negative sign of the value.)

FROM TYPE	TO TYPE	NATURE OF CONVERSION
char, short, int	*int, long*	Widening; sign bit extended to keep negative values negative
int, long	*char, short, int*	Truncation; high-order bytes discarded, low byte(s) kept

The modifier *unsigned* with a data type means that the variable being declared will never be negative. This permits *unsigned* variables to have positive values twice as large as their *signed* counterparts. If you assign a negative value to an *unsigned* variable, that variable ends up with a large positive value that has the same internal bit representation as the negative value. Conversely, the assignment of a large *unsigned* value to a variable of a *signed* type may result in that variable being assigned a negative value.

The following program demonstrates the effects of the sign, truncation, and widening conversions we've just discussed on a *short* integer named *short_var*:

```
/* Convert a short int copy of -3 to other integral types. */

main()
    {
    short short_var = -3;
    unsigned short uns_short_var = short_var;
    char char_var = short_var;                      /* Truncate: 2 bytes to 1. */
    unsigned char uns_char_var = short_var;
    long long_var = short_var;                      /* Widen: 2 bytes to 4. */
    unsigned long uns_long_var = short_var;

    printf("short_var = %d, uns_short_var = %u\n", short_var, uns_short_var);
    printf("char_var = %d, uns_char_var = %u\n", char_var, uns_char_var);
    printf("long_var = %ld, uns_long_var = %lu\n", long_var, uns_long_var);
    }
```

Here is the output from this program:

```
short_var = -3, uns_short_var = 65533
char_var = -3, uns_char_var = 253
long_var = -3, uns_long_var = 4294967293
```

Let's look more closely at the effects of type conversion on C's two floating-point data types, *double* and *float*. Variables declared as type *double* are double-precision and consume 8 bytes of memory. Type *float* variables are single-precision and occupy only 4 bytes of memory. Conversion of data from *float* to *double* simply adds insignificant zero digits after the last digit of the fractional portion and causes no change in value. Conversion from *double* to *float*, however, truncates some of the least significant digits and narrows the range of possible values considerably.

The Microsoft C compiler converts a *double* value to *int* type by first converting the *double* to *float*, then converting the *float* value to *long*. Unfortunately, this intermediate conversion may result in the loss of more precision than with some other C compilers that convert directly.

The conversion of integral data to floating-point data is as simple as adding *.0* after the integer being converted, assuming that the floating-point type has enough significant digits to hold the entire integer.

Now that you know *how* various conversions are performed, let's look at the rules for *when* they take place.

Conversion Rules

The rule for conversion in assignment expressions is that a copy of the value on the right-hand side of the assignment operator is converted to the type of the variable on the left-hand side. In the following example, the converted value of *small* is assigned to the variable *big*:

```
short small;
long big;

small = 32;
big = small;            /* The short value 32 of small is converted to the */
                        /*   long value 32L and then assigned to big.       */
```

The rules governing data conversions prior to the evaluation of an expression, known as the *usual arithmetic conversions,* are more complex. One or both of two kinds of conversion may take place prior to an expression's evaluation: *widening* ensures that operands are wide enough to be operated on; *type balancing* converts the narrower of the widened operands to the same data type as the wider. (Width of a data type simply means the number of bytes of memory a value of that type occupies.) Once both operands are wide enough and of the same type, the operation specified by the operator is executed.

Widening conversions for expression evaluation in C programs follow these rules:

- ▶ All *char* or *short* operands are converted to *int*.

- ▶ All *float* operands are converted to *double*.

- ▶ All *unsigned char* and *unsigned short* operands are converted to *unsigned int*.

Type-balancing rules for expression evaluation are applied in the following order *after* the widening conversion is completed:

- ▶ If one operand is *double*, the other operand is converted to *double* and the result is *double*.

- ▶ Otherwise, if one operand is *unsigned long*, the other operand is converted to *unsigned long* and the result is *unsigned long*.

- ▶ Otherwise, if one operand is *long*, the other operand is converted to *long* and the result is *long*.

- ▶ Otherwise, if one operand is *unsigned int*, the other operand is converted to *unsigned int* and the result is *unsigned int*.

The Assignment Operators

We talked about assignment earlier, in relation to grouping and conversions. Now let's look at this operation in greater detail.

The simple assignment operator of C is the single equal sign (=). It is used to set the value of a variable. (C also has a set of shorthand assignment operators that we'll discuss later in this chapter.) The actual value assigned to the variable on the left side of the assignment operator is not just the value on the right side of the operator: It is the value on the right side *converted* to the data type of the variable on the left side. All assignment operators have equal and very low precedence, and group from right to left.

A powerful and unusual feature of the assignment operators is that they give assignment expressions a type and value that can be used in a larger expression. Multiple assignments and embedded assignments in a statement are permitted precisely *because* assignment expressions have a value, as in the following example:

```
main()
{
long big;                                                   /* 4-byte integer */
short little;                                                /* 2-byte integer */

big = little = 131073;                                        /* multiple assignment */
printf("#1: big = %ld, little = %d\n", big, little);
big = (little = 50) * 1000;                                   /* embedded assignment */
printf("#2: big = %ld, little = %d\n", big, little);
}
```

These lines actually produce the following output:

```
#1: big = 1, little = 1
#2: big = -15536, little = 50
```

Notice that the multiple assignment in the example program causes *big* to be 1. This is because *131073* is first assigned to *little*, but *little* is type *short* and can hold at most 32767, so *little* receives only the low-order 2 bytes of *131073*, which contain *1*. Because assignment groups data from right to left, the value *1* is then assigned to *big*, even though *big* is wide enough to have held the original *long* value of *131073*.

The statement with the embedded assignment needed the parentheses in order to overcome the precedence of multiplication over assignment. Without the parentheses, *little* would be assigned the low-order 2 bytes of *50000*, and then that value would be assigned to *big*.

The variable on the left side of an assignment operator *must* be a scalar variable or an element of an array (that is, it must refer to a manipulatable region of storage), and is called an *lvalue* (pronounced *ell-value*). The name of an array alone, without an index expression in square brackets, is not an *lvalue* and therefore cannot be assigned to.

Assignment Shorthand Operators

The assignment shorthand operators are a more terse and efficient way of expressing some assignment expressions. They are used when the variable being assigned to also appears in the expression on the right-hand side of the statement.

Shorthand assignment is more efficient than simple assignment and should be used wherever possible. Let's look at a few examples of shorthand assignments that produce the same results as the simple assignments in the right-hand column:

SHORTHAND ASSIGNMENT	SIMPLE ASSIGNMENT
num += 3;	*num = num + 3;*
*val *= num + 4;*	*val = val * (num + 4);*
*ans /= div *= div;*	*ans = ans / (div = div * div);*

Here is the complete list of assignment shorthand operators, including the bitwise operators, which we'll discuss in greater detail in Chapter 20:

TYPE	OPERATORS
Arithmetic	+= , -= , *= , /= , %=
Bitwise	<<= , >>= , &= , ^= , |=

Sequence Guarantees and the Comma Operator

C makes a rather fine distinction between order of evaluation of the terms of an expression and order of the operations that combine those terms. For example, the next statement calls three functions:

```
ans = func_one(num) + func_two(num) * func_three(num);
```

The *return values* from functions *func_two* and *func_three* are multiplied and then added to the return value from *func_one*. The order of operations on the return values is controlled by the precedence of multiplication over addition, but C makes no sequence guarantee about the order in which the *operands* of the multiplication and addition are evaluated. In other words, you cannot depend upon *func_two* being called before *func_three*, nor in fact upon any of these three functions being called in any particular order. To assume an order would be dangerous, since other compilers (or a new release of your present compiler) might generate a different order of calls.

Now, if the functions called in an expression are truly independent of one another, then the order of calls doesn't matter, but if one function writes to a file another function will read, or if two functions share some common data in memory, then they are dependent and the order of calls becomes important.

One way to guarantee sequence in C is to put the function calls in separate statements, so that you gain control over the order in which they are called, like this:

```
hold = func_one(num);
ans = func_two(num);
ans *= func_three(num);          /* equivalent to ans = ans * func_three(num) */
ans += hold;                     /* equivalent to ans = ans + hold           */
```

Another approach is to use the *comma* operator to join two expressions into a single expression. The comma operator guarantees to evaluate the expressions from left to right. The type and value of the result are the type and value of the rightmost expression, the last one to be evaluated. For example, to exchange the

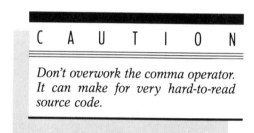

C   A   U   T   I   O   N

Don't overwork the comma operator. It can make for very hard-to-read source code.

values of the variables *curr* and *prev* in a single statement using the comma operator, you could use this code:

```
temp_swap = prev, prev = curr, curr = temp_swap;
```

The Increment and Decrement Operators

Assignment expressions are not the only expressions that can change the value of a variable. Two other operators also have that ability.

The *increment* operator adds 1 to the value of a variable. Increment is written as a pair of pluses (+ +) before or after the variable name, with no spaces between. It is a unary operator, meaning that it acts on only a single operand. The action of the increment operator depends upon whether it is applied to its operand as a prefix or as a postfix:

```
++posit;                         /* increment operator as a prefix  */
posit++;                         /* increment operator as a postfix */
```

Both statements achieve the same result: The new value of the variable *posit* is equal to its old value plus 1. But if you use increment as a prefix, the variable is incremented before its value is used in the surrounding expression. If you use it as a postfix, the increment occurs after the variable being incremented is used and before the next sequence-guarantee point. Here are a couple of examples:

```
count = 1;
flag = count++;                     /* equivalent to flag = 1, count = 2; */
flag = ++count;                     /* equivalent to count = 3, flag = 3; */
```

The *decrement* operator is used to subtract 1 from its operand. The syntax and behavior of the decrement operator, a pair of minuses ($--$), are the same as for the increment operator.

Increment and decrement both assign back into their operands, which means that their operands must be *lvalues* or your compiler will reward you with an error message:

```
--(qty * 3);                        /* Will produce error message:           */
                                    /* ERROR: LVALUE REQUIRED, WILL NOT COMPILE */
```

Use of the variable being incremented or decremented a second time in the same expression, before a sequence guarantee, creates ambiguous code that will behave differently in different environments, so don't do it! For example, the following two statements could set *junk* to 1 or 3, depending upon whether or not *bad* is incremented before the second *bad* is multiplied by 2.

```
bad = 0;
junk = ++bad + 2 * bad;
```

One-Dimensional Arrays

An array is a variable that holds one or more values in ordered sequence. These values are called *elements,* and they must all have the same data type. To declare a variable as an array, you supply an integer-constant array dimension in square brackets (*[]*) after the name of the variable. You may not declare an array's dimension with an expression containing a variable: Only constant expressions are permitted. Arrays can be multidimensional and of any type (we'll discuss those later), but for now we'll stick with simple one-dimensional arrays.

Let's look at the 30-element array of *short* integers named *orders* and the 81-byte *char* array named *buf.* They're represented diagrammatically like this:

```
short orders[30];
```

orders[0]	orders[1]		orders[29]

```
char buf[81];
```

buf[0]	buf[1]	buf[2]	buf[3]		buf[79]	buf[80]

You'll notice that the *index* (the subscript in the square brackets) of the first element of the array is always 0, not 1 (arrays are referred to as *zero-origin*), so the index of the last element of an array is one less than the declared dimension of the array.

If you forget that the index of the first element of an array is zero, you may fall victim to a class of errors called "off by one." Not using the zeroth element of an array is harmless (and can sometimes even yield more efficient code because it eliminates repeated addition and subtraction of 1 to compensate for the zero origin), but if you try to use an element beyond the declared dimension of the array, you risk a nasty bug—one that will not be reported to you by the compiler or even be evident during execution. Since your programs are not blocked from accessing nonexistent array elements, no error message is produced, but other types of program errors usually result. Checking for indexes that exceed array bounds is an option provided by many languages, but it is not present in C at this time (for efficiency reasons), which is unfortunate, because it would be nice run-time protection to have in the C debugging environment.

The subscript operator (*[]*) is used to access a single element of an array. All array accesses in C must be element by element; no C operator will examine or change more than a single element of an array at a time in any statement. A loop is usually set up when you need to operate on all elements of an array. (However, you can call library functions like *strcpy()* and *strncpy()* to copy arrays using a single statement.)

As you can see from the following examples, you may use the subscript operator for array accessing on either side of an assignment operator, and you may use any kind of integral expression as the index:

```
curr_order_count = orders[order_num];
orders[order_num] = 0;
first_char = buf[0];                       /* The ZEROth element is first. */
last_char = buf[80];                 /* The index of the last element is */
                                     /*    the array dimension minus 1.    */
```

This next array assignment statement is a candidate for the *= shorthand operator:

```
ar[5 * x - y * y] = ar[5 * x - y * y] * 4;
```

The subscript *[5 * x − y * y]* is evaluated twice here, but the following shorthand assignment evaluates the array subscript only once, with exactly the same results:

```
ar[5 * x - y * y] *= 4;
```

The increment and decrement operators are also very useful in array operations. This next example demonstrates how the position of the increment operator affects evaluation of the index:

```
pos = 1;
arr[pos++] = 11;              /* equivalent to arr[1] = 11, pos = 2; */
arr[++pos] = 33;              /* equivalent to pos = 3, arr[3] = 33; */
```

Buffers and Strings

The dimension of an array is used to reserve storage for the values of its elements. Your code often will use only some of the elements from the beginning of an array, so you'll need a way to keep track of how many data elements have actually been used. There are two groups of utility functions in the standard library to help you with this task for character arrays. Let's look at each of them separately.

One option is to designate a special element value, such as zero, to mark the end of the data elements in an array. The one-dimensional character array called a string uses a null character ('\0') to mark the end of its data. (Of course, this means that the string itself can never contain a null character.)

The other option is to use the character-array buffer, which will hold as many of any character (including the null) as you like. However, you must store the length of your buffer in a separate variable, whose data type is usually *short* or *long*. The length of the buffer should never exceed the dimension of the array.

C gives the programmer control over which of these options is used with character arrays. Buffer-oriented library functions are quicker because they don't have to keep checking for null characters. But if you use buffers for faster data access, you increase memory requirements, because you must store a length for each buffer. If you use strings, you have a more standard, portable set of library functions to work with, and there is no need to clutter up your program with a bunch of string-length variables, but program execution may be a little slower.

As I've already mentioned, by C convention the null character is used to mark the end of the contents of a string: That is, a string is a *null-terminated array* of characters. (The value of the null character is numerically zero.) The following example builds a null-terminated string named *text* and uses the *%s* format to display it:

```
main()
{
    char text[3];                    /* Declare 3-element char array.       */

    text[0] = 'h';                   /* Single quotes make a char constant. */
    text[1] = 'i';                   /* 2nd character has element index 1.  */
    text[2] = '\0';                  /* Null character ends text string.    */
    printf("%s\n", text);            /* Show each character before the null. */
}
```

This program outputs just one word:

```
hi
```

Since C has no operators that can act on whole strings, the compiler provides library functions instead. All library string functions expect, and depend upon, the presence of a null character to mark the end of each string. The string *hi* in the preceding example could have been copied to the string variable *text* and then changed to *higher* by using the library

string copy and concatenation function calls (all Microsoft C standard
library string functions have names that begin with *str*):

```
char text[81];

    /* ... */
strcpy(text, "hi");                     /* Copy 'h', 'i', '\0' to text.   */
strcat(text, "gher");                   /* Add 'g', 'h', 'e', 'r' to text. */
                                        /* Now text equals "higher".      */
```

Obviously, this is quicker and easier than assigning each element in *text*,
as we did in the first example.

Library *buffer* functions treat the null character just like any other
character, but they require that buffer lengths be passed as additional arguments. For example, this call to the library buffer function *memcpy* copies
6 bytes from the 7-byte string *"higher"* to *buf* (the buffer-oriented library
functions have names that begin with *mem*):

```
memcpy(buf, "higher", 6);
```

Now that you've learned some basic techniques for creating variables
and managing data in C, we can turn to the statements that control the flow
of execution in C programs. There is quite a bit to discuss, so we'll devote
a separate chapter to the subject.

The Flow of Control

Statements are normally executed in the order they are entered in the program, unless a control-flow statement causes execution to jump to a different location. Machine languages have just a few simple control-flow commands, but higher-level languages like C have more variety, to facilitate modular block-structured programming. Let's look at C's control-flow commands individually.

The if Statement

The *if* statement uses the value of a conditional expression to determine whether or not to execute another statement, or to choose which of two statements to execute. Here are the two forms of *if* syntax:

```
if (condition_expression)                        /* Is expression non-zero? */
    statement_1                              /* Then execute statement_1. */

if (condition_expression)                        /* Is expression non-zero? */
    statement_1                              /* Then execute statement_1. */
else                                  /* Otherwise execute else's statement_2. */
    statement_2
```

In the first example, *statement_1* is executed if *condition_expression* is non-zero; otherwise the program moves on to the next executable line of code. In the second example, *statement_1* is executed if the value of *condition_expression* is non-zero; otherwise the optional *statement_2* is executed.

Before we talk further about *if* statements, let's look at how condition expressions are evaluated.

Comparing Two Values

C has six relational operators (see Chapter 3, Figure 3-1) that return the result of a comparison test on their two operands:

SYMBOL	MEANING	SYMBOL	MEANING
==	Equal	>=	Greater than or equal
!=	Not equal	<	Less than
<=	Less than or equal	>	Greater than

If the condition tested for is true, then the integer *1* is the value of the relational expression; otherwise the value is *0*: *1* means true; *0* means false. Here are a few examples of relational expressions and their values:

EXPRESSION	VALUE OF EXPRESSION
3 == 5	*0*
2 != −3	*1*
1.32 <= 1.31	*0*
'A' < 'Z'	*1*

The relational operators are useful only for comparing scalar (non-array) values or single elements of an array. Two of the standard library's string functions, which we'll discuss in a moment, may be called to compare arrays of characters.

Logical Operators and Expressions

C's three logical operators are used to combine true and false values, such as those from relational expressions. The result of any logical operation will be either *1* for true or *0* for false. C's logical operators are:

OPERATOR	NAME	EXAMPLE	RESULT
&&	Logical *AND*	*p && q*	*1* if both *p* and *q* are non-zero, else *0*
||	Logical *OR*	*p || q*	*1* if either *p* or *q* is non-zero, else *0*
!	Logical *NOT*	*!p*	*0* if *p* is non-zero, else *1*

The *&&* and *||* operators also possess two special features:

> ▶ Left-to-right sequence guarantee and sequence point.

> ▶ Short circuit: Second operand not evaluated unless needed.

Left-to-right sequence guarantee means that the left operand is always evaluated before the right operand. The order of evaluation can be important with operands that call functions or have side effects applied to them. (Side effects are changes an operator causes to the value of a variable. The *assignment, increment,* and *decrement* operators produce side effects.) Most operators don't have a sequence guarantee. For example, the next statement adds the return values from functions *func_1* and *func_2*; however, we can't rely upon which function might be called first.

```
sum = func_1(num) + func_2(num);                    /* no sequence guarantee */
```

The fact that the *&&* and *||* operators are sequence points simply means that all outstanding side effects will be applied to the first operand before the second is evaluated. In other words, the side effects are completed *before* the operation is executed. Let's look at an example. The next code segment tests for a newline at the end of the string *text* and increments *full_lines* if the character is found:

```
if (text[pos++] == '\n' && text[pos] == '\0')
    ++full_lines;
```

The *&&* sequence point guarantees that the *pos++* increment in the first expression will happen *before text[pos]* is compared with the '*\0*' in the second expression.

The *&&* and *||* operators have an interesting and very useful conditional aspect, as you can see from the following segment:

```
if (elem_count < array_dim && array[elem_count] > 0)
    ++positives;
```

If the first expression, *elem_count < array_dim,* is false (*0*), then the second expression, *array[elem_count] > 0,* is not evaluated! This is the short-circuit feature. It's very practical and efficient, because if the value of the first expression in a logical *AND* condition is *0,* the result of the entire

expression must be *0*, regardless of the value of the second expression. The
|| (logical *OR*) operator short-circuits if its first operand is *non*-zero, because
the result of the entire expression will have to be *1*, regardless of the value
of the second operand.

Comparing Two Strings

The library functions *strcmp()* and *strncmp()* are used to compare all
or parts of two strings:

FUNCTION	ACTION
strcmp(s1, s2)	Compares two strings and returns *0* if strings *s1* and *s2* are equal; >0 if *s1* $>$ *s2*; <0 if *s1* $<$ *s2*.
strncmp(s1, s2, n)	Compares up to *n* characters of two strings and returns same values as *strcmp()*.

In the following example, the strings *curr_name* and *prev_name* are
compared; if they are equal, a message is printed.

```
char curr_name[40], prev_name[40];

/* ... */
if (0 == strcmp(curr_name, prev_name))
    printf("Current and previous equal.\n");
```

In the next example, the third, fourth, and fifth characters of the
string *part_id* are compared with *"BAA"* to see whether they are higher in
the ASCII coding sequence. If they are greater than or equal to *"BAA"*, a
message is printed.

```
char part_id[20];                                    /* part number */

if (strncmp(&part_id[2], "BAA", 3) >= 0)
    printf("3rd, 4th, and 5th characters in part_id >= BAA.\n");
```

Notice the unary *address-of* operator (&) used before *part_id[2]*
in the *if* statement. The library string functions *strcmp()* and *strncmp()*
(among others) expect two *arrays* of characters to be passed. But passing
an array argument does not transfer the entire array to the called function;
it transfers only the memory address of the first byte of the array. Used as
an argument to a function, or within another expression, the name of an

array is therefore equivalent to the address of its zeroth element (more on this in Chapter 15). For example, the address of the first character of a string named *part_id* could be expressed in two ways:

```
&part_id[0]                                    /* Avoid this method. */
part_id                             /* This is the preferred method. */
```

To pass the address of the third character of *part_id* as an argument, you would use:

```
&part_id[2]              /* Remember: part_id[0] is the first character. */
```

The combination of relational operators and library functions should give you plenty of comparison tools to work with, but if they still aren't enough to do what you have in mind, you can always write your own specialized functions.

Compound Statements as Blocks

To control execution of a set of statements using an *if* or other control-flow statement, you must surround the set with a pair of curly braces (*{}*). We call such a set of one or more statements surrounded by curly braces a *compound statement.* A compound statement is, for purposes of syntax, considered a single statement. No semicolon is needed to end a compound statement, since the closing curly brace (*}*) does that job, as in this next example:

```
if (condition)                              /* Is condition non-zero? */
    {
    statement_1;                 /* Yes. Execute statements 1 and 2. */
    statement_2;
    }
else
    {
    statement_3;                  /* No. Execute statements 3 and 4. */
    statement_4;
    }
```

The value of this syntax will become very apparent in this next section, where we look at controlled statements that are themselves control-flow statements.

Nesting and Chaining

One of the powerful aspects of C syntax is that it allows for statements within statements. The *if* and optional *else*, together with the statements they control, actually form a single statement. But either of the statements controlled by *if...else* may also be an *if...else* statement. When an *if...else* statement is controlled by a surrounding *if...else* statement, like the one here, it is known as a *nested if* statement:

```
if (expression_1)                       /* Style rule:                    */
    {                                   /*    Surround nested if with {} to */
    if (expression_2)                   /*    prevent accidental mismatch of */
        statement_1;                    /*    an else with the wrong if.    */
    else
        statement_2;
    }
else
    statement_3;
```

If *expression_1* is zero, *statement_3* is executed and not *statement_1* or *statement_2*. If *expression_1* is non-zero and *expression_2* is non-zero, then *statement_1* is executed and not *statement_2* or *statement_3*. If *expression_1* is non-zero and *expression_2* is zero, then *statement_2* is executed and not *statement_1* or *statement_3*.

The *else if* construct is used to choose one of a set of actions based on conditions that are tested in a given order (hence the term *chaining*). The *else if* is not actually a new statement; it's merely a construct that bends the indenting rules in order to resemble the *case* statement found in some other programming languages (the *switch* statement is C's *case* construct).

```
/* Case-like if statement */        /* Equivalent else-if construct */

if (expression_1)                    if (expression_1)
    statement_1;                         statement_1;
else                                 else if (expression_2)
    {                                    statement_2;
    if (expression_2)                else if (expression_3)
        statement_2;                     statement_3;
    else                             else
        {                                statement_4;
        if (expression_3)
            statement_3;
        else
            statement_4;
        }
    }
```

Loop Statements

The *if* statements we've been discussing are used to conditionally execute one or more statements just once. But what if you want one or more statements to be conditionally executed over and over, as long as a condition expression remains non-zero? Let's take a look at how C handles such *loops.*

The while Statement

Loop statements are used to execute a statement repeatedly as long as a condition expression, known as the *loop test,* is non-zero. The statement that is executed repeatedly is called the *loop body.* The loop body may be a simple or compound statement or the null statement, about which you will learn more shortly. Here is the syntax of the *while* loop statement:

```
/* The while loop:  If the condition_expression test is */
/*   non-zero, then execute body_statement and repeat.  */

while (condition_expression)
   body_statement;
```

The *while* statement tests the condition at the top of the loop before executing the body of the loop. If the *while* test is non-zero, then the body is executed once and the test is repeated. If the test is non-zero again, then the body is executed once more and the test is repeated. This process continues until the test expression evaluates as zero, in which case the loop terminates and the statement following the end of the loop is executed.

We've seen how the function *scanf( )* can be used to input long integers (Chapter 2), but so far we've ignored the return from *scanf( )*, which is the count of the pieces of data successfully input according to the format specifiers in the format string. Now let's see how we can make use of that return value in a program that acts like an adding machine: It accepts as input as many long integers as you care to supply, and outputs their total.

```
/* Adding machine: This program will input and add long integers. */

#include <stdio.h>

main()
   {
   long number, total = 0;

   printf("Enter numbers to add, or q to quit.\n#: ");
   while (1 == scanf("%D", &number))
      {
      total += number;
      printf("#: ");
      }
   printf("Total: %ld\n", total);
   }
```

The interaction produced if you use this program to add *123* and *987* looks like this:

```
Enter numbers to add, or q to quit.
#: 123
#: 987
#: q
Total: 1110
```

The *while* loop makes its test (in this case, on the value *scanf()* returns) before each execution of the loop body, but suppose you want to make the test *after* execution of the body. Let's see how this can be done.

The do...while Statement

The *do...while* loop test is made *after* the body is executed, at the *bottom* of the loop, so a *do...while* loop will always execute at least once. Here is the syntax of the *do...while* loop:

```
/* The do...while loop:  Execute loop body. If the  */
/*    condition_expression is non-zero, then repeat. */

do
   body_statement;
while (condition_expression);    /* Caution: Don't forget the semicolon here. */
```

Let's see how we can modify our adding-machine program to use the *do...while* construct.

```
/* Adding machine, using do...while. */

#include <stdio.h>

main()
   {
   long number, total = 0;
   int more = 1;                                  /* Initialize true/false flag. */

   printf("Enter numbers to add, or q to quit.\n");
   do
      {
      printf("#: ");
      if (1 == scanf("%D", &number))
         total += number;
      else
         more = 0;
      }
   while (more);
   printf("Total: %ld\n", total);
   }
```

(The *do...while* loop test, *(more)*, could also have been written as
(more == 1) or *(more != 0)*, with no change in the program's behavior.)

Both the *while* and the *do...while* loops are simple combinations
of a loop test and a loop body. However, there is one other type of loop,
the *for* loop, that has additional components.

The for Statement

The *for* loop is used to count from a starting value to an ending value,
or until some condition becomes false. To accomplish this, the *for* loop has
two features not found in the *while* loop: an *initializing expression* and a
step expression.

```
for (init_expression; test_expression; step_expression)
   body_statement;
```

The *for* initializing expression is evaluated once and only once, as the
first action of the loop. The loop test is made at the top of the loop *after* the
initializing expression is evaluated. If the test is non-zero, the loop body is
executed and then the step expression is evaluated. (Even though initialization has already been performed, if the test fails on the first pass through
the *for* loop, the body is not executed and control passes out of the loop.)

The second and all subsequent iterations of the *for* loop repeat the
pattern: test, body, step. The loop terminates when the test is zero. Like the
while loop, the *for* loop guarantees that the condition was non-zero immediately before each execution of the loop body. This next example shows a

for loop that counts from 1 to 3 and prints the value of *loop_counter* (the body of the loop):

```
main()
  {
  short loop_counter;                                    /* Declare counter. */

  /* Count from 1 to 3. */
  for (loop_counter = 1; loop_counter <= 3; ++loop_counter)
     printf("%d\n", loop_counter);
  printf("After loop, %d\n", loop_counter);
  }
```

Notice that *loop_counter*'s value after the loop is executed for the last time equals the first value that caused the loop test to fail, so *four* lines are output by the segment above:

```
1
2
3
After loop, 4
```

Which loop statement is right for a given job? Well, the choice is really pretty straightforward. The *for* loop is always preferable if the loop requires initialization, a step expression, or both. However, if neither is needed, use a *while* loop, unless the test must be made after the body of the loop, in which case use a *do...while* loop.

The Null Statement

The following code segment strips leading spaces off the character string named *text*. Notice that the body of the first *for* loop is a *null statement,* created by the semicolon indented alone on the line following the *for* expressions: That is, the semicolon creates an empty statement that serves as the loop body. This construct is useful when all the conditional work is really done by the test and step portions of the loop.

```
/* Loop until a nonspace character (may be null) is found. */

for (last_space = 0; text[last_space] == ' '; ++last_space)
   ;                                       /* null statement for loop body */

/* strlen() returns the index of text's null character. */
len_text = strlen(text);                   /* Get string length of text. */

/* Loop: move characters back to replace leading spaces. Notice the use */
/*    of the comma operator to perform two initializations and two step  */
/*    expressions in each loop.                                       */
for (from_pos = last_space, to_pos = 0;    /* loop initializer */
   from_pos <= len_text;                   /* loop test */
   ++from_pos, ++to_pos)                   /* loop step */
      text[to_pos] = text[from_pos];       /* loop body */
text[to_pos] = '\0';                       /* new end of string for text */
```

Actually, all three expressions that follow the keyword *for* are optional, but if they are omitted, the semicolons are still required as placeholders. For example, the next code segment has a *for* loop with no initializing expression. It inputs a number to start from and then counts down to zero.

```
main()
   {
   short count_down;

   printf("Enter number to count down from: ");
   scanf("%hd", &count_down);
   for (; count_down >= 0; --count_down)                    /* no initializer */
      printf("%d\n", count_down);
   }
```

If you were to enter *4* at the prompt, the output from this segment would look like this:

```
Enter number to count down from: 4
4
3
2
1
0
```

The switch Statement

The *switch* statement is used to transfer program control to a labeled *case* statement within the compound statement that follows it. The C *switch* statement behaves much like the *case* statements other languages use: It lets you choose among an arbitrary number of actions on the basis of the value of an integer expression that is matched against the *case label constants.* (No two case label constants may have the same value in a *switch.*) If no label is equal to the *switch* expression, program control is transferred to the *default:* label, if one has been supplied. Otherwise, control passes to the next executable C statement after the body of the *switch.*

The *switch* statement is executed starting from the matching label and continuing until control is explicitly transferred out of the *switch* by the *break* statement, which causes the program to jump to the first statement after the body of the *switch*. Without an intervening *break* statement, control simply flows into the *case* following the one that matched successfully.

```
/* Prompt for command; then call appropriate function to do it. */

main()
    {
    short command;
    int rtn;

    do                                                /* Loop until quit command given. */
        {
        printf("CUSTOMER DATA MANAGEMENT MENU\n\n");
        printf("1. List\n2. Add\n3. Change\n4. Quit\n\t#: ");
        rtn = scanf("%hd", &command);
        if (rtn == 0)
            command = 0;                                            /* unknown command */
        else if (rtn != 1)                                      /* End of file reached. */
            command = 4;                                                      /* Quit. */
        switch (command)
            {                                          /* Begin switch statement body. */
            case 1:                                                             /* List. */
                list_cust();                               /* Call list_cust function. */
                break;                      /* Don't allow add_cust call after list. */
            case 2:                                                              /* Add. */
                add_cust();
                break;
            case 3:                                                         /* Change. */
                change_cust();
                break;
            case 4:                                                            /* Quit. */
                break;                               /* Do nothing in this case. */
            default:                              /* Bad command; ring bell. */
                printf("Unknown command: %d\7\n", command);
                break;                      /* Here to prevent problems if new cases */
                                            /*    are added later.                  */
            }                                   /* end switch statement body */
        }                                      /* end do...while loop body */
    while (command != 4);                       /* Repeat if not quitting time. */
    }                                           /* end of main() function */
```

(In order to compile this program successfully, the functions *list_cust, add_cust,* and *change_cust* must also have been written. The writing and calling of other functions is covered in Chapter 5.)

The *switch* statement is more efficient than the equivalent *else if* construct, but the *else if* construct is more flexible and cannot always be replaced by a *switch*. For example, if tests must be made in a specific order or if two expressions containing variables must be compared, then *else if* is required.

Common Control-Flow Blunders

The syntax of control-flow statements is easy to learn, but the bugs described in this next section are just as easy to create. We're going to look at several examples of incorrect code. *Please don't imitate them* in programs you write. Just learn to recognize and avoid them. Each code segment has at least one thing wrong with it. The text following the segment explains what is wrong, but try to figure it out for yourself before you read the explanation: You'll find you learn more that way.

The following code segment produces only the single line of output *loop_counter = 6*. Why?

```
for (loop_counter = 1; loop_counter <= 5; ++loop_counter);
    printf("Loop counter = %d\n");
```

Only one line is output because the call to *printf()* is not *inside* the body of the loop. The loop body thus becomes the null statement created by the misplaced semicolon at the end of the first line of code. That semicolon is the mistake.

How many times will the following loop body be executed? What criticisms (if any) can you make about this piece of code?

```
short a[100];
short p;
long t;

for (t = p = 0; p <= 100; ++p)
    t += a[p];
```

This loop executes 101 times, which causes the statement

```
t += a[100];
```

to be executed once, since the last time the loop body is executed, the variable *p* equals 100. Unfortunately, *a[99]* is the last element of the array *a*. *Off by one!* In addition, the variable names used in this segment are too short and lack meaning, making the code difficult to understand, and the elements of the array have never been assigned values, so the total is meaningless anyhow. (Since the total is never displayed, maybe that's not really a problem in this particular case.)

The next segment of code will not compile. It will cause a fatal error. Why?

```
if (curr_val > max_val)
    max_val = curr_val;
    total += curr_val;
else if (curr_val < min_val)
    small_tot += min_val;
```

Here the *if* was intended to control the two statements that follow it. The curly braces that should surround the pair of statements to make them a compound statement are missing. This blunder creates what we call a *dangling else*, which will make the compiler very unhappy. The code should correctly read:

```
if (curr_val > max_val)
    {
    max_val = curr_val;
    total += curr_val;
    }
else if (curr_val < min_val)
    small_tot += min_val;
```

This next goof is a subtle one, and it has caught most C programmers at least once, just as it's going to catch you someday, so watch out for

```
if (array_index = last_element)
    printf("At last element.\n");
```

The mistake is that the single = assignment operator was used where the double == equality operator was intended. As the segment stands, *array_index* is assigned the value of *last_element,* and as long as that value is non-zero, the *if* condition will be considered true and *printf()* will be called.

C compilers ignore indenting: They skip over comments and white space as if they weren't there. So incorrect indenting can fool *you* but not the compiler, as in the next example. This segment of code will subtract *qty_on_order* from *qty_on_hand* whenever the stock of the item is less than the quantity on order and the item isn't backordered, rather than only when *qty_on_hand* is greater than or equal to *qty_on_order*:

```
/* Line 1 */     if (qty_on_hand < qty_on_order)
/* Line 2 */         if (qty_back_ordered > 0)
/* Line 3 */             printf("HELP!!!");
/* Line 4 */     else
/* Line 5 */         qty_on_hand -= qty_on_order;
```

Faulty indenting makes the *else* on line 4 appear to match the *if* on line 1. But the rule is that, when an *else* is used, it matches the *closest* preceding un-*else*d *if* statement, which in this case is on line 2. A style rule that requires use of braces around all nested *if*s can prevent this problem.

```
if (qty_on_hand < qty_on_order)
   {                                            /* Protect nested if. */
   if (qty_back_ordered > 0)
      printf("HELP!!!");
   }                                            /* Mark end of nested if. */
else
   qty_on_hand -= qty_on_order;
```

This next piece of code prints *Got one!* no matter what the value of *num*. Can you see why?

```
if (num == 1 || 18 || 37)
   printf("Got one!\n");
```

The *if* test in this example is equivalent to *((num == 1) || 18 || 37)*. Obviously, something is wrong with the use of the logical *OR* (||) operator. The correct code reads:

```
if (num == 1 || num == 18 || num == 37)
   printf("Got one!\n");
```

Statements to Handle with Care

We know that the flow of control through a function should generally be from top to bottom, down the page of a listing, and that C's *if, switch,* and loop statements provide neat mechanisms for altering this flow of control without letting things get too out of hand. But C also has three less benign statements that alter control flow: *break, continue,* and *goto.* Abuse of these three statements leads to programs that are difficult to read, write, or modify, so be very, very cautious with them.

The *goto* statement is Enemy #1 and should simply never be used. A few *goto*s sprinkled around can turn a readable program into a bowl of spaghetti. Those *goto*s that jump to earlier lines create hidden loops: Replace them with one of C's loop statements. And *goto*s that jump to later lines can generally be replaced by *if*s or *switch*es. If after all I've said you still want to learn more about the syntax of *goto, goto* your manual...!

The *continue* statement is Enemy #2. It is used to jump to the end of the loop body and begin the next iteration. This amounts to conditionally executing the rest of the loop body after the *continue* statement. The readable way to accomplish conditional execution of a set of statements at the end of a loop body is to make them into a compound statement (using {}), and then control the block with an *if* statement.

```
/* Avoid using continue. */         /* Use an if instead. */
while (more_to_do)                   while (more_to_do)
   {                                    {
   ...statements                        ...statements
   if (expression)                      if (!expression)
      continue;                            {
   ...statements                           ...statements
   }                                        }
                                        }
```

Enemy #3 is two-faced. You've seen the friendly side of *break* used when coding a *switch* statement: It causes the program to jump to the statement following the end of the innermost surrounding *while, for, do...while,* or *switch* statement. But sometimes *break* isn't the best way to accomplish what you want. Look at this example:

```
/* Avoid using break. */            /* Use an if instead.          */
while (more_to_do)                   while (more_to_do)
   {                                    {
   ...statements                        ...statements
   if (expression)                      if (!expression)   /* Use ! */
      break;                               {
   ...statements                           ...statements
   }                                        }
                                        else
                                           more_to_do = NO;
                                        }
```

Does the use of break on the left side look more readable at first glance? It certainly may. However, if each set of statements contains 15 lines, then *break* becomes hidden and the fact that the second group of statements is executed only if *expression* is non-zero is hard to see.

Now that you have a pretty thorough understanding of C statements and data handling, let's start pulling it all together into functions. In the next chapter, we'll talk about the structure and management of functions and the techniques for joining functions to form complete programs.

5

Functions: The Backbone of C

A function is an independent set of statements executed to perform a specific task. All C programs are built from functions: a *main()* function, the functions that *main()* calls, and the functions that these functions call. As we discussed in Chapter 1, the philosophy underlying all C programming is that you can speed program development and reduce maintenance by building large programs from smaller, self-contained functions, each of which does a single job well.

Your program can include functions you write, compiler library functions called by your code, and library functions called by other library functions. It's important to plan your functions as useful building blocks. Make their purposes simple and clear, so you can concentrate on how to combine them to do a job, without worrying about the details of how each performs its specific task.

This chapter is about the control-flow and data-management aspects of a function's personality, and (briefly) about the compilation and linking processes that take functions from source form to executable program.

Functions and Control Flow

To call a function, just use its name followed by a pair of parentheses, as in this call to the Microsoft library function *abort()*, which terminates program execution:

```
abort();
```

You may call a function from as many other functions as you like. The function call may be followed by a semicolon, making it an executable statement, or the call may be part of a larger expression that expects the called function to return some value. Let's look first at functions that don't return a value, so you can become familiar with the syntax and appearance of functions in general.

When a function is called, control transfers to the beginning of the function's body and statements are executed one by one from that point until the program encounters a return statement or the closing brace of the called function. Control then returns to the calling function, which resumes execution with the next command after the subfunction call. Here is a simple example of a *main()* function with a single subfunction named *subf()*:

```
main()
  {
  printf("Begin main.\n");
  subf();                                  /* Call function subf(). */
  printf("End main.\n);
  }
subf()                                     /* Define function subf(). */
  {
  printf("Function subf() called.\n");
  }
```

and here is the output they produce by calling the library function *printf()*:

```
Begin main.
Function subf() called.
End main.
```

Function bodies may not be nested. The closing curly brace of one function *must* precede the beginning brace of the function that follows it. For example, in the preceding program, the body of *subf()* was not defined until after *main()* was closed with a *}*.

The order of functions in a source file makes no difference to C, but it can make a difference to the programmer hunting through a printed listing to find a particular function. One practical approach to organizing functions in your source file is to put the high-level functions first, followed by the low-level functions. Or you may prefer to arrange the functions alphabetically by name, especially if there are many of them. A comment section at the start of your program with the names of all functions contained in the source file is also helpful.

Functions and Data

There are several paths through which data can flow between functions in C programs:

▶ The calling function can pass argument values to the called function.

▶ The called function can return a single value to the calling function.

▶ Functions can share a single copy of variables that have been properly declared.

Variables declared within a function are known only within that function, so you may use the variable names from one function again in another function without any fear of conflict between variables with the same name. (Some exceptions do exist, such as the variables of shared data-storage classes mentioned earlier, but we'll look at those in Chapter 7.)

Function Arguments

The arguments passed from a calling function supply data and option information to the called function. The parentheses after the function name contain these arguments, which are simply a list of expressions separated by commas. This next statement calls *printf()* and passes it four arguments:

```
printf("%d * %d = %d\n", var, num, var * num);
```

Copies of the values of the arguments are passed to the parameter variables declared in the code for the function being called. The value of the first argument is passed to the first parameter, the second argument to the second parameter, and so on.

Most functions expect a specific number of arguments, each of a specific type. In response to ANSI's *Proposed C Standard,* several C compilers now use the source code's function declarations to verify that the correct numbers and types of arguments are being passed in function calls. This feature is a great help to programmers in catching argument-passing bugs before they can create problems during program execution.

Returning Data from a Function

A function that returns a value is called by using its name, followed by parentheses, within a larger expression. (You'll recall that we used the function name followed by parentheses and a semicolon to call functions that do *not* return a value. Some languages refer to these latter as subroutines and those that do return a value as functions, but in C *both* are called functions.)

Every function except *main()* has the option of executing a return statement followed by an expression. The return expression's value is sent back to the calling function by the same reference that called the subfunction: That is, only one call is needed to accomplish both data transfers. The two functions in the following program, *main()* and *avg_3_ints()*, let you see both sides of this return-value mechanism. (Notice the space after the reserved word *return*. We'll discuss this style rule in Chapter 9.)

```
/* Obtain an int return value: the average of three integers. */

main()
    {

    /* Pass avg_3_ints return value as an argument to printf(). */
    printf("Average of 13, 22, 31 = %d\n", avg_3_ints(13, 22, 31));
    }

/* avg_3_ints returns the average of the 3 integers passed. */
int avg_3_ints(int_one, int_two, int_three)    /* Define function avg_3_ints. */
int int_one, int_two, int_three;                    /* Declare parameter types. */

    {
    return ((int_one + int_two + int_three) / 3);
    }
```

The program's single line of output reads:

```
Average of 13, 22, 31 = 22
```

The data type of a function's return value is known as the *return type* of the function. To call a function that returns data of any type other than *int,* the calling function must explicitly declare the return type in order to be sure of obtaining the return value correctly. The following statement, which we'll use in a program later in this chapter, declares the return type of the function *avg_3_longs* to be *double*:

```
double avg_3_longs();
```

You can use arguments to return more than one value to the calling function, but you'll need to understand pointers to write such functions. We'll go into this in detail in Chapter 15.

Defining Functions

The first line of a function is called the *function definition* because it defines the return type and the parameter names. Good style dictates that you *always* specify the return type in a function definition. For functions that do not return a value, just use *void* as the return type, to indicate that no value is being returned.

In the following example, the function *avg_3_longs*, listed minus its body, is defined to return type *double*. The function's second line declares the parameter types, in this case all *long:* This must be done before the function's opening curly brace.

```
double avg_3_longs(long_one, long_two, long_three)
long long_one, long_two, long_three;

{
/* ... */
}
```

Coding Calling and Called Functions

In the following program, the subfunction *avg_3_longs()* declared in the *main()* function expects to receive three *long* arguments, and returns a *double* value that is the average of the three arguments:

```
/* Prompt for 3 long integer numbers and print their average. */

main()
{
    double avg_3_longs(long, long, long);        /* Declare subfunction. */
    long first, second, third;            /* Declare numbers prompted for. */
    double average;                       /* Declare average of the numbers. */

    printf("Enter 3 numbers: ");

    /* Check scanf() return value for 3 good numbers. */
    if (3 != scanf("%ld %ld %ld", &first, &second, &third))
        printf("\nBad input data\7\n");
    else                                  /* Input data are OK, so proceed. */
        {
        average = avg_3_longs(first, second, third);            /* Call. */
        printf("\nThe average of %ld, %ld, and %ld is %f.\n",
            first, second, third, average);
        }
}                                         /* end of the main() function */
```

(continued)

```
/******************************************************************************/
/*  avg_3_longs() is a function that returns type double.                     */
/*  The three parameters, all type long, are numbers to be averaged by        */
/*  totaling them and dividing by 3.0.                                        */
/******************************************************************************/
double avg_3_longs(long_one, long_two, long_three)

/* Parameters MUST be declared BEFORE the function's starting {, as follows: */
long long_one, long_two, long_three;              /* Declare 3 longs to average. */

    {

    /* Non-parameter variables MUST be declared AFTER the function's */
    /*    starting {, as follows:                                    */
    double average;                               /* Holds computed average to return. */

    average = ((long_one + long_two + long_three) / 3.0);
    return (average);                             /* Return value to caller. */
    }
```

A typical interaction with this program would work like this:

```
Enter 3 numbers:    11 22 33
The average of 11, 22, and 33 is 22.000000.
```

But if the user entered bad or incomplete data, the results would look like this instead:

```
Enter 3 numbers:    11 twenty two 33
Bad input data
```

You'll notice that we needed two statements within *main()* to correctly call our subfunction *avg_3_longs*. The first declared the return type to be *double* and the parameters to be three *long* integers. The second actually called *avg_3_longs* and saved the return value in *average*:

```
double avg_3_longs(long, long, long);

    /* ... */
average = avg_3_longs(first, second, third);
```

Function declarations do not always need to describe all parameters. Let's take a look at two that don't:

```
short func_one(short, , short);
long func_two(double, );
```

In the first declaration, the pair of commas indicates that no type checking is to be performed on the second argument to *func_one*. The declaration of *func_two*'s parameter types ends with a comma, which means that the first parameter is type *double,* but no type checking is to be performed for any subsequent arguments.

	COMMAND		PURPOSE
	`A>MSC CMD.C;`		Compile *cmd.c*.
FIGURE 5-1	`A>MSC SUB.C;`		Compile *sub.c*.
	`A>LINK CMD + SUB;`		Link object modules.
Typical C	`A>CMD`		Execute program.
compilation/	`A>EDLIN SUB.C`		Modify *sub.c* based on results.
modification	`A>MSC SUB.C;`		Recompile *sub.c*.
sequence	`A>LINK CMD + SUB;`		Link modified object modules.
	`A>CMD`		Execute modified program.

Joining Functions to Form Programs

As I mentioned at the beginning of this chapter, C builds programs by combining functions that perform specific tasks. These functions need not even reside in the same source file. The factors you'll need to consider when deciding how to organize functions into source files are discussed in detail in Section II.

For now, let's suppose that our program consists of two source files, *cmd.c* and *sub.c,* each containing several functions. These two files are created with a text editor and compiled separately. Then the object files generated by the compiler are joined by the linker. The sequence shown in Figure 5-1 demonstrates the use of the compiler commands and the *EDLIN* editor to compile, execute, modify, and recompile our program. Notice that *cmd.c* was not recompiled, because it was not modified.

The linker searches all available libraries for functions you call. If it can't find the called function in either the object files you specify or the libraries it was told to search, it will return a fatal error message stating that an undefined symbol named *_function name* was found.

A library is simply a special file that holds a collection of functions in compiled (object) form. It is a good place to collect the utility functions shared by the members of a team working on the same application, or basic functions that will be used company-wide in a variety of applications. The *LIB* command allows you to construct new libraries as needed, or add new functions to existing libraries.

You now know enough C to write lots of basic C applications code, but there are still some technical points we need to cover before you'll be ready to develop an effective interactive business application. I'll present these in Section II.

Section II discusses C programs as data: ways programs can store and access data both within and outside themselves. Chapter 6 teaches you how to use the compiler's preprocessor commands to help make your programs more portable and easier to maintain. Chapter 7 looks at the storage classes a variable may have, and their effects on its lifetime, scope, and behavior. Chapter 8 deals with accessing data outside your program—data in the command line and in environment variables controlled by the operating system—and with filter programs that can be chained together using pipes. Chapter 9 summarizes coding styles and standards for C programs.

SECTION II

The C Preprocessor

6

The C preprocessor is a program with its own command language. It is used to expand C programs into full code before compilation. The preprocessor allows programmers to write C source code that is readable, portable, easily modified, and terse. We'll see how in a minute.

The C preprocessor is actually a text-processing program, separate from the C language. It is invoked as the first pass the compiler makes through your source code. The preprocessor takes text files (either source programs or straight text) as its input and produces an expanded text file as its output. It has commands that allow the programmer to include outside files, substitute text, expand macros, and conditionally exclude lines of text.

Preprocessor Syntax

Preprocessor syntax is well standardized among the numerous C compilers. Microsoft's C compiler also incorporates some ANSI enhancements that increase the readability and usefulness of its preprocessor commands by making them more closely resemble C control-flow statements.

All preprocessor commands begin with a pound sign (#), followed by a lowercase name. Only one command may appear on a line (as with C statements, the backslash indicates statements that are continued on the following line).

Preprocessor Debugging

In order to debug your source code or view the effects of pre-processing, you will need to halt compilation after the preprocessing pass and capture the output.

Let's suppose you want to examine the preprocessor's effect on the file *ordentry.c*. You would just use the following form of the compilation command to instruct the preprocessor to save its output in the file *ordentry.i*:

```
MSC ORDENTRY.C /P /C;
```

The */P* option instructs the compiler to save the results of preprocessing in a file with the same base name as the source file, with the *.i* extension instead of *.c*. The */C* option causes the compiler to preserve program comments in the output (they are normally stripped out).

The #define Command

The *#define* command is used to cause all uses of an identifier in the C source code to be replaced by text defined in the preprocessor. The syntax is *#define IDENTIFIER definition_text*. The definition text may be an expression, a part of a statement, or one or more complete statements.

It is always preferable to use defined constants in C source code, in place of ordinary constants or variables whose values never change. The use of *#defined* symbols can increase readabilty, portability, and ease of maintenance. You don't need to include the expanded code every time a defined symbol is used, and you can change all occurrences of the defined symbol in the entire program with just one change at the preprocessor level. In addition, carefully chosen identifier names add to the clarity of your code by reflecting the purpose of each defined constant.

The *#define* command is followed by the name being defined and the text that is to replace it. This is direct text-for-text replacement; no expression evaluation takes place. For clarity, good C programming style dictates

> **C A U T I O N**
>
> *The preprocessor does not replace #defined symbols within quotes, in character constants, or included as part of a longer name.*

the use of uppercase for defined symbols and lowercase for variable names. The command below defines *NMONTHS* to be the number *36*:

```
#define NMONTHS 36
```

(Read as "pound define NMONTHS as 36.") This definition replaces all subsequent uses of the symbol *NMONTHS* in the input program with *36*. The following examples will make this clearer. If these lines are input to the preprocessor,

```
#define NMONTHS 36
#define L_CUST_NAME 30

    /* ... */
long sales_history[NMONTHS];
char cust_name[L_CUST_NAME + 1];

    /* ... */
for (month = 0; month < NMONTHS; ++month)
    total_sales += sales_history[month];
```

this output will be generated:

```
long sales_history[36];
char cust_name[30 + 1];

for (month = 0; month < 36; ++month)
    total_sales += sales_history[month];
```

The use of *#defined* symbols makes this code easy to read, and only the line *#define NMONTHS 36* needs to be modified to change the number of months of sales history totaled everywhere in the input program. The loop in the example will continue to execute for all months specified, without further modification.

C O M M E N T

Notice the numeral 1 added to the length of the string cust_name. *This is to make room for the terminal null character, so that the full 30 characters can be used for the name.*

This next example clearly demonstrates the value of *#defined* constants in creating more self-documenting source code:

```
#define MAX_CREDIT 249999

if (order_amt > MAX_CREDIT)                          /* more readable */
    /* ... */
if (order_amt > 249999)                  /* less readable and less clear */
    /* ... */
```

Obviously this is a help to you in writing the program now, but it will be an even greater help to the programmer maintaining the system months or years down the line.

Definitions with #defined Symbols

The preprocessor makes a single pass through its input file, but individual lines are repeated until all *#define*d symbols are fully expanded. This may take several passes through the line, since a definition may itself contain other *#define*d symbols. For example, if both *MIDSCREEN* and *SCRNLEN* are *#define*d, with *MIDSCREEN* *#define*d as half of *SCRNLEN*'s value, it will take the preprocessor at least two passes to expand every statement that uses *MIDSCREEN*.

```
#define SCRNLEN 24               /* Note use of defined symbol SCRNLEN */
#define MIDSCREEN (SCRNLEN / 2)  /*   in definition of MIDSCREEN.      */
```

Definitions to Avoid

There are some types of definitions that look just fine but can get you into real trouble, so here are a few DON'Ts:

▶ Avoid circular definitions in which the symbol being *#define*d appears in its own definition. In the following example, the symbol *INFINITY* expands endlessly, and at the very least will tie the preprocessor in knots:

```
#define INFINITY (INFINITY + 1)                 /* Becomes: var = */
var = INFINITY;              /* ...(((INFINITY + 1) + 1) + 1)... */
```

▶ Omit definitions that don't add clarity. They force the reader to look elsewhere to learn the meaning of the symbol. For example, the following definition doesn't tell us a thing:

```
#define TWELVE 12                                /* Yes, I know. */
```

▶ Along the same lines, avoid confusing definitions. You may know that the following definition means that all 12-month contracts carry 14-percent interest, but anyone else reading your code would be very confused indeed:

```
#define TWELVE 14                           /* That's news to me. */
```

▶ Avoid using definitions that make a program no longer look like C. For instance, you have the ability to *#define BEGIN {* and *#define END }* and then use *BEGIN* and *END* in place of *{* and *}*. This is perfectly legal, but another C programmer would find it both confusing and pointless.

Macro Definitions

A macro is a *#define* command that substitutes arguments into the definition text. It is used like a function, to make one command execute many commands by passing outside arguments to internal parameters. But the preprocessor expands a macro in place, to actually become the code the macro represents. The overhead of calling and returning from a function is saved, but the tradeoff lies in the additional code generated by the preprocessor each time a macro is invoked in the source program.

The full macro syntax is *#define MAC_NAME(parameter_list) definition_text.* In the following example, the macro *AVG3* uses the functions *avg_3_ints()* and *avg_3_longs()* from the last chapter to compute the average of three values, *regardless of their data types,* a feat impossible with a function:

```
#define AVG3(a, b, c) (((a) + (b) + (c)) / 3)
```

This invocation of *AVG3* combines constants and variables of several data types:

```
result = AVG3(3.89, 23L * num, var);
```

When *AVG3* is expanded by the preprocessor, it will look like this:

```
result = (((3.89) + (23L * num) + (var)) / 3);
```

Macro definitions must be only a single line long; however, that line can be continued by ending it with a backslash (\). No spaces are allowed between the name of the macro and the opening parenthesis that follows. For both style and safety, enclose the entire definition and every use of a macro parameter in the definition text in a pair of parentheses. This will help you avoid the precedence problems that can occur when the macro is invoked as part of a larger expression. Use ONLY uppercase for macro names, to avoid confusing them with functions, whose names are in lowercase.

Macros and functions.   In C, a macro has some important differences from a function that performs the same job:

▶ A macro is generic and will accept different data types for arguments, unlike functions, which are less flexible. For instance, the *AVG3* macro can take arguments that are *char, short, long, float,* or *double.*

▶ Macros execute faster than their equivalent functions, because function-call and return processing is not required.

▶ Macros are more difficult to debug than functions. In fact, they should be written first as functions, debugged, and then converted to macros.

▶ A macro can contain many statements, but if you use a 10-statement macro 100 times, you will add 1000 statements to your program. If you call a 10-statement function 100 times, your program gains only 110 statements.

▶ Macros, unlike functions, must be passed exactly the number of arguments they expect. Beware of side effects on macro arguments, and don't call a function as an argument in order to use the function's return value. The reason is simple: The side effect or function may execute twice and create problems.

Types of macros.   Macros fall into three categories, based on the nature of their expansion: expression macros, statement macros, and block macros. The type of macro determines the context in which it may appear. For instance, an expression macro may be called many times in a statement, but a statement macro may not be used as part of an expression because statements have no value.

Here's an example of the kind of situation where a statement macro *is* very useful:

```
#define ADD_SAFE(a, b, sum, errfn)       \
    {                                      \
    sum = (a) + (b);                       \
    if ((a) > 0 && (b) > 0 && sum <= 0)    \
        errfn(a, b);                       \
    else if ((a) < 0 && (b) < 0 && sum >= 0) \
        errfn(a, b);                       \
    }
```

The *ADD_SAFE* macro provides a safer form of integer addition than the + operator, because *ADD_SAFE* checks for overflow, whereas ordinary addition does not. If overflow is detected, the program calls the *errfn()* function, whose name you pass as an argument.

<table>
<tr><td>C   O   M   M   E   N   T</td></tr>
</table>

Where you have a choice, use expression macros rather than statement macros, because expression macros have a value and can be used like functions that return a value.

If a macro expands into one or more statements, as in the preceding example, it is wise to enclose it in a pair of curly braces ({}). This forces the macro to be a single (though perhaps compound) statement and thus prevents the nesting problems that may arise if the macro is invoked as the body of a loop or as the target of an *if* statement.

The use of macros and ordinary *#define*s can save repeated typing of frequently used code segments or expressions, as you can see from this next example using the *AVG3* macro *#define*d earlier:

```
#define PRN(name, val) printf("The value of %s is %d.\n", name, val)
PRN("income average", AVG3(income, yr1_inc, yr2_inc));
```

The #if Compilation Command

Conditional compilation commands can be used to control C source and preprocessor commands. The conditional commands cause selected source lines to be compiled or skipped over, depending upon the value or existence of a *#define*d symbol or macro.

The *#if* command controls the lines of C source and preprocessor command text between itself and the associated *#endif* command, like this:

```
#if restricted_constant_expression
    /* ...text to be conditionally compiled... */
#endif
```

If the *restricted_constant_expression* after *#if* is non-zero, the lines after the *#if* command are preserved for compilation; otherwise they are ignored and the preprocessor continues with the line following the *#endif*.

A *restricted constant expression* is a special type of constant expression. It may contain any constants (except *enum* constants), combined by operators (except *sizeof, cast, comma,* and *assignment*) to form an expression that is evaluated at compilation. The restricted constant expression may also contain the expression *defined(IDENTIFIER),* which is evaluated as true if the *IDENTIFIER* has been *#defin*ed as a constant or macro. For example, these three lines will cause *draw (10, 20, 30, 40);* to be compiled only if the symbol *GRAPHICS* is already *#defin*ed:

```
#if defined(GRAPHICS)
   draw(10, 20, 30, 40);
#endif
```

I've already mentioned that you can disable, rather than delete, lines of C code and preprocessor commands that have been entered in a program but are not yet fully functional, so that they will be ignored while you debug another section of the code. Unfortunately, the comment delimiters /* and */ will not comment out code that itself contains comments, because the first */ the preprocessor encounters will be regarded as the end of the comment and everything after it will be treated as potentially executable code. But *#if* offers an easy solution to the problem: Just use *#if 0* to ensure that the surrounded lines will not be compiled.

```
#if 0
   /* ...lines the compiler will forever ignore... */
#endif
```

Among the preprocessor commands that would need to be ignored in certain situations are *MSC's* memory-related keywords *near, far,* and *huge.* These keywords are valuable because their use in declarations allows C programs to take advantage of all installed memory on a PC, rather than just the 64K bytes of program and 64K bytes of data allowed by many earlier compilers. However, they are *not* standard and therefore may have to be removed in order to use certain C compilers that run on 32-bit systems, especially systems with virtual-memory capability. You can use the following command sequence to globally disable these keywords, replacing them with empty strings (provided the name *BIGMEMORY* is already *#defin*ed):

```
#if defined(BIGMEMORY)
   #define near
   #define far
   #define huge
#endif
```

Chaining and Nesting

You may frequently find yourself in a situation where several alternatives must be considered before a routine is executed. This can be handled by chaining or nesting *#if* statments to cover all required conditions.

The following example of chaining preserves one of the four sets of C command lines (source or preprocessor) and skips over the other three:

```
#if restricted_constant_expression
    /* ...lines of C source or preprocessor commands... */
#elif restricted_constant_expression
    /* ...lines of C source or preprocessor commands... */
#elif restricted_constant_expression
    /* ...lines of C source or preprocessor commands... */
#else
    /* ...lines of C source or preprocessor commands... */
#endif
```

The lines preserved are the ones following the first *#if* or *#elif* whose restricted constant expression is non-zero (and therefore true). The preprocessor's *#elif* command behaves like C's *else if* construct. Should all tests fail, the lines after the optional *#else* at the end are picked for output.

Each *#if* in a nest or chain construct must be paired with an *#endif,* *#elif,* or *#else* to mark the end of its range of control. Like C's *else if* construct, the *#elif* is optional, and may be repeated as many times as you like. If used, the optional *#else* must follow the last *#elif* command and must itself be followed by *#endif.*

The following code for an application designed to run in three different environments is a good example of nesting syntax:

```
/* Prepare to display a message for the user to read. */

#if defined(GRAPHICS)
    #if defined(HIGHRES)            /* Is display high resolution? */
        grmove(88, 90);            /* Move high-resolution cursor. */
    #else                      /* If not, it must be medium resolution. */
        grmove(44, 90);            /* Move medium-resolution cursor. */
    #endif                      /* NOTE: grmove is not in a library. */
#elif defined(CRT)           /* If not GRAPHICS, then must be text. */
    CUR_MV(8, 30);                  /* Move screen text cursor. */
#else                        /* This must be a hardcopy terminal */
    printf("\n\n");              /*    (no cursor), so skip two lines. */
#endif
```

Embedded Test Drivers and Debugging Code

It is important to save embedded test drivers and debugging code.
Test-driver code demonstrates correct calls to the function being tested, as
well as the proper return value, given the arguments being passed. You
should retain the driver in the source file with the function it verifies, and
when you add new function capabilities, you should also add the appropriate new tests to the driver.

The easiest way to save test drivers and debugging code is to conditionally compile them. The following example compiles *linelen()*'s test
driver if the symbol *DBGMAIN* is defined. You can define *DBGMAIN* (or any
identifier) either by using the */D* switch plus the identifier name (with no
space between) in the *MSC* compile command, as we do here, or by using
a separate *#define* command.

```
/* TO COMPILE FOR DEBUG:  MSC LINELEN.C /DDEBUG /DDBGMAIN; */
/******************************************************************************/
/* linelen() is the line-length function. It returns the number of        */
/* characters before '\n' in the line, or -1 if '\0' is found before '\n'. */
/******************************************************************************/

int linelen(line)
char line[];                                        /* the string to be processed */

    {
    short len;

    for (len = 0; line[len] != '\0' && line[len] != '\n'; ++len)

#if defined(DEBUG)
        printf("\nDEBUG: line[%d] = %c (hex: %x)\n",
            len, line[len], line[len]);                 /* DEBUG output */
#else
        ;                                               /* no DEBUG; a null loop body */
#endif
    return (line[len] == '\n' ? len : -1);   /* Returns -1 if '\0' before '\n'.*/
    }

#if defined(DBGMAIN)
    #define TESTFOR(cond, msg) if (!(cond)) \
    printf("\7\n***TEST FAILED: %s\n", (msg))

    /******************************************************************************/
    /* Test driver to test the linelen() function.                              */
    /******************************************************************************/

    main()
        {
        TESTFOR(linelen("12\n") == 2, "linelen #1");
        TESTFOR(linelen("\n") == 0, "linelen #2");
        TESTFOR(linelen("") == -1, "linelen #3");
        printf("linelen tests complete\n");
        }
#endif
```

In the previous example, the tests were compiled with both *DBGMAIN* and *DEBUG* defined (*DEBUG* controls the debugging output from the *printf()* function), producing this output:

```
DEBUG: line[0] = 1 (hex: 31)
DEBUG: line[1] = 2 (hex: 32)
linelen tests complete
```

New ANSI Command Syntax

The *#ifdef* (if defined) and *#ifndef* (if not defined) commands with which some of you may be familiar have been rendered semi-obsolete by the new ANSI *#if defined(ID)* syntax you saw in some of the preceding examples. Both the old and the new forms of the *defined* command are followed by the names of identifiers and both will compile code after them if *ID* is *#define*d as a macro or a symbol:

```
#if defined(ID)   ←→   #ifdef ID
```

The advantage of *#if defined(ID)* is that it permits the use of the new *#elif* command to make an *else if* construct. Before this ANSI modification, the processing of alternatives always involved sometimes-messy sets of nested *#if*s.

The old *#ifndef* command has not been replaced and has no new syntax. Even though we can now use the *#elif* construct to take care of most alternatives, *#ifndef* still has a definite place in our preprocessor vocabulary. For instance, some C compilers, including Microsoft's, give a diagnostic message if you *#define* a symbol that is already *#define*d. You can get around this by using the preprocessor's *#ifndef* command to test for the existence of a prior definition:

```
#ifndef YES
    #define YES 1
    #define NO 0
#endif
```

Undefining Variables

Some preprocessors require that a symbol be undefined before it can be defined with a new value. The *#undef* command accomplishes this by removing the existing definition of the symbol. This command sequence checks to see whether *ENDSTEPS* is already defined, undefines it if necessary, and then redefines it with the new value *5*:

```
#if defined(ENDSTEPS)
    #undef ENDSTEPS
#endif

#define ENDSTEPS 5
```

Header Files

Definitions included in a special source file called a header file can be used by C functions in many different source files. This means that you won't have to duplicate common definitions in every file in an application. Some header files, such as *stdio.h* and *ctype.h,* come with your compiler, as part of the standard library. (For good style, header-file names should end with the *.h* extension.) Others may be associated with a corporate or project library. Or you may want to develop your own. More on all that later. First, let's learn how to use these files to simplify C programming.

The #include Command

The preprocessor's *#include* command makes the contents of a header file available to C source files by simply replacing each *#include* command in a source program with the contents of the header file it names.

For good style, *#include* commands should be placed at the beginning of the C source file, after the initial comments describing the file, but before the first function.

There are two forms of syntax for the *#include* command. Your choice depends upon where the *#include*d file is to be searched for. (If the path is complete and unambiguous, then no search is needed and the forms are equivalent.)

COMMAND	ACTION
#include "pathname"	Searches current directory first, then standard places if needed.
#include <pathname>	Searches standard places only.

Use the $<\ldots>$ form for header files that are to be used systemwide; they may be included from many directories to compile a wide variety of applications. Use the " " form for files that are intended only for a specific program or for personal use.

To create a path to the default directory or the "standard search places" for header files, use the MS-DOS *SET* command. For example, the following statement makes \ *INCLUDE* on drive B the directory where the compiler looks for header files:

```
SET INCLUDE = B:\INCLUDE
```

To override this setting, use the *MSC* command's */I pathname* switch, which causes the designated path name to be searched *before* the standard places. The following MSC command will search *A:\SPECDIR* for header files before searching *B:\INCLUDE*:

C A U T I O N

A #included file may itself contain other #include commands. Although such nesting of header files is legal, it is a questionable practice, since the danger of invisible changes in a hidden header file cannot be ignored.

```
MSC SPEC.C /I A:\SPECDIR
```

The *MSC /X* switch prevents the standard places from being searched at all.

Headers and Library Functions

Let's take a minute to clarify the difference between header files and library files, since some people confuse the two. A header file is a text file that contains C source and preprocessor commands to be compiled when the header file is *#included* in a C source file. A library file is an object file that contains a collection of already-compiled modules for frequently used functions. Libraries are searched by the linker for functions you call but did not write. Remember: Libraries are used by the linker; header files are used by the preprocessor.

To add to the confusion, most libraries also have associated header files to hold *#defines*, declarations of library-function parameter and return types, and related information needed by functions in the library. Let's look briefly at two of these.

```
/*static char *SCCSID = "@(#)stdio.h:1.4";*/
/*
 * stdio.h
 *
 * defines the structure used by the level 2 I/O ("standard I/O") routines
 * and some of the associated values and macros.
 *
 * Copyright (C) Microsoft Corporation, 1984
 */

#define  BUFSIZ   512
#define  _NFILE   20
#define  FILE     struct _iobuf
#define  EOF      (-1)

#ifdef M_I86LM
#define  NULL     0L
#else
#define  NULL     0
#endif

extern FILE {
     char *_ptr;
     int   _cnt;
     char *_base;
     char  _flag;
     char  _file;
     } _iob[_NFILE];

#define  stdin    (&_iob[0])
#define  stdout   (&_iob[1])
#define  stderr   (&_iob[2])

#define  _IOREAD   0x01
#define  _IOWRT    0x02
#define  _IONBF    0x04
#define  _IOMYBUF  0x08
#define  _IOEOF    0x10
#define  _IOERR    0x20
#define  _IOSTRG   0x40
#define  _IORW     0x80

#define  getc(f)    (--(f)->_cnt >= 0 ? 0xff & *(f)->_ptr++ : _filbuf(f))
#define  putc(c,f)  (--(f)->_cnt >= 0 ? 0xff & (*(f)->_ptr++ = (c)) : \
                     _flsbuf((c),(f)))

#define  getchar()  getc(stdin)
#define  putchar(c) putc((c),stdout)
```

(continued)

FIGURE 6-1 | *The* stdio.h *header file included with the*
              Microsoft C compiler

The *stdio.h* and *ctype.h* header files.   The most frequently used library
header file is *stdio.h*, listed in its entirety in Figure 6-1. It contains definitions
needed for standard I/O functions that you call, such as single-character input
and output using the macros *getchar( )* and *putchar( )*.

```
#define  feof(f)       ((f)->_flag & _IOEOF)
#define  ferror(f)     ((f)->_flag & _IOERR)
#define  fileno(f)     ((f)->_file)

/* function declarations for those who want strong type checking
 * on arguments to library function calls
 */

#ifdef LINT_ARGS            /* arg. checking enabled */

void clearerr(FILE *);
int fclose(FILE *);
int fcloseall(void);
FILE *fdopen(int, char *);
int fflush(FILE *);
int fgetc(FILE *);
int fgetchar(void);
char *fgets(char *, int, FILE *);
int flushall(void);
FILE *fopen(char *, char *);
int fprintf(FILE *, char *, );
int fputc(int, FILE *);
int fputchar(int);
int fputs(char *, FILE *);
int fread(char *, int, int, FILE *);
FILE *freopen(char *, char *, FILE *);
int fscanf(FILE *, char *, );
int fseek(FILE *, long, int);
long ftell(FILE *);
int fwrite(char *, int, int, FILE *);
char *gets(char *);
int getw(FILE *);
int printf(char *, );
int puts(char *);
int putw(int, FILE *);
int rewind(FILE *);
int scanf(char *, );
void setbuf(FILE *, char *);
int sprintf(char *, char *, );
int sscanf(char *, char *, );
int ungetc(int, FILE *);

#else                       /* arg. checking disabled - declare return type */

extern FILE *fopen(), *freopen(), *fdopen();
extern long ftell();
extern char *gets(), *fgets();

#endif   /* LINT_ARGS */
```

FIGURE 6-1 | *The* stdio.h *header file included with the
Microsoft C compiler (continued)*

The *getchar()* macro returns the next character that is input as an
integer. The *#define*d symbol *EOF*, whose value is −1, is then compared
with *getchar()*'s returned character for end-of-file determination. The

putchar() macro prints whatever character is passed to it. Let's look at an example to see how this works:

```
/* Program to copy input to output, one character at a time. */
#include <stdio.h>                      /* Needed for getchar(), putchar(), EOF. */
main()
   {
   int char_input;                              /* character that was input, or EOF */
                          /* Copy all input characters to output, one by one. */
   while ((char_input = getchar()) != EOF)
      putchar(char_input);
   }
```

This little program copies each input character to output, until the end-of-file marker is reached.

The library header file *ctype.h* holds macros that determine the "type" of a character: upper/lowercase, printable, decimal digit, and so forth. (The names of these macros often begin with *is: isupper, isdigit,* and *isalpha.*)

Header files for applications.   We've just talked about the header files *stdio.h* and *ctype.h* as examples of frequently used standard-library header files. These library files provide you with a great deal of programming power, but you will still need to create your own header files for the specific applications you develop. For instance, the header files *stddefs.h, projutil.h,* and *ordentry.h* that I will refer to in later chapters do not come with your compiler. They are files I've created for use in application development. (You'll find the complete listings of these header files in Chapter 10.)

My header files all contain similar kinds of information, so why do I have three of them, instead of just one large one? That's easy: Because the contents of the files are grouped according to the scope of the data.

FILE NAME	CONTENTS
stddefs.h	Company-wide standard definitions and types used by nearly all programs
projutil.h	Project utility definitions used by programs that call functions in the project utility library
ordentry.h	Application-specific definitions used only for order-entry programs

What does and does not belong in your header files? Once again, this is really a question of good programming style. Header files should contain preprocessor commands, declarations of function parameter and return types, and some things we haven't discussed yet: structure definitions, *typedef* type-synonym statements, and external non-defining declarations.

Header files should *not* contain executable C statements, except in the form of preprocessor macros (therefore, header files should not generate object code when compiled). Nor, it follows, should they *#include* entire outside functions. Instead, compile the outside functions separately and then use the linker to join them once they are in object form. That way, if you have to modify one function, you won't need to recompile any un-modified functions along with it.

To Share or Not to Share

7

One of the first decisions you'll need to make when you design a C program is whether you want data in some variables to be available to more than one function. This requires an understanding of the way C handles such data.

When a variable is assigned a value in a BASIC program, the variable remains in existence from then on, and may be used by any subsequent portion of the program. In fact, the lifetime of *all* BASIC variables extends beyond execution of the BASIC program: That is, after the program has finished running, you can print the values of your variables as they were when the program ended—very handy for debugging.

FORTRAN, on the other hand, uses separately compiled routines, with each routine's variables isolated from those in other routines, regardless of name. The programmer must specifically define areas in memory called common blocks to hold data to be shared by *all* routines in a program. This is clearly an improvement over BASIC, since it permits the programmer to limit the number of places in a program that can access a given variable.

C, like FORTRAN, has storage classes that allow variables to be shared by several functions, but C gives even greater control over data because the programmer can declare variables to be shared by *some, but not all* functions in a program.

Since C has provided this added control, use it wisely: Don't make data more widely shared than necessary. If you make all variables global, C will be no more powerful in this respect than good old BASIC. And if a variable can be accessed even where it is not used, you will still have to examine that part

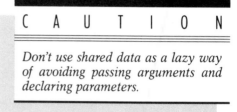

Don't use shared data as a lazy way of avoiding passing arguments and declaring parameters.

of the program for bugs if the variable's value becomes incorrect. So rather than make your C variables global, use arguments to functions to pass data, thereby restricting the data path to the calling and called functions.

Storage Class of a Variable

Storage class is a characteristic of all C variables. A variable's storage class is controlled by both the placement of its declaration in the program and the use of one, and only one, of the storage-class keywords shown in Figure 7-1.

The complete syntax for declaring a variable includes its storage class, data type, name, and optional initializer, followed by a semicolon:

```
static double rate = 0.15;
```

You will also see the storage-class terms *GLOBAL*, *SEMIGLOBAL*, and *IMPORT* *#define*d in the *stddefs.h* header file from our order-entry application (Chapter 10):

COMMAND	MEANING
#define GLOBAL	Define a global variable.
#define SEMIGLOBAL static	Define a semiglobal variable.
#define IMPORT extern	Refer to a semiglobal or global variable defined elsewhere.

These are not C terms. They are terms I have defined to make the storage class of a variable clearer than it would be from the normal reserved storage-class keywords. (The definition of *GLOBAL* in the preceding example is not an error. *GLOBAL* is defined there as an empty string: That is,

KEYWORD	DESCRIPTION
auto	Internal to function or block where declared
register	Like *auto*, but faster memory access
extern	Globally shared by all functions
static	Internal to function or block, or shared by some functions

FIGURE 7-1

C's storage classes and their scopes

the term *GLOBAL* is deleted wherever it is used. This has the same effect as defining all *GLOBAL* variables as *extern*.) We'll discuss these special classes in detail later in the chapter.

Scope of a Variable

The scope of a variable is the set of statements (functions or blocks) in which the variable's name may be used to obtain its value. For example, an *auto* variable declared within a block can be accessed only by statements within that block. (All variables you have seen declared so far have had the default storage class *auto*.) The storage for an *auto* variable declared in a *block* is allocated when the block is entered and released when the block is exited. The next time the block is entered, the variable will not "remember" its old value, because a different location may be allocated to it. This is exactly the same as the behavior of an *auto* variable declared at the start of a *function*. (If you refer to a variable outside its scope, you will get a compilation error.)

C O M M E N T

It is good programming style to use the most restricted scope possible for each of your variables.

Resolution of Name Conflicts

A name conflict can arise if two variables have the same name and overlapping scopes. The variable the program will reference where a name conflict occurs is the one with the more restrictive scope. For example, if a block-scope variable appears in a function with a function-scope variable of the same name, the program will reference the block-scope variable during execution of the block.

You'll see a potential name conflict for the variable *overlap* in the next example. The *overlap* variable is declared as type *char* in the *main()* function, except within the block, where it is declared as an array with 10,000 elements of type *short*. The *overlap* variable the program references in the block is the array of type *short*, because the block scope is narrower than the function scope:

```
main()
   {
   char overlap = 'A';

   /* ... */
   overlap = 'Z';
      {                                       /* Begin block and begin scope overlap. */
      short overlap[10000];

      overlap[0] = 9;

      /* ... */
      printf("1: overlap[0] = %d\n", overlap[0]);
      }                                        /* End block and end scope overlap. */
   printf("2: overlap = %c\n", overlap);
   }
```

The output from the program will look like this:

```
1: overlap[0] = 9
2: overlap = Z
```

C   O   M   M   E   N   T

Well-written programs never use the same name for two different items of data.

This rule for scope-of-variable conflicts applies to data in all the storage classes we're about to look at. We'll begin with the most restrictive class (*auto*) and work our way out to the least restrictive (*GLOBAL*).

The auto Storage Class

The keyword *auto* is used to declare a variable as having *automatic* storage class. Automatic variables are temporary variables internal to a specific function or to a block within a function. They are temporary because their lifetime begins when the function or block is entered and ends when that function is exited or the end of the block is reached.

Because *auto* is the most frequently used storage class, it is the default class for variables declared within the body of a C function or block, as well as for a function's parameters. It is seldom specifically declared. For example, these two declarations inside a function or block are equivalent:

```
short item_num;
auto short item_num;
```

The storage reserved to hold the value of a variable for its lifetime is said to be *allocated* to that variable. Use of the *auto* storage class conserves memory because only the *auto* variables in the functions on the active calling stack need to have memory allocated to them. That is, if a second-level function is executing, only its own *auto* variables and those of the main function occupy memory; *auto* variables declared in other functions do not have memory allocated to them at this stage in the program's execution.

Initializing an auto Variable

All *auto* variables are allocated, and may be initialized, upon each entry to the declaring function or block. The value of an *auto* variable not explicitly initialized is undefined. This means that whatever value happens to already be stored in that memory location remains, which may produce problems during program execution.

Expressions used to initialize *auto* variables may include calls to functions that return values, as in this next example:

```
short max_len = strlen(ltoa(max_val, buf, 10));
short min_len = strlen(ltoa(min_val, buf, 10));
```

The initializers used here demonstrate the flexibility of *auto* variables: *max_len* and *min_len* are initialized to the number of digits in the *long* integers *max_val* and *min_val*, respectively, by converting the values of *max_val* and *min_val* to string form with the library function *ltoa* (*ltoa* converts *long* to ASCII) and then using the library function *strlen()* to return the length of the string.

Initializing variables unnecessarily is a waste of execution time and a source of confusion to the program reader. For example, in the segment

```
short cnt = 0;

for (cnt = 1; cnt <= max_cnt; ++cnt)
```

cnt = 0 is useless, because the zero is never used.

C forbids initialization of an *automatic array*. This rule follows naturally from the fact that C will not assign a value to more than a single element during assignment or initialization. For example, *char msg[8] = "illegal";* is an illegal statement within a function and won't compile. To assign values to the elements of an *auto* array, you must assign the values one at a time (in an initialization loop, for instance).

The static Storage Class

We've seen that lifetime is an important characteristic of a storage class. For *auto*, life begins when you enter the declaring function or block and ends when you leave it. But what if you want some variables to be available a little longer? Well, the *static* storage class has a much longer lifetime—in fact, the entire time the program is executing.

Once again we're faced with a trade-off, this time between longer lifetime and increased memory requirements. All *static* variables have memory allocated to them as long as the program is running, which means that there must be enough memory available to hold *all* the *static* data at one time.

The life of a *static* variable begins with initialization, which takes place only once during execution of the program, and ends when the program terminates. Its value is stored in the same location throughout the duration of the program.

The scope of a *static* identifier is the function or block in which it was declared. However, unlike *auto* data, *static* values are remembered when the scope is left and reentered, as long as program execution isn't terminated.

Initializing static Scalars and Arrays

Initialization of *static* data takes place once and only once, before execution of the *main()* function begins. All *static* variables not assigned a specific value, including *static* arrays, are initialized by default to zero.

Variables with *static* storage class may be initialized by *constant expressions only*; you cannot call functions or refer to other variables to initialize *static* scalars or arrays.

C O M M E N T

It is good style to explicitly initialize all static arrays and scalars.

To explicitly initialize a *static* array, you may supply a comma-separated list of constant expressions in curly braces, like this:

```
static short leap_yrs[5] = {1980, 1984, 1988, 1992, 1996};
```

Arrays of character data (strings) are initialized with text inside double quotes. A double-quoted string constant is equivalent to a constant array with one more element than the number of characters inside the double quotes. This additional element is the null character (\0), which marks the end of the array. Both of these next two declarations initialize a four-character array named *country* with the text *"USA"*:

```
static char country[4] = "USA";
static char country[4] = {'U', 'S', 'A', '\0'};
```

It is an error to supply *more* initializers than there are array elements, but if *fewer* initializers are supplied than the number of elements the array was declared to have, the compiler automatically initializes the remaining elements to zero:

```
/* Fills array with: 87346, 96437, 0L, 0L, 0L. */
/* Note: Our company is only two years old.    */
static long last_five_years_sales[5] = {87346, 96437};
```

It would be easy for someone reading a C program to miss the fact that some of the variables are initialized to zero if those initializers don't appear in the declaration. To initialize to zero with good style, be explicit:

```
static long expense_category_totals[12] = {0};
```

How to Not Count Characters

We all hate to count characters in the text of a message we want
to output, so here's a way to avoid it, at least some of the time. You can use
empty brackets (*[ ]*) in the declaration of a *static* array, with the dimension
omitted; the array's dimension will then be taken to be the number of initializers provided. In the following declaration, the dimension of *msg[ ]*
is automatically set to 24:

```
static char msg[] = "C counts my characters.";                    /* empty [] */
```

The SEMIGLOBAL Storage Class

The particular types of data we have looked at so far are called
internal because the scope is restricted to the body of a function or a block
within a function. But C also has storage classes that are less restrictive.
The first of these *external* classes we'll look at is called *external static*. This
class permits data to be shared among a few specified functions that are
part of a single program.

As I mentioned earlier, in order to make it easier to manage and
debug *external static* data in our order-entry application, I've defined two
more descriptive symbols to replace these reserved terms (see *stddefs.h*,
Chapter 10). The first, *SEMIGLOBAL,* is used to declare a variable as having
external static storage class (as opposed to internal) and is placed *outside*
any function body. The second, *IMPORT,* is used *within* a function to tell
the program to look outside the function for the variable's definition. The
two terms are used together (see also *GLOBAL*), as you'll see later in
this chapter.

```
#define SEMIGLOBAL static          /* Used to define a semiglobal variable. */
#define IMPORT extern              /* Used to refer to a semiglobal or global */
                                   /*    variable defined elsewhere.          */
```

Here are some examples of the types of *SEMIGLOBAL* declarations
used in the C order-entry application:

```
/* These declarations are outside of any function body. */

SEMIGLOBAL char company[L_COMPANY + 1] = "";
SEMIGLOBAL char is_resale[L_IS_RESALE + 1] = "n";
SEMIGLOBAL short ship_weights[MAX_ITEMS] = {0};
SEMIGLOBAL short tot_weight = 0;
SEMIGLOBAL char scrn_title[] = "*** ENTER NEW ORDER ***";
```

These are known as *defining declarations* because they cause storage to be allocated to hold the values of the shared data they declare. Defining declarations always appear outside the body of any function and, for good style, should have initializers. The scope of any variable declared outside a function is all of the source file that follows the defining declaration.

This ability to share data is a legitimate reason for grouping certain functions together in a single source file, where they will all be compiled together (their *internal* variables will still remain independent of each other). Otherwise, each function should be stored in a separately compiled source file.

The GLOBAL Storage Class

Most programming languages provide a global (fully shared) storage class of data known simply as *external* or *common* data. In C, this class is called *extern*. Data classified as *extern* are accessible to all functions in the entire program, so you would use this storage class for data needed by many functions in more than one source file.

You'll recall that in *stddefs.h*, I've simply used an empty string to define the term *GLOBAL* for use with *extern* data. Since defining declarations are placed outside any function, this has the effect of causing the storage class to default to *extern*.

A word of caution, however: Tracing the source of shared-data bugs is difficult in applications with large amounts of global data. With so many places to look, debugging can become prohibitively time-consuming. If possible, group functions that need to share data into one source file and use the *SEMIGLOBAL*, rather than the *GLOBAL*, storage class.

The defining declaration of a *GLOBAL* identifier may be accompanied by an initializer. As a matter of good style, every *extern* identifier should have one and only one defining declaration in the entire set of source files that will be compiled and linked to form a program. Here is the defining

declaration for *bell_ok,* the only item of *GLOBAL* data in our order-entry
application. Notice its position *before* the *main()* function in the source file.

```
/* Declare data shared among functions in all source files (GLOBAL). */
GLOBAL bflag bell_ok = YES;                          /* It's OK to ring bell. */
main()
   {
```

(The term *bflag* in this definition is a synonym data type from *stddefs.h.*
A *bflag* variable is a 1-byte flag designated to hold true/false data in the
form 1 or 0.)

Importing Outside Variables

It is good style to specifically *IMPORT* any outside (*GLOBAL* or
SEMIGLOBAL) shared data that a function accesses. We've already defined
the symbol *IMPORT* to be the keyword *extern,* so declarations that begin
with *IMPORT* clearly designate their variables as shared quantities, to be
imported from outside (and above) this function. Most compilers require
that every variable *IMPORT*ed into a function have a defining declaration
on the outside. (The Microsoft compiler is an exception: It will create a
defining declaration if none is found.)

The following declarations, called *referencing declarations,* are used
to access the shared data in the order-entry example from inside a hypo-
thetical function called *inp_sale():*

```
void inp_sale()
   {
   IMPORT bflag bell_ok;                             /* IMPORT a GLOBAL. */
   IMPORT char company[];                            /* IMPORT 5 SEMIGLOBALs. */
   IMPORT char is_resale[];
   IMPORT short ship_weights[];
   IMPORT short tot_weight;
   IMPORT char scrn_title[];

   short step;
   short ipart;
```

Let's examine this code segment in more detail. I've included a bit more than just the *IMPORT* declarations, in order to show you where the *IMPORT*s are placed: They should be the first declarations after the opening brace of the function, and are followed by the *internal* declarations, if any. Notice that *IMPORT*ed array declarations, like *static* array declarations, may use empty brackets (*[ ]*) rather than a specific dimension constant.

Referencing declarations are required in each function that needs to access external data, *unless* the function follows the defining declaration in the same source file. Referencing declarations appear inside the function, begin with the symbol *IMPORT* or the keyword *extern*, and do not have initializers. Use of empty brackets (*[ ]*) for the first dimension is again both permitted and recommended in the referencing declarations of external arrays.

C O M M E N T

Even where not required, good style dictates that you always use referencing declarations, since they document part of a function's external interface: that is, the way the function interacts with its environment.

```
void err_warn(first, second)
char first[], second[];                    /* two parts of diagnostic message */

    {
    IMPORT bflag bell_ok;                  /* referencing declaration */
    short first_len = strlen(first);
    short second_len = strlen(second);
```

External referencing declarations are also permitted outside a function in order to make an *external* identifier visible to all functions in the source file. This saves repeated typing, but at the cost of readability. This type of declaration is commonly (and acceptably) hidden away in one of the header files used to declare the parameter and return types of all functions in a library. The order-entry application's project-utility header file, *projutil.h*, is a good example of this approach. This file contains, among other things, the referencing declarations for our project-utility library functions. When the header file is *#include*d at the beginning of a source file, outside any function, all its return-type and parameter-type declarations become available throughout the source file. (This also allows the compiler to check calls to these functions.)

```
/* If IMPORT is not already #defined, do it now. */

#ifndef IMPORT
    #define IMPORT extern
#endif

    /* ... */
/* Declare project-utility function return and argument types.          */
/*   If your C compiler does not support the declaration of argument types, */
/*   supply empty () after function name, rather than the types listed here. */
/*   These declarations make it possible to call any of these functions from */
/*   anywhere within the source file after this header file (projutil.h)     */
/*   is #included. The call will be checked for the proper number and types  */
/*   of arguments and use of return values.                             */

IMPORT void beg_scrn(char[], char[], char[], char[]);
IMPORT stepcode prompt(char[], char[], short, short, flag, short, short);
IMPORT stepcode nprompt(long *, char[], long, long, flag, short, short);
IMPORT void tput(short, short, char[]);
IMPORT void ntput(short, short, long, short);
IMPORT flag match(char[], char[]);
IMPORT void err_warn(char[], char[]);
IMPORT void err_exit(char[], char[]);
IMPORT void strrjust(char[], short);
IMPORT void logentry(char[]);
```

Cartridge and Other ROM-Based Software

The following warning applies to only a small group of programmers: those who write C programs that will be ROM-based (for instance, cartridge software).

Ordinarily, when you ask the operating system to use a program, a copy of that program is loaded from disk into RAM and then executed. ROM-based software, however, executes directly from ROM; no loading takes

> **C A U T I O N**
>
> With *ROM-based software*, static *and* external *data won't be initialized.*

place. You'll recall that the *static* and *extern* initializers are applied at load-time; in this case we have no loading, hence no initialization. Therefore, initial *static* and *extern* values for a ROM-based application *must* be assigned explicitly in a non-declaration statement.

The register Storage Class

I've left the discussion of *register* storage until last because it's seldom used in interactive applications. Why so? Well, the explanation is really pretty straightforward. Shorter, faster machine-level instructions are used on data in registers, which reduces code size and improves the efficiency of the CPU in most environments. But the delays encountered in interactive processing are usually caused by the slowness of I/O, not by the CPU, so registers don't help much in these programs.

When *register* storage *is* used, what kinds of data should be placed in registers? Primarily, frequently accessed variables such as loop counters. Parameters may also be declared to have *register* storage class. For portability, use registers only with *char, short,* and *int* data, never with *long, float,* or *double.*

Microsoft's C compiler supports the *register* storage class, though many others do not at this time. Two registers are available per function or block, and additional register requests are legal. Registers are the same size as an *int* variable: either 2 or 4 bytes, depending upon the CPU chip.

How many *register* declarations are permitted in a function or block? As many as you like, because the compiler is free to ignore them. Requests for *register* storage are just that: "requests." You are not promised a register, and if denied a register, the declared variable automatically reverts to the *auto* storage class, with no change in results. And although C can use registers, it is unable to access a *specific* register that a system programmer might want to examine or set. In C, the compiler chooses which registers it will use. The only way around this is to write an assembler function to set the register.

In all other respects, the behavior of the *register* storage class is identical with that of the *auto* storage class: That is, initialization, scope, and lifetime are the same.

To declare a variable with *register* storage class, just begin the declaration with the keyword *register*:

```
register short loop_counter;          /* Variable loop_counter resides */
                                      /*    in a register.             */
```

Summary of Storage Classes

A variable is *allocated* when memory is obtained to hold its value and *freed* when that memory is returned to the system's control for other use. The *lifetime* of a variable is the period between these two events. There are two possible lifetimes for a variable:

FORM	ACTION
EACH	Allocates storage on entry to declaring block or function; frees storage on leaving block or function (value is lost).
ONCE	Allocates storage once, before execution; allocated storage location used for full life of the program.

A variable may be *initialized* when memory is allocated to it. Two forms of variable initialization are possible in C:

FORM	ACTION
EACH	Initializes on each entry to declaring function or block; scalars initialized to expressions; arrays not initialized.
ONCE	Initializes only once, before the program begins execution; scalars and arrays initialized to constants only.

The *scope* of a variable is the set of statements where the name of the variable may be used to obtain a value. Reference to a variable outside its scope is an error. C supports three levels of variable-name scope:

LEVEL	DESCRIPTION
INTERNAL	Name is known only in declaring function or block.
SEMIGLOBAL	Name is shared among functions following the declaration in the same source file.
GLOBAL	Name is shared among all functions in a program that *IMPORT* the name *or* that follow the defining declaration of the name in the same source file.

STORAGE CLASS	INITIALIZATION	ALLOCATION	SCOPE
auto	EACH	EACH	INTERNAL
register	EACH	EACH	INTERNAL
static (internal)	ONCE	ONCE	INTERNAL
static (external)	ONCE	ONCE	SEMIGLOBAL
extern	ONCE	ONCE	GLOBAL

FIGURE 7-2 | *Acceptable combinations of initialization, allocation, and scope*

Storage classes do not exist for all possible combinations of initialization, allocation, and scope characteristics. Figure 7-2 lists the acceptable storage classes.

The types of shared data used by an application influence how the functions in that application are organized into source files. We'll look at the development of source-file structure in Chapters 9 and 10, but first we need to learn how to access data *outside* C programs by using the operating-system command line and C's run-time support.

Data Outside the Program

8

So far we've spent quite a bit of time discussing how C handles the storage and sharing of data in the various components of a source program. But your C program can also access data from external sources: command-line and operating-system environment variables, and data stored in other files. Let's talk about each of these outside sources separately.

Environment Variables

Environment variables are strings created with the MS-DOS *SET* command or the library function *putenv()*. Environment data last through-out your session at the computer (or until specifically changed), because the data are owned by the operating system, not the program. To learn the value of an environment variable, call the library function *getenv()*, like this:

```
putenv("UNAME = GREG");              /* Assign GREG to environment variable UNAME. */
                                     /*    MS-DOS equivalent:  SET UNAME GREG       */
printf("UNAME = %s\n", getenv("UNAME"));      /* Display contents of UNAME. */
```

(The UNIX and XENIX operating systems also have environment vari-ables, but instead of calling *putenv()* to set variables in these systems, you access the environment data table directly.)

The Program Command Line

The command line (the line of text that commands the operating system to execute your program) is a source of high-level data for some programs. For instance, you can pass argument or option data to the *main()* function from the command line, and since the command-line interface to *main()* is implemented on nearly all C compilers, portability isn't an issue.

The syntax of the MS-DOS *DIR* command is a good illustration of the use of command-line interfaces. In fact, *DIR* could easily have been written in C:

```
DIR [<filespec>] [/W] [/P]
```
      File name   Options

Command name

As you can see from this example, three types of information can be included on a command line:

▶ The name of the file that holds the executable program. This must be the first word on the command line (MS-DOS lets you omit the *.exe* file-name extension).

▶ Command-line arguments. These optional strings of text are passed to your *main()* using the *array of pointers* data structure (see Chapter 15).

▶ Standard input/output redirections. These come last on the command line, and are also optional.

Command-Line Arguments

In a sense, command-line arguments are a unique storage class made up of read-only data. Text in the command line is separated into words, which are then grouped into a list to pass to *main()*, which is free to ignore these arguments if they aren't appropriate to the environment.

What kind of data are passed to *main()* in this manner? Well, command-line arguments are typically limited to file names or option strings (sometimes known as *flags* or *switches*), which often appear cryptic. Menus are a friendlier alternative to the command line: They *show* you the options you otherwise are forced to memorize. But menus are slower than the command-line interface, so experienced programmers seldom use them.

Standard Input/Output Redirection

The last entries on the command line are the standard file-redirection commands we discussed briefly in Chapter 2. Standard input data are normally obtained by waiting for the user to type at the keyboard. Standard output normally appears on the screen. The redirection commands permit a program to input data from another source, such as a disk or modem, and output data to a different destination, such as a printer or disk file. This ability to redirect program input and output without changing the program itself gives C a device-independent edge over many other languages.

C's standard library output functions will send output to *any* device. What device that is depends upon file-redirection instructions to a small piece of object code called the *C run-time header,* which is responsible for calling your *main()* function as a subfunction. The C run-time header opens three standard files for *main():*

NAME	DESCRIPTION
stdin	Standard input file, normally from the keyboard
stdout	Standard output file, normally to the screen
stderr	Standard error (output) file, normally to the screen

An interactive program reads from the standard input file to obtain data from the user and writes to the standard output (or standard error) file to display a message for the user. If you redirect the standard output of a program to a disk file, the redirected output will be saved in that file, but won't appear on the screen. The fact that the user will not see this redirected output as it is produced accounts for the standard error file: Data written to *stderr* will appear on the screen, even if *stdout* is redirected elsewhere, so that the user can see any error messages.

An interactive program becomes non-interactive when its standard *input* is redirected to a disk file. In that case, each time your program needs to input a line of text, it reads a line from the disk file. The advantage to this kind of redirection is that responses can be stored in advance and output can be saved for later viewing.

Filter Programs

Programs that get data from standard input, process the data, and
write the results to standard output are called filter programs. Command-
line redirection permits filter programs to be used in a variety of ways.

Let's use a practical example to demonstrate how the redirection
commands work. A filter program that creates line-numbered listings can
be very useful to C programmers, since the compiler's diagnostic messages
use line numbers to refer to objectionable lines in the source code. Here's
a short program, *listing.c*, that will produce such a numbered listing:

```
/*****************************************************************************/
/* Output a line-numbered program listing of the program read from          */
/* standard input to standard output.                                       */
/*****************************************************************************/

#include <stdio.h>

main()
    {
    char line[512];                          /* Holds one source line. */
    short line_number;                          /* Holds line count. */

    /* List next line of input until EOF reached, */
    /*    at which time gets() returns zero.       */
    for (line_number = 1; gets(line); ++line_number)
       printf("%3d %s\n", line_number, line);
    printf("\n\n\n\n\n\n");                    /* Skip some lines at end. */
    }
```

The interactive use of this listing program, without any redirections,
looks a little odd. When you execute the program, each line you type is
echoed back to you on the screen with a line number as a prefix, and you
must press ^Z (^D with some operating systems) alone on a line to signal
the end of the standard input file. (Calls to *gets()* after the end of standard
input return a zero, which causes the *for* loop to terminate.) Here is a
sample of the results of interactive use of our listing program without any
I/O redirection:

```
B>LISTING
first line of input
   1  first line of input
last line of input
   2  last line of input
^Z

B>
```

Seems rather pointless, doesn't it? (Actually, it's an easy way to give
listing a quick test.) The program becomes more useful, however, when file

redirections are applied. The source code for our listing program is saved in the file *listing.c*. Now suppose we use the < symbol to redirect standard input to be read from the file or device named:

```
B>LISTING < LISTING.C
```

This command produces our listing program from *listing.c* in the following format (no, the program didn't chop four spaces off each line; I did that so the output would fit the book's page width!):

```
 1 /**********************************************************************/
 2 /* Output a line-numbered program listing of the program read from    */
 3 /* standard input to standard output.                                 */
 4 /**********************************************************************/
 5
 6 #include <stdio.h>
 7
 8 main()
 9    {
10    char line[512];                              /* Holds one source line. */
11    short line_number;                             /* Holds line count. */
12
13    /* List next line of input until EOF reached, */
14    /*    at which time gets() returns zero.       */
15    for (line_number = 1; gets(line); ++line_number)
16        printf("%3d %s\n", line_number, line);
17    printf("\n\n\n\n\n\n");                       /* Skip some lines at end. */
18    }
```

The > sign redirects the program's standard output to the file or device named after the symbol. For example, this next command produces a numbered listing of the data in *listing.c* and stores the output in a file named *listing.lst*:

```
B>LISTING < LISTING.C > LISTING.LST
```

(Here's a trick to help you remember which symbol applies to input and which to output. Think of > and < as arrowheads that point toward or away from the command. The > points away from the command, so it controls the command's output. The < points toward the command, so it controls the command's input.)

The >> redirection command redirects standard output to the *end* of the file named after the symbol. There is no risk of losing data using >>, because new lines are simply appended after the last line of the existing file. (With both > and >>, the operating system automatically creates an empty file if the file to hold the output does not already exist.) To

C A U T I O N

Use > with great caution, because its first action is to delete all data in the file named after the symbol. Nothing will ruin your day faster than wiping out a valuable data file because you confused > with <!

line-number a series of files with *listing* and save the output from all of them in a single file named *c.lst,* you could use the following commands:

```
B>LISTING < BEG_SCRN.C > C.LST
B>LISTING < ERR_EXIT.C >> C.LST
B>LISTING < ERR_WARN.C >> C.LST
```

The >> guarantees that the second and third files will not overwrite the first when they are output.

Pipes That Join Commands

No, this isn't a plumbing class, but data *should* flow like water, so the analogy is instructive. The pipe redirection command is a single vertical bar (|) placed between two commands. It causes the standard output of the first command (on the left side) to be redirected and used as the input for the second command. For example, this MS-DOS command causes the output from the *DIR* command to be piped into *listing*:

```
DIR *.C | LISTING
```

The output from *listing* appears on your screen as a line-numbered directory of all files with the *.c* extension.

Pipes under the UNIX and XENIX operating systems execute both commands in parallel, passing the output from the first command to the second command immediately, as it is produced, whereas MS-DOS creates a temporary file for the output of the first command and then uses that file as standard input to the second command.

Standard Files in Interactive Applications

The names of our three standard files—input, output, and error—carry definite implications about how those files are intended to be used. But some programs, such as the order-entry application in Section III, use these files in ways that do not exactly follow the sense of their names. Let's see why this is so.

Interactive programs produce two kinds of output: prompt messages that ask for data to be entered by the user (output on the screen) and data received from the user to be saved for additional processing later. The problem is where to output the validated user entries. If all the program's output is written to the *stdout* file, then the validated user data will be mingled with screen-control characters and prompt messages.

One way to keep these two types of output separated is to write the validated data to disk, using a file other than the standard ones. We'll see how to do that in Section V. For now, just be aware that the disadvantage of this method is that you can no longer use standard file-redirection commands on those data.

A second and more satisfactory solution uses the standard error file (*stderr*) to output prompt messages, diagnostic messages, and screen-control commands (clear screen, move cursor, and the like), leaving the standard output file (*stdout*) free to be used for one purpose only: storage of the validated data resulting from program processing. This approach allows us to redirect application data without simultaneously redirecting display text.

In order to send output to the standard error file in this way, you will first need to *#include <stdio.h>* at the start of your source file, so that *stderr* will be available to every function in your file. Then use one of the following library functions to send output to *stderr*:

FUNCTION	EXAMPLE
`fprintf(stderr, format_string, arg_1, arg_2, ...);`	`fprintf(stderr, "Enter a number\ from %d to %d:", low, high);`
`fputs(data_string, stderr);`	`fputs("Enter customer name: ",stderr);`
`fputc(data_char, stderr);`	`fputc('\7', stderr);`

The first function in the example, *fprintf()*, behaves just like *printf()*, except that one new argument, the file variable *stderr*, must precede the rest. (We'll look at file variables more extensively in Section V.) The second function, *fputs()*, resembles the function *puts()* used to output a string to standard output. Unlike *puts()*, however, *fputs()* does not output a newline (\n) after the string. The third function, *fputc()*, is used to output a single character to *stderr*.

Well, that about winds up our quick tour of C basics. You now know enough C to begin analyzing the code for the order-entry application program, so let's quickly review the conventions for C coding style (Chapter 9), and then move on to the advanced topics I've been promising.

Coding Style and Standards

9

Before we actually begin working with the order-entry system that forms the heart of this book, we need to spend a few minutes discussing the style rules and standards that are so important in creating readable, maintainable C software.

Well-written, clearly structured code is always a pleasure to read. Poorly written code can be a headache, or worse. The following rules have become conventions in C programming, and blessed are they who adhere to them consistently.

Surround operators that take two operands with spaces.

Do not put a space between a unary operator and its operand.

Do not put a space between a function name and its opening parenthesis.

Put one space after reserved keywords.

Indent blocks uniformly, using the tab key rather than the spacebar.

Put braces alone on a line, indented in alignment with the block they create.

Code only one statement per line.

Skip a line after the last declaration.

When you plan the structural components of your program, keep in mind the following suggestions:

COMPONENT	STRUCTURE
Identifier names:	Be consistent: Use the same name for the same purpose throughout the program.
	Be meaningful: Choose a variable name that explains the meaning of the value, and avoid short names that only a cryptographer could decipher.
	Be accurate: Make sure the variable name is always truthful about the nature of the value.
Functions:	Make them tools that do only one job, but do it very well.
	Limit function bodies to one page (about 60 lines).
Comments:	Begin each source file and each function with a comment stating its purpose.
	Document all external interfaces with comments.
	Explain complex or tricky code segments with step-by-step comments.
	Include explanatory comments with each declaration, as needed.
goto statements:	Don't use them.

Source-File and Function Formats

Once you've designed the flow of data between functions, you need to decide how those functions should be organized to make the flow not just possible, but also easy to understand. The following "generic" example shows a typical organization for C source files. It is logical and readable, and helps make program development and maintenance easier.

```
/* BEGIN SOURCE FILE:   FILENAME.C */
/*****************************************************************************/
/* Comments describing functions and data in source file.                 */
/*****************************************************************************/

#include commands
#define commands

Structure and union tag declarations (described later)
Type synonym statements using typedef
GLOBAL (external) defining declarations (with initializers)
SEMIGLOBAL (external static) defining declarations (with initializers)

Functions
    Source files that contain no functions and hold only GLOBAL defining
    declarations are permitted.
```

As we've seen, C source files most often contain just a single function. This is preferred style. Place more than one function in a source file only when those functions share some *SEMIGLOBAL* (*external static*) data. Here is the recommended style for the layout of each function in a source file:

```
/*****************************************************************************/
/* Comments describing the function, its uses, and interfaces.               */
/*****************************************************************************/

return_type function_name(parameter list)
parameter declarations
    {
    IMPORT (extern) referencing declarations
    internal declarations

    function body statements
    }
```

The style rules presented in this chapter aren't just arbitrary. They're designed to make your life as a C programmer easier—just how *much* easier you'll see in the next chapter, where we begin analyzing the order-entry source listings.

Section III focuses on the actual development of our product: THE ORDER-ENTRY APPLICATION PROGRAM. The user interface is the heart of this highly interactive business application. Chapter 10 contains the application design and the source code for the program, with detailed comments explaining each function. Chapter 11 discusses the code used to manage the prompt screens that make up the user interface. Chapter 12 covers screen output, with emphasis on library and order-entry display functions, and Chapter 13 deals with strict but "friendly" control of user input.

SECTION III

The Order-Entry
Application Program

In this chapter, we will discuss the design for the Software Vendor Order-Entry Application, and then look at the complete source listings. This program is real: It does let you enter orders for software. The source files compile without any diagnostics at the default warning level (level 1; see the *MSC* command's /W option).

We'll discuss each of the application's functions and data structures in detail in the chapters following the listings (check the colored reference numbers beside each file). For now, let's concentrate on the system design and the organization of the files.

Application Design

Let me set the scene for the design and development of the order-entry application, which we are going to use in our own business, not market as part of our product line.

As software entrepreneurs, we are already aware of the deficiencies of running a business manually, with old-fashioned paper-and-pencil records, so naturally we want to automate right from the start. And as experienced software engineers, we know the value of early user involvement and feedback in the design process, so *before* we begin to design the application, we interview everyone who will be using the system, to obtain as much information as possible about their requirements and work styles. We come up with a list something like this:

USER	NEED(S)
System manager	Access control for system security.
	Maximum input controls, to minimize user problems.
	Error log to aid in system maintenance.
Sales personnel	No data-entry experience.
	Clear and uniform prompts, efficient defaults, and recognizable numeric displays.
	Input control and diagnostic messages.
	Ease of correction within fields, between fields, and between screens.
Warehouse personnel	Easy-to-read list of items and quantities to be shipped.
	Complete shipping information, including address, carrier, and shipping charges.
Accounting personnel	Complete billing address and telephone contact.
	Resale information.
	Appropriate tax rate, if not for resale.
	Customer's payment terms and credit limit.
Company accountant	Record of sales, by item, for profit-loss analysis.
	Detailed resale records, for sales-tax reporting.
	Totals by month/quarter, for IRS reporting.
	Transaction log, for audit trail.
Sales manager	Record of sales by product, for planning.
	Demographic information (location, type and size of business, etc.), for marketing strategies.
	Customer addresses and telephone numbers, for advertising.
	To know how customers heard about company.
	Record of each salesperson's performance.

When we are satisfied that we have a clear and detailed understanding of the requirements of all these different individuals, we actually begin designing the system.

We then call a second meeting with the users to review the first cut of the design and decide upon any necessary modifications. We prepare a set of sample data screens, as they will be seen by the salespeople taking orders (see Figure 10-1), and submit them for approval.

Identify
user

id_user()

```
                         *** ENTER NEW ORDER ***
                              SALESPERSON




                     Office       _____
                     Salesperson  _____
                     Password

            Instructions for Commands Available at Prompts:

            ^R = (control-R) Re-prompt for previous.
            ^E = Erase data field, make it empty.
            ^X = Exit and cancel order.

            Press ^X to exit, or another key to continue: _
```

Identify
customer

id_cust()

```
User                     *** ENTER NEW ORDER ***                    Company
                              IDENTIFY
            Customer Name       _____
            Company Name        _____
            Phone Number
            Ship to Name        _____
                    Company     _____
                    Street      _____
                    2nd Street  _____
                    City        _____   State __  Zip ____
            Bill to Name        Bill same address? <y/n>  y
                    Company     _____
                    Street      _____
                    2nd Street  _____
                    City        _____   State __  Zip ____
            Resale?       n     Resale Permit Number  _____
            Advertising Ref     _____
```

ENTER
NEW ORDER

main()

Get
order

ord_itms()

```
User                     *** ENTER NEW ORDER ***                    Company
                              ENTER ITEMS
            Customer Name    John Doe

            Company Name     XYZ Corporation

            Part Number      Description                Qty  Unit-Price
            _____     Order-Entry Software Package  1  $   123.45
            _____




                                           Order Total  $   123.45
```

Get shipping
and billing data

ship_pay()

```
User                     *** ENTER NEW ORDER ***                    Company
                              SHIP, TAX, PAY
            Customer Name    John Doe

            Company Name     XYZ Corporation

            Shipping Weight      123
                    Carrier  _____   Ship Charge  $_____

            Sales Tax Percent  ___                        $    .00

            Payment Terms Code  _____
                                           Item Total  $   123.45
                                           Order Total $   123.45
      Comment  _____
      Is order OK? <y/n>  y
```

Write order
to output

wrt_ord()

```
BEGIN ORDER 10001
TM Thu May 09 14:53:53 1985
OF Company
SL User
CN John Doe
CO XYZ Corporation
SN John Doe
SC XYZ Corporation
ST
SS
SZ
PN S1234
QY 1
PR 12345
TL 12345
TX 0
SH ups
SA 0
WT 123
PA
END ORDER 10001
```

FIGURE 10-1 | *Top-level structure of the order-entry application*

SOURCE FILE	FUNCTION	LEVEL	PURPOSE
stddefs.h		header	Holds company-wide definitions, synonym types, macros.
ordentry.h		header	Holds order data-field definitions.
ordentry.c		high	Declares *GLOBAL* data and controls entire application.
ordbuild.c		middle	Declares *SEMIGLOBAL* data; holds middle-level functions.
	id_user()	middle	Identifies user/salesperson.
	id_cust()	middle	Identifies customer.
	ord_itms()	middle	Inputs items to order.
	ship_pay()	middle	Inputs shipping and payment data.
	wrt_ord()	middle	Writes the order to *stdout*.
get_addr.c	*get_addr()*	low	Prompts for an address.
pnt_id_c.c	*pnt_id_cust()*	low	Paints customer ID screen.
pnt_ship.c	*pnt_ship_pay()*	low	Paints shipping and payment screen.
stubs.c	*inv_find()*	low	Finds a part in inventory.
	pw_find()	low	Finds a user's password.
	order_num()	low	Creates next order number.
	logentry()	low	Saves a message in the log file.

(continued)

FIGURE 10-2 *Organization of order-entry source listings*

After our users have accepted the screen formats, we begin designing our program structure. We agree that the logical approach is to write a separate function to manage each input screen, one to manage the final order output, and a main routine to control the interactions among them. The tree diagram in Figure 10-1 shows the top-level design we decide upon for our program.

Now we pseudocode each of the functions and plug them back into our tree, to be sure all necessary interactions are provided for. We repeat this procedure for all levels of the application. The requirements of the top-level functions dictate the specifications for the lower-level functions,

SOURCE FILE	FUNCTION	LEVEL	PURPOSE
projutil.h		header	Holds declarations and symbols used with the project utility library.
prompt.c	*prompt()*	lib	Inputs a string from user; verifies match, checks length.
nprompt.c	*nprompt()*	lib	Inputs a *long* integer from user; validates range.
fprompt.c	*fprompt()*	lib	Inputs a double-precision floating-point number from user; validates range.
tput.c	*tput()*	lib	Displays a string at specified row and column.
ntput.c	*ntput()*	lib	Displays a *long* integer, right justified, at specified row and column.
ftput.c	*ftput()*	lib	Displays a double-precision floating-point number, right justified on the decimal point, at specified row and column.
beg_scrn.c	*beg_scrn()*	lib	Clears screen and prints screen headings.
match.c	*match()*	lib	Verifies that a string matches a pattern string.
strrjust.c	*strrjust()*	lib	Right justifies a string, filling with blanks.
err_warn.c	*err_warn()*	lib	Displays a two-string diagnostic warning message and return.
	err_exit()	lib	Displays a serious diagnostic message and exits application.

FIGURE 10-2 | *Organization of order-entry source listings (continued)*

rather than the reverse. (These lower-level functions fall into two categories: those specific to the order-entry application, and general-purpose utility functions that can be called in other applications we write in the future.)

Finally, we write, compile, test, and debug our program, get final approval from our users, and install the system. We're ready to do business!

Organization of Listings

Figure 10-2 shows how the application source-file listings are organized. The source file *ordbuild.c* contains more than one function because the functions share data; *errwarn.c* contains two functions that act as a team; and *stubs.c* contains all the incomplete functions. All other source files hold only a single function (see Chapter 9 on style). The functions in *stubs.c* are only partially developed at this stage, because we haven't yet discussed some of the material that needs to go in them. These stubs are still useful for debugging the rest of the application, however, and will be replaced later by fully operational versions.

Project Utility Library Functions

The source files with level *lib* hold general-purpose utility functions that are not specific to our order-entry application. You will find them very useful for writing many of your own applications. (Programs that call any of these functions should *#include projutil.h*, which contains the declarations and definitions used in conjunction with the project utility functions.)

General-purpose functions like these may be compiled to object form and combined in a single file called a *library* (see Chapter 9). Building such libraries of commonly used utility functions makes it easy to link them with other functions you write. (With Microsoft's C, use the *LIB* command to build and maintain libraries for use with the *MSC LINK* command.)

Header Files

Most header files, like *projutil.h*, are written to be used in conjunction with a specific set of related functions. The related function declarations should also be included in these header files, to permit the compiler to check your function calls for the proper number and types of arguments, as well as to handle the return values correctly. (You will find it much easier to call the associated functions if you supply meaningful and descriptive names for constants passed as arguments.)

Header files may also be organized with groups of people in mind, rather than groups of related functions: for example, you the author alone, programmers on the same project, or all programmers throughout the company. The *stddefs.h* file is an example of this last type. If you *#include <stddefs.h>* at the start of a program, you can avoid coding *#define* commands for long lists of frequently used single-purpose definitions.

C A U T I O N

In order to enable type-checking with the standard I/O functions, you must #define LINT_ARGS. This causes the section of stdio.h *that contains the declarations for these functions to be compiled whenever you #include the* stdio.h *header file.*

Printing Program Listings

You can create line-numbered source listings for the order-entry program by using the listing filter program we looked at in Chapter 8. The commands to prepare the individual listings look like this:

```
LISTING < ORDENTRY.C > PRN:
LISTING < ORDBUILD.C > PRN:
```

The file named after the < redirection for standard input is the file to be listed. The > *PRN:* redirects the standard output to the printer.

An alternate way of making these line-numbered listings is to use the >> output-redirection command to gather all listing output into a single file (for example, *ordentry.lst*) before printing:

```
LISTING < ORDENTRY.C  >  ORDENTRY.LST
LISTING < ORDBUILD.C  >> ORDENTRY.LST
COPY ORDENTRY.LST PRN:
```

(The spaces around the redirection symbols in the preceding examples are optional.)

Compiler Error Messages

As I said earlier, all of the order-entry source files compile without errors at the default warning level. Therefore, if you *do* receive any error messages from the compiler, it's most likely the result of a typing error. Unfortunately, however, the error messages that the compiler generates don't always spell out exactly what the error is. For instance, if you make a typing error on one line, the compiler might not detect and report an error until the next line. And even then, the error it does report could be very misleading.

Let's look at a few intentional errors, to get a feel for the kinds of error messages that are generated and why:

```
 1   #include <stdio.h>
 2   #include <stddefs.h>
 3
 4   void tput(row, col, text)
 5   short row, col;
 6   char text[];
 7
 8      {
 9      CUR_MV(row, col);
10      fputs(text, stderr);
11      }
```

All of the errors are errors of omission. I have deleted the highlighted characters one at a time and recompiled *tput()* after each deletion, to generate the individual error messages. For example, when I deleted the *w* on line 5, I received this message:

```
tput.C(5) : 'ro' : ignored
```

In this case, the message makes it very clear what the problem is: The compiler is ignoring the identifier *ro* because it is not used in the function. A quick scan of the source code makes this typographical error practically jump out at us.

But it's not always that easy. The next error message is reported when I delete the semicolon from the end of line 5:

```
tput.C(6) : type 'char' unexpected
```

Wait a minute! The compiler is telling me I have an error on line 6, but that line looks fine. Hmmm ... Remember, the compiler recognizes the *semicolon* as the end of a statement, and basically ignores a *newline* character in the source code. So the compiler is actually trying to make sense of the line:

```
short row, col char text[];
```

It doesn't know what to do with the type specifier *char* in the middle of this line, and it tells me so.

The same type of error on line 9 will produce an equally disconcerting message about line 10:

```
tput.C(10) : syntax error: identifier 'fputs'
```

This time the error is created by deleting the semicolon from line 9. Instead of telling me that it didn't expect the identifier *fputs,* the compiler reports a syntax error. Obviously, just because the compiler reports an error on a certain line, that doesn't mean the problem is in that line!

Another thing I should point out here is that there could very well be a large number of error messages generated from a single mistyped statement. For instance, if you misspell an identifier in a function declaration, it will generate an error message wherever the function is called.

Here's how to isolate the real problem: If during compilation you suddenly see hundreds of error messages scrolling up the screen, press ^C and restart the compiler. Be ready to press ^S as soon as you see the first error message. This will suspend compilation so that you can read the first message and record the line number on which it occurred. Then press ^Q to continue. After compilation is complete, go back and look at your source code, at the first line specified by the compiler. If you do not find the error on that particular line, scan the lines immediately preceding it and you will probably find a simple typing error.

In this last example, I've left off the closing brace. During compilation, I received this error message:

```
tput.C(12) : syntax error EOF
```

Now something *really* seems funny here. The compiler is telling me that I have an error in line 12, but there *is* no line 12 in this source listing. Ah, but there is, as far as the compiler is concerned. It contains the end-of-file (*EOF*) marker. Since the compiler expects a closing brace *before* the invisible *EOF,* it tells me I have a syntax error. Once again, the problem is a bit puzzling at first glance, but actually quite simple to correct.

The Header Files

The order-entry application uses three header files, each containing definitions, declarations, and the like, grouped according to scope of use.

Company-Wide Header: *stddefs.h*

This file combines definitions used frequently by all the programmers. It contains several debugging and screen-control macros. (The screen-output capabilities assume you are working with the ANSI.SYS terminal driver.)

STDDEFS.H ▶Pages 161, 190

```
/* HEADER FILE: STDDEFS.H */
/**************************************************************************/
/* stddefs.h: standard defined symbols for general company use. The file */
/*    stdio.h should be #included with this file if DEBUG macros or screen- */
/*    control definitions will be used.                                  */
/**************************************************************************/
```

(continued)

STDDEFS.H (continued)

```
/* Symbols related to definition and use of shared data. Declarations of   */
/*   data with storage class static or external should begin with these    */
/*   shared-data modifiers:                                                 */
/*      GLOBAL begins defining declarations for external data; data are     */
/*        shared by all functions that IMPORT the data.                     */
/*      SEMIGLOBAL begins defining declarations for static external data;   */
/*        data are shared by functions in the same source file that IMPORT  */
/*        the data.                                                         */
/*      IMPORT begins non-defining declarations of GLOBAL and SEMIGLOBAL    */
/*        data. A defining declaration allocates new, initialized storage.  */
/*        Non-defining declarations refer to data defined elsewhere, to     */
/*        allow examination or modification of those data.                  */
#define GLOBAL
#define SEMIGLOBAL static
#define IMPORT extern

/* Data types that are synonyms of other types. */
typedef unsigned char unchar;                    /* unsigned characters */
typedef unsigned short unshort;              /* unsigned short integers */
typedef unsigned long unlong;                 /* unsigned long integers */
typedef char byte;                       /* byte: 1-byte number (0 to 127) */
typedef char bflag;                        /* bflag: 1-byte true/false flag */
typedef int flag;                        /* flag: int-sized true/false flag */

/* Constants for true or false data, to be used in conjunction    */
/*   with synonym types flag (int sized) and bflag (char sized). */
#ifndef YES                      /* If not already defined, then define YES, NO. */
#define YES 1
#define NO 0
#endif

/***********************************************************************/
/* Symbols related to standard library function.                       */
/***********************************************************************/

/* Status of SUCCEED or FAIL passed to exit(); aborts program. */
#define SUCCEED 0
#define FAIL 1

/* File handles (descriptor numbers) for standard files to be  */
/*   used with the low level I/O functions read() and write(). */
#define STDIN 0
#define STDOUT 1
#define STDERR 2

/***********************************************************************/
/* DEBUG macros either produce debug output or disappear, depending upon */
/*   whether or not DEBUG is defined. All take two arguments: a message  */
/*   to display and a value. The type of the value determines which macro */
/*   will be correct to use. Pass a string that uniquely identifies this  */
/*   debug call as the first argument, id.                                */
/*                                                                        */
/*      SDBG(id, str)              Shows string str and its length.       */
/*      LDBG(id, long)             Shows long.                            */
/*      IDBG(id, int)              Shows int.                             */
/*      UIDBG(id, unsigned_int)    Shows unsigned int.                    */
/*      CDBG(id, char)             Shows ASCII and hex for a char.        */
/*      DDBG(id, double)           Shows double.                          */
/*                                                                        */
/*   Note: #include <stdio.h> should precede this file.                   */
/***********************************************************************/
```

(continued)

STDDEFS.H (continued)

```
#if defined(DEBUG)                           /* Is this a DEBUG compilation? */

/* Definitions for macro expansion prefix and suffix text. */
/* Arguments to CUR_MV control screen position of debug output.          */
/* Replace "stderr" with "stdout" if debug output redirection is needed. */
#define DBG_BGN (CUR_SAVE, CUR_MV(24, 0), CLR_LINE, fprintf(stderr,
#define DBG_END ), getch(), CUR_REST)

#define SDBG(id, str) DBG_BGN "SDBG! %s = %-.50s, L = %d _\b", \
   (id), (str), strlen(str) DBG_END
#define LDBG(id, lngv) DBG_BGN "LDBG! %s = %ld _\b", \
   (id), (lngv) DBG_END
#define IDBG(id, intv) DBG_BGN "IDBG! %s = %d _\b", \
   (id), (intv) DBG_END
#define UIDBG(id, uint) DBG_BGN "UIDBG! %s = %u _\b", \
   (id), (uint) DBG_END
#define CDBG(id, chr) DBG_BGN "CDBG! %s = %c, (\\x%02x) _\b", \
   (id), (chr), (chr) DBG_END
#define DDBG(id, dblv) DBG_BGN "DDBG! %s = %E _\b", \
   (id), (dblv) DBG_END
#else                        /* Not in DEBUG mode; make DEBUG macros disappear  */
                             /*   by defining them with null expansions.        */
#define SDBG(a, b)
#define LDBG(a, b)
#define IDBG(a, b)
#define UIDBG(a, b)
#define CDBG(a, b)
#define DDBG(a, b)
#endif


/****************************************************************************/
/* Screen and Cursor-Control Commands:                                      */
/* CUR_MV(r, c)   Move cursor to row r (1-25), column c (1-80).             */
/* CUR_UP(n)      Move cursor up n lines (ignored if at top).               */
/* CUR_DN(n)      Move cursor down n lines (ignored if at bottom).          */
/* CUR_RT(n)      Move cursor right n spaces (ignored at right margin).     */
/* CUR_LT(n)      Move cursor left n spaces (ignored at left margin).       */
/* CUR_SKIP       Send newline.                                            */
/* CUR_SAVE       Save cursor position.                                    */
/* CUR_REST       Restore cursor position.                                 */
/* CLR_SCRN       Clear screen and move cursor to home.                    */
/* CLR_LINE       Erase from cursor to end of line.                        */
/* CLR_EOS(r, c)  Erase from row r, col c to screen end, leave cursor at r,c. */
/* BELL           Ring bell once by sending control-g.                     */
/*                                                                          */
/* NOTE: Definitions below are for ANSI.SYS terminal driver.               */
/****************************************************************************/

#define CUR_MV(row, col) fprintf(stderr, "\33[%d;%dH", row, col)
#define CUR_UP(num) fprintf(stderr, "\33[%dA", num)
#define CUR_DN(num) fprintf(stderr, "\33[%dB", num)
#define CUR_RT(num) fprintf(stderr, "\33[%dC", num)
#define CUR_LT(num) fprintf(stderr, "\33[%dD", num)
#define CUR_SKIP fputs("\n", stderr)
#define CUR_SAVE fputs("\33[s", stderr)
#define CUR_REST fputs("\33[u", stderr)
#define CLR_SCRN fputs("\33[2J", stderr)
#define CLR_LINE fputs("\33[K", stderr)
#define CLR_EOS(r, c) {byte i_; CUR_MV(r,c); \
   for (i_=r; i_<=25; ++i_) CLR_LINE, CUR_DN(1); CUR_MV(r,c); }
#define BELL fputc('\7', stderr)
```

Project Utility Header: *projutil.h*

This file defines synonym data types and declares function argument
and return types for the project utility library functions. The file is used by
programmers in our project group.

PROJUTIL.H   ►**Pages 161, 162**

```
/* HEADER FILE: PROJUTIL.H */
/*********************************************************************/
/* projutil.h: project utility library function header file. #include this   */
/*   file near the start of source files containing functions that will call */
/*   any of the project utility functions listed below.                      */
/*********************************************************************/

/*********************************************************************/
/* Project Utility Function Summary:                                         */
/*                                                                           */
/*      prompt()        Input a string, check match, check length.           */
/*      nprompt()       Prompt for a long int, echo right justified.         */
/*      fprompt()       Prompt for a double, echo right justified.           */
/*      tput()          Print a string at specific screen row and column.    */
/*      ntput()         Print a long integer right justified on screen.      */
/*      ftput()         Print a double right justified on screen.            */
/*      beg_scrn()      Clear screen; print four headings at screen top.     */
/*      match()         Compare a data string against a match string.        */
/*      strrjust()      Right justify a string, padding with blanks.         */
/*      err_warn()      Print a warning message, input Escape.               */
/*      err_exit()      Call err_warn(), then terminate program.             */
/*      logentry()      Append message text to log file.                     */
/*                                                                           */
/* To learn more about these functions, read their source code.             */
/*********************************************************************/

/* If IMPORT is not already #defined, then do it now. */
#ifndef IMPORT
#define IMPORT extern
#endif

/* Type stepcode is a synonym data type defined below. The typedef statement */
/*   makes stepcode equivalent to type char. Type stepcode declares return    */
/*   values from the functions prompt(), nprompt(), and fprompt().            */
typedef char stepcode;

/* Declare project utility function return and argument types: If your       */
/*   (non-Microsoft) C compiler does not support the declaration of          */
/*   argument types, supply empty () after the function's name.              */
/* These declarations make it possible to call any of these functions from   */
/*   anywhere within the source file after this header file is #included.     */
/*   The call will be checked for the proper number and types of arguments    */
/*   and proper use of the return value.                                      */
IMPORT stepcode prompt(char[], char[], short, short, flag, short, short);
IMPORT stepcode nprompt(long *, char[], long, long, flag, short, short);
IMPORT stepcode fprompt(double *, char[], double, double, short,
    short, flag, short, short);
IMPORT void tput(short, short, char[]);
IMPORT void ntput(short, short, long, char[], short);
IMPORT void beg_scrn(char[], char[], char[], char[]);
IMPORT void ftput(short, short, double, short, char[], short);
```

(continued)

PROJUTIL.H (continued)

```
IMPORT flag match(char[], char[]);
IMPORT void strrjust(char[], short);
IMPORT void err_warn(char[], char[]);
IMPORT void err_exit(char[], char[]);
IMPORT void logentry(char[]);

/* Argument constants and control symbols for prompt(). */
#define PRMTBSIZ 161                          /* prompt buffer size */
#define MAND 1                        /* for fifth argument: mandatory input */
#define OPT 0                         /* for fifth argument: optional input */


#define C_MASK '_'                    /* character to repeat for prompt field */

/* User command characters for prompt(). */
#define C_NULL '\x05'                 /* ERASE ENTRY: '\x05'is control-E. */
#define C_BACK '\x12'                  /* BACK UP: '\x12' is control-R. */
                                       /*   Move back to previous prompt. */
#define C_CANC '\x18'                  /* CANCEL: '\x18' is control-X. */
                                       /*   Cancel order and program. */


/* These are the possible return values from prompt() that a */
/*    variable with synonym type stepcode may take.          */
#define STEPOK 0                   /* Data were entered; may be null if OPT. */
#define STEPBACK 1                 /* C_BACK was entered; back up a prompt. */
#define STEPCANC 2                 /* C_CANC was entered; cancel transaction. */

/* Note this statement:                                                     */
/*    enum stepcode {STEPOK, STEPBACK, STEPCANC};                           */
/* This enumeration does almost the same job as the typedef synonym type    */
/*    stepcode and the symbols STEPOK, STEPBACK, and STEPCANC. The          */
/*    difference is that a variable of synonym type stepcode is not an      */
/*    enumerated constant and so may be incremented and decremented. The    */
/*    increment and decrement operators are used here to compute the next   */
/*    step to perform. At some future time, ANSI may decide to permit ++    */
/*    and -- on enumerated type variables.                                  */
```

Order-Entry Header: *ordentry.h*

This file holds definitions of type synonyms and of symbols that define the sizes or limits of data fields in an order. It is specific to the order-entry application. (In a database-management system, this kind of information would be stored in the data-dictionary files.)

C A U T I O N

Redefinition of a field or addition of a new field in the order-entry application may make it necessary to recompile source files that use this header file.

ORDENTRY.H   ▶Page 129

```
/* HEADER FILE: ORDENTRY.H */
/************************************************************************/
/* ordentry.h: header file for the order-entry application.           */
/************************************************************************/

/* Type money is defined as a synonym of type long for amounts */
/*    of money in cents up to + or - $21,474,836.47.           */
typedef long money;

/* Order data maximum field widths defined for data input by prompt(). */
#define L_USER 25
#define L_PASSWORD 8
#define L_OFFICE 25
#define L_CUST_NAME 30
#define L_COMPANY 30
#define L_PHONE 14
#define L_SHIP_NAME 40
#define L_SHIP_CMPY 40
#define L_SHIP_STRT 40
#define L_SHIP_STRT2 40
#define L_SHIP_CITY 15
#define L_SHIP_STATE 2
#define L_SHIP_ZIP 5
#define L_BILL_SAME 1
#define L_BILL_NAME 40
#define L_BILL_CMPY 40
#define L_BILL_STRT 40
#define L_BILL_STRT2 40
#define L_BILL_CITY 15
#define L_BILL_STATE 2
#define L_BILL_ZIP 5
#define L_IS_RESALE 1
#define L_RESALE_ID 17
#define L_ADV_REF 40
#define L_PARTS 15
#define L_PART_DESC 30
#define L_PRICES 11
#define L_TAX_AMT 11
#define L_SHIP_CAR 19
#define L_PAY_TERMS 10
#define L_COMMENT 69

/* Maximum number of items on an order. */
#define MAX_ITEMS 10

/* Maximum numeric values input by nprompt() and fprompt(). */
#define H_QUANTITY 999L
#define H_SHIP_AMT 30000.0
#define H_TAX_PCNT 99.9
```

The Top Level: *main()*

The source file *ordentry.c* is the location of the *main()* function that directs the entire order-entry process.

ORDENTRY.C   ▶Page 160

```c
/* SOURCE FILE: ORDENTRY.C */
/********************************************************************/
/* The main() function for the Software Vendor Order-Entry Program. Each  */
/*   case commands a significant step in order entry, such as prompting for */
/*   a screen of data or sending order data to a file.              */
/* The action after the completion of a step will be one of the following: */
/*   Cancel the order.                                              */
/*   Back up to the previous step.                                  */
/*   Go on to the next step.                                        */
/* The action is controlled by the user's use of special command characters */
/*   that are described further in the header file projutil.h.      */
/********************************************************************/

#include <stddefs.h>                    /* needed for GLOBAL, IMPORT, and YES */
#include "projutil.h"     /* needed for prompt() symbols STEPOK, STEPBACK, and */
                          /*   STEPCANC, and synonym type stepcode        */

/* Declare data shared among functions in all source files (GLOBAL). */
GLOBAL bflag bell_ok = YES;                       /* It's OK to ring bell. */

main()
    {

    /* Declare subfunction return and parameter types. */
    IMPORT stepcode id_user(void), id_cust(stepcode);
    IMPORT stepcode ord_itms(stepcode), ship_pay(stepcode);
    IMPORT stepcode wrt_ord(void);
    short step;
    stepcode step_rtn;      /* step_rtn is the return value from a step. It is */
                            /* passed to the next step. It may equal:       */
                            /*   STEPOK    Step complete; go on to next step. */
                            /*   STEPBACK  Back up to closest previous step. */
                            /*   STEPCANC  Cancel order entry (quit).        */

    enum prompts {ID_USER, ID_CUST, ORD_ITMS, SHIP_PAY, WRT_ORD,
        ENDSTEPS};

    for (step = 0, step_rtn = STEPOK; step != (short) ENDSTEPS &&
        step_rtn != STEPCANC; )
        {
        switch (step)
            {
            case ID_USER:                       /* Identify user (salesperson). */
                step_rtn = id_user();
                break;
            case ID_CUST:                          /* Identify customer. */
                step_rtn = id_cust(step_rtn);
                break;
            case ORD_ITMS:                      /* Input order detail items. */
                step_rtn = ord_itms(step_rtn);
                break;
```

(continued)

ORDENTRY.C (continued)

```
            case SHIP_PAY:                  /* Input shipping info, tax, pay terms. */
               step_rtn = ship_pay(step_rtn);
               break;
            case WRT_ORD:                              /* Write order; update files. */
               step_rtn = wrt_ord();
               break;
         }

         /* Determine next step based on return from last one. */
         if (step_rtn == STEPOK)                        /* Was last step successful? */
            ++step;                                     /* Yes; go on to next step. */
         else if (step_rtn == STEPBACK && step > 0)
            --step;                                     /* No; back up to previous step. */
      }
   }
```

The Middle Level: *ordbuild.c*

The source file *ordbuild.c* contains the second-level functions, called directly from *main()*, that control data input and output. These functions make extensive use of *SEMIGLOBAL* data (*external static* storage class) to share the fields in an order. This file is as long as your longest application source file should ever be: about 500 lines.

ORDBUILD.C   ▶Page 165

```
/* SOURCE FILE: ORDBUILD.C */
/***************************************************************************/
/* Functions for order-entry prompt screens and for saving data. These are  */
/*    the middle-level functions that call the low-level display and prompt  */
/*    functions to input screens of order data. They are in one source file  */
/*    to permit order data in memory to be shared by them, but not by other  */
/*    functions linked into the order-entry program.                         */
/***************************************************************************/

#include <stdio.h>
#include <stddefs.h>
#include "projutil.h"
#include "ordentry.h"

/* Semiglobal data shared by functions in this source file only. */
/* Data items are fields of an order. */
SEMIGLOBAL char user[L_USER + 1] = "";
SEMIGLOBAL char office[L_OFFICE + 1] = "";
SEMIGLOBAL char cust_name[L_CUST_NAME + 1] = "";
SEMIGLOBAL char company[L_COMPANY + 1] = "";
SEMIGLOBAL char phone[L_PHONE + 1] = "";
SEMIGLOBAL char ship_name[L_SHIP_NAME + 1] = "";
SEMIGLOBAL char ship_cmpy[L_SHIP_CMPY + 1] = "";
SEMIGLOBAL char ship_strt[L_SHIP_STRT + 1] = "";
SEMIGLOBAL char ship_strt2[L_SHIP_STRT2 + 1] = "";
SEMIGLOBAL char ship_city[L_SHIP_CITY + 1] = "";
SEMIGLOBAL char ship_state[L_SHIP_STATE + 1] = "";
```

(continued)

ORDBUILD.C (continued)

```
SEMIGLOBAL char ship_zip[L_SHIP_ZIP + 1] = "";
SEMIGLOBAL char bill_same[L_BILL_SAME + 1] = "y";
SEMIGLOBAL char bill_name[L_BILL_NAME + 1] = "";
SEMIGLOBAL char bill_cmpy[L_BILL_CMPY + 1] = "";
SEMIGLOBAL char bill_strt[L_BILL_STRT + 1] = "";
SEMIGLOBAL char bill_strt2[L_BILL_STRT2 + 1] = "";
SEMIGLOBAL char bill_city[L_BILL_CITY + 1] = "";
SEMIGLOBAL char bill_state[L_BILL_STATE + 1] = "";
SEMIGLOBAL char bill_zip[L_BILL_ZIP + 1] = "";
SEMIGLOBAL char is_resale[L_IS_RESALE + 1] = "n";
SEMIGLOBAL char resale_id[L_RESALE_ID + 1] = "";
SEMIGLOBAL char adv_ref[L_ADV_REF + 1] = "";

/* Variables "parts" and "part_descs" are 2-dimensional character arrays. */
SEMIGLOBAL char parts[MAX_ITEMS][L_PARTS + 1] = {""};
SEMIGLOBAL char part_descs[MAX_ITEMS][L_PART_DESC + 1] = {""};

SEMIGLOBAL long quantities[MAX_ITEMS] = {0};
SEMIGLOBAL short ship_weights[MAX_ITEMS] = {0};
SEMIGLOBAL short tot_weight = 0;
SEMIGLOBAL money prices[MAX_ITEMS] = {0};
SEMIGLOBAL money part_total = 0;
SEMIGLOBAL char ship_car[L_SHIP_CAR + 1] = "";
SEMIGLOBAL money ship_amt = 0;
SEMIGLOBAL double inp_ship_amt = 0.0;
SEMIGLOBAL double tax_pcnt = 0.0;
SEMIGLOBAL money tax_amt = 0;
SEMIGLOBAL char pay_terms[L_PAY_TERMS + 1] = "";
SEMIGLOBAL char comment[L_COMMENT + 1] = "";
SEMIGLOBAL byte last_part = 0;                    /* index of last part on order */

/* Shared data not part of an order. */
SEMIGLOBAL char scrn_title[] = "*** ENTER NEW ORDER ***";
```
▶Page 166
```
/****************************************************************************/
/* id_user() identifies the user (salesperson or data-entry clerk). The user */
/*    enters office code, name, and password. The password is then verified.  */
/****************************************************************************/

stepcode id_user()
    {
    IMPORT char user[];
    IMPORT char office[];
    IMPORT char scrn_title[];

    /* pw_find() is called to verify user and look up user data. */
    flag pw_find(char *, char *, char *);
    char password[L_PASSWORD + 1];
    stepcode step_rtn;
    short ichar;

    /* Paint screen: Show headings for data to prompt for. */
    beg_scrn("", scrn_title, "", "SALESPERSON");
    tput(10, 20, "Office");
    tput(12, 20, "Salesperson");
    tput(14, 20, "Password");
```

(continued)

ORDBUILD.C (continued)

```
   do                              /* Loop until data entered or order canceled. */
      {

      /* Input name of office seller is working in. */
      step_rtn = prompt(office, "L", 3, L_OFFICE, MAND, 10, 32);
      if (step_rtn == STEPBACK)
         err_warn("Office must be supplied:", "");
      }
   while (step_rtn == STEPBACK);
   if (step_rtn != STEPCANC)                                    /* Prompt for user. */
      do                              /* Loop until data entered or order canceled. */
         {
         user[0] = '\0';                             /* DON'T show last user id. */
         step_rtn = prompt(user, "L", 2, L_USER, MAND, 12, 32);
         if (step_rtn == STEPBACK)
            err_warn("I must know who you are:", "");
         }
      while (step_rtn == STEPBACK);
   if (step_rtn != STEPCANC)                          /* Input password without echo. */
      {
      CUR_MV(14, 32);
      for (ichar = 0; ichar < L_PASSWORD &&
         (password[ichar] = getch()) >= ' '; ++ichar)
         ;
      if (password[ichar] >= ' ')
         ++ichar;
      password[ichar] = '\0';
      if (!pw_find(office, user, password))
         {
         err_warn("Access denied:", user);
         step_rtn = STEPCANC;
         }
      else                                           /* Display instructions. */
         {
         tput(17, 17, "Instructions for Commands Available at Prompts:");
         tput(19, 20, "^R = (control-R) Re-prompt for previous.");
         tput(20, 20, "^E = Erase data field, make it empty.");
         tput(21, 20, "^X = Exit and cancel order.");
         tput(23, 17, "Press ^X to exit, or another key to continue: _\b");
         if (getch() == C_CANC)
            step_rtn = STEPCANC;
         }
      }
   return (step_rtn);
   }
```

▶Page 172

```
/*****************************************************************************/
/* id_cust() prompts for customer identification information: customer name, */
/*    company, phone, shipping/billing addresses, resale number, and         */
/*    advertising reference.                                                 */
/*****************************************************************************/

stepcode id_cust(step_rtn)

   /* If screen is backed into, step_rtn == STEPBACK; */
   /*    otherwise step_rtn == STEPOK                 */
   stepcode step_rtn;
```

(continued)

ORDBUILD.C (continued)

```
{
/* Shared data accessed in this function. */
IMPORT char office[], user[], cust_name[], company[], ship_name[],
    ship_cmpy[], ship_strt[], ship_strt2[], ship_city[], ship_state[],
    ship_zip[], bill_name[], bill_cmpy[], bill_strt[], bill_strt2[],
    bill_city[], bill_state[], bill_zip[], adv_ref[], is_resale[],
    resale_id[], scrn_title[];
stepcode get_addr(stepcode, short, char[], char[], char[],
    char[], char[], char[], char[]);
void pnt_id_cust(void);
short step;

/* Names of case labels for data-field prompts. */
enum prompts {NAME, COMPANY, PHONE, SHIP_ADDR, BILL_ADDR,
    RESALE, ADV_REF, ENDSTEPS};

/* Begin new screen. */
beg_scrn(user, scrn_title, office, "IDENTIFY");
pnt_id_cust();                                      /* Paint screen. */
tput(4, 30, cust_name);
tput(6, 30, company);

/* Begin at last prompt if screen backed into. */
step = (step_rtn == STEPOK) ? 0 : (short)ENDSTEPS - 1;

/* Note: (short) is a cast operator used to make a type short copy of the */
/*    value of the enum constant ENDSTEPS. Not using a cast gives a        */
/*    warning message.                                                     */

/* Loop: Input each field of this screen. */
for (step_rtn = STEPOK; step_rtn != STEPCANC &&
    (step < (short)ENDSTEPS) && (step >= 0); )
    {
    switch (step)                       /* Select next field to prompt for. */
        {
        case NAME:                                /* Get customer name. */
            step_rtn = prompt(cust_name, "L", 3, L_CUST_NAME, MAND, 4, 30);
            break;
        case COMPANY:                             /* Get company name. */
            step_rtn = prompt(company, "L", 3, L_COMPANY, OPT, 6, 30);
            break;
        case PHONE:                               /* Get customer phone number. */
            step_rtn = prompt(phone, "P", 7, L_PHONE, OPT, 7, 30);
            break;
        case SHIP_ADDR:                           /* Get address to ship to. */
            if (ship_name[0] == '\0')             /* No address input yet? */
                {                       /* Then set default name and company. */
                strcpy(ship_name, cust_name);
                strcpy(ship_cmpy, company);
                }

            /* Prompt for address data. Call get_addr(). */
            step_rtn = get_addr(step_rtn, 9, ship_name, ship_cmpy, ship_strt,
                ship_strt2, ship_city, ship_state, ship_zip);
            break;
        case BILL_ADDR:                           /* Get address to send bill to. */
            tput(15, 30, "Bill same address? <y/n>    ");
            step_rtn = prompt(bill_same, "Q", 1, L_BILL_SAME, MAND, 15, 56);
            CUR_MV(15, 30);                       /* Move cursor to     */
            CLR_LINE;                             /*   erase question. */
```

(continued)

ORDBUILD.C (continued)

```
                if (step_rtn == STEPOK && strchr("Nn0", bill_same[0]))
                    step_rtn = get_addr(step_rtn, 15, bill_name, bill_cmpy,
                            bill_strt, bill_strt2, bill_city, bill_state, bill_zip);
                else if (step_rtn == STEPOK)
                    bill_name[0] == '\0';                    /* Bill same address. */
                break;
            case RESALE:                                /* Is purchase for resale? */
                step_rtn = prompt(is_resale, "Q", 1, L_IS_RESALE, MAND, 21, 25);
                if (step_rtn == STEPOK && strchr("Yy1", is_resale[0]))
                    step_rtn = prompt(resale_id, "L", 3, L_RESALE_ID, OPT, 21, 53);
                break;
            case ADV_REF:                   /* How did customer hear about product? */
                step_rtn = prompt(adv_ref, "L", 1, L_ADV_REF, OPT, 23, 30);
                break;
            }

        /* Determine next step based on return from last one. */
        if (step_rtn == STEPOK)                           /* Last was successful? */
            ++step;                                  /* Yes; go on to next step. */
        else if (step_rtn == STEPBACK)
            --step;                                  /* No; back up to last step. */
        }
    return (step_rtn);
    }
```
▶Page 176
```
/*****************************************************************************/
/* ord_itms() prompts repeatedly for part numbers and quantities of each    */
/*     item ordered by customer. Displays price and shipping weight of each. */
/*****************************************************************************/

stepcode ord_itms(step_rtn)
stepcode step_rtn;
    {
    IMPORT char user[], office[], scrn_title[];
    IMPORT char parts[][L_PARTS + 1];
    IMPORT char part_descs[][L_PART_DESC + 1];
    IMPORT long quantities[];
    IMPORT short ship_weights[];
    IMPORT money prices[];
    IMPORT byte last_part;
    IMPORT money part_total;
    flag inv_find(char[], char[], money *, short *);
    short step;
    char dbuf[14];                  /* dummy string to pass to ftput() and ntput() */
    byte ipart, part_cnt;
    byte row;                                        /* line number on screen */
    bflag part_found, more_items = YES;          /* part_found not initialized */
    enum prompts {PART_NUM, QUANTITY, ENDSTEPS};

    /* Paint screen. */
    beg_scrn(user, scrn_title, office, "ENTER ITEMS");
    tput(4, 10, "Customer Name");
    tput(4, 30, cust_name);
    tput(6, 10, "Company Name");
    tput(6, 30, company);
    tput(9, 10, "Part Number      Description");
    tput(9, 59, "Qty  Unit-Price");
    tput(22, 51, "Order Total");
```

(continued)

ORDBUILD.C (continued)

```
    step = ipart = 0;                              /* initializer for loop */
    for (step_rtn = STEPOK; step_rtn != STEPCANC &&
        ipart < MAX_ITEMS && ipart >= 0 && more_items; )
        {
        row = ipart + 11;                               /* row to prompt on */
        switch (step)
            {
            case PART_NUM:                              /* Get next part number. */
                do                              /* while part entered and not found */
                    {
                    step_rtn = prompt(parts[ipart], "L", 1, L_PARTS, OPT, row, 10);

                    /* Got a part number and it checks out? */
                    part_found = (step_rtn == STEPOK) && inv_find(parts[ipart],
                        part_descs[ipart], &prices[ipart], &ship_weights[ipart]);

                    /* Check for end of order. */
                    if (step_rtn == STEPOK && parts[ipart][0] == '\0')
                        more_items = NO;

                    /* If part not found, then tell user. */
                    else if (!part_found && step_rtn == STEPOK)
                        err_warn("No such part:", parts[ipart]);
                    else if (part_found)     /* Show description and price of part. */
                        {
                        tput(row, 27, part_descs[ipart]);
                        tput(row, 64, "$");
                        ftput(row, 65, (double) prices[ipart] / 100.0, 2,
                            dbuf, L_PRICES);

                        /* Default quantity is 1. */
                        if (!quantities[ipart])
                            quantities[ipart] = 1;
                        }

                    /* Indent avoids confusion of do...while with while loop. */
                    } while (step_rtn == STEPOK && !part_found && more_items);
                break;
            case QUANTITY:                              /* Get quantity for part ordered. */
                step_rtn = nprompt(&quantities[ipart],
                    "#", 0L, H_QUANTITY, MAND, row, 59);
                break;
            }
        if (step_rtn == STEPOK)                          /* Update total on screen. */
            {

            /* Has number of parts on this order increased? */
            if (ipart > last_part && ipart < MAX_ITEMS && quantities[ipart] > 0)
                last_part = ipart;                       /* Yes, add another part. */

            /* Sum the prices times quantities of parts ordered. */
            for (part_total = part_cnt = 0; part_cnt <= last_part; ++part_cnt)
                part_total += prices[part_cnt] * quantities[part_cnt];
            tput(22, 64, "$");
            ftput(22, 65, (double) part_total / 100.0, 2, dbuf, L_PRICES);
            }
```

(continued)

ORDBUILD.C (continued)

```
      /* Determine next part to prompt for and next step. */
      if (step == (short)PART_NUM)                   /* Just got a part number. */
         {
         step = (short)QUANTITY;                       /* Next get a quantity. */
         if (step_rtn == STEPBACK)
            --ipart;
         }
      else                                            /* Just got a quantity. */
         {
         step = (short)PART_NUM;                     /* Next get a part number. */
         if (step_rtn == STEPOK)
          ++ipart;
         }
      }
   return (step_rtn);
   }
```
►Page 181
```
/*****************************************************************************/
/* ship_pay() prompts for shipping carrier, shipping charges, sales-tax      */
/*    rate, and payment terms. Input these data after items are entered.     */
/*****************************************************************************/

stepcode ship_pay(step_rtn)

   /* If screen is backed into, step_rtn == STEPBACK; */
   /*    otherwise step_rtn == STEPOK.                */
   stepcode step_rtn;
   {
   IMPORT char office[], user[], cust_name[], company[],
      ship_car[], pay_terms[], comment[], scrn_title[];
   IMPORT money part_total, tax_amt, ship_amt;
   IMPORT double inp_ship_amt, tax_pcnt;
   IMPORT char is_resale[];                          /* Yes means no sales tax. */
   IMPORT byte last_part;
   IMPORT short ship_weights[];
   IMPORT short tot_weight;
   short step;
   char dbuf[14];
   byte ipart;
   enum prompts {SHIP_CAR, SHIP_AMT, TAX, PAY_TERMS, COMMENT, ENDSTEPS};

   /* Verify that something has been ordered; else return STEPBACK. */
   if (quantities[0] == 0 || parts[0][0] == '\0')
      {
      err_warn("Nothing ordered:", "");                    /* Give diagnostic. */
      return (STEPBACK);                          /* Back up to previous screen. */
      }

   /* Begin new screen. */
   beg_scrn(user, scrn_title, office, "SHIP, TAX, PAY");
   pnt_ship_pay();                                           /* Paint screen. */
   tput(4, 30, cust_name);
   tput(6, 30, company);
```

(continued)

ORDBUILD.C (continued)

```
/* Sum ship weights and show total (weights in ounces). */
for (ipart = tot_weight = 0; ipart <= last_part; ++ipart)
   tot_weight += ship_weights[ipart];
ntput(9, 30, (long) tot_weight, dbuf, 10);              /* Show total weight. */

/* Begin at last prompt if screen backed into. */
step = (step_rtn == STEPOK) ? 0 : (short)ENDSTEPS - 1;
for (step_rtn = STEPOK; step_rtn != STEPCANC &&
   (step < (short) ENDSTEPS) && step >= 0; )
   {
   switch (step)
      {
      case SHIP_CAR:                              /* Get shipping carrier. */
         step_rtn = prompt(ship_car, "L", 1, L_SHIP_CAR, OPT, 11, 30);
         break;

      case SHIP_AMT:                       /* Get shipping charges, if */
         if (ship_car[0] != '\0')          /*    a carrier was entered. */
            step_rtn = fprompt(&inp_ship_amt, "F", 0.20,
               H_SHIP_AMT, 11, 2, OPT, 11, 65);
            ship_amt = (money) (inp_ship_amt * 100.0);
         break;
      case TAX:                                  /* Get sales-tax percentage. */

         /* If sale is for resale, then don't add sales tax. */
         if (strchr("Yyl", is_resale[0]))
            tax_pcnt = 0.0;
         else                       /* Prompt for local tax rate, if any. */
            step_rtn = fprompt(&tax_pcnt, "F", 0.0,
               H_TAX_PCNT, 4, 2, OPT, 14, 30);
         if (step_rtn == STEPOK)
            tax_amt = (tax_pcnt * part_total) / 100;
         tput(14, 64, "$");
         ftput(14, 65, (double) tax_amt / 100.0, 2, dbuf, L_TAX_AMT);
         ftput(18, 65, (double) part_total / 100.0, 2, dbuf, L_PRICES);
         ftput(20, 65, (double) (part_total + tax_amt + ship_amt) / 100.0,
            2, dbuf, L_PRICES);
         break;
      case PAY_TERMS:                            /* Get payment terms code. */
         step_rtn = prompt(pay_terms, "L", 1, L_PAY_TERMS, MAND, 17, 30);
         break;
      case COMMENT:                          /* Get order comment (if any). */
         step_rtn = prompt(comment, "L", 1, L_COMMENT, OPT, 22, 11);
         break;
      }

   /* Determine next step based on return from last one. */
   if (step_rtn == STEPOK)                       /* Last was successful? */
      ++step;                                    /* Yes; go on to next step. */
   else if (step_rtn == STEPBACK)
      --step;                                    /* No; back up to last step. */
   }
return (step_rtn);
}
```

(continued)

ORDBUILD.C (continued)

▶Page 183

```
/***************************************************************************/
/* wrt_ord() writes an order to standard output after asking if all is OK. */
/* The order number is assigned from a counter.                            */
/***************************************************************************/

/*  File data to be output are written to the standard output file (stdout). */
/*     This permits data to be redirected at the command line. For example:  */
/*        ORDENTRY > SS841225.ORD          Creates new file;                 */
/*                                           note date encoded in name.      */
/*        ORDENTRY >> NEWORDS.DAT          Appends data to file.             */
/*        ORDENTRY | ORDSAVE | ORDPRINT    Serves as source for a pipeline.  */
/*                                                                           */
/*  This standard file use scheme gives flexibility in the way the program   */
/*     may be used. Text and control characters are output to the standard   */
/*     error file (stderr), so they won't appear in the redirected output.   */

stepcode wrt_ord()
    {

    /* IMPORT all the fields of the order. */
    IMPORT char office[], user[], cust_name[], company[], ship_name[],
        ship_cmpy[], ship_strt[], ship_strt2[], ship_city[], ship_state[],
        ship_zip[], bill_name[], bill_cmpy[], bill_strt[], bill_strt2[],
        bill_city[], bill_state[], bill_zip[], adv_ref[], resale_id[];
    IMPORT char is_resale[];                       /* Yes means no sales tax. */
    IMPORT char parts[][L_PARTS + 1];
    IMPORT long quantities[];
    IMPORT money prices[];
    IMPORT byte last_part;
    IMPORT short tot_weight;
    IMPORT char ship_car[], pay_terms[], comment[];
    IMPORT money part_total, tax_amt, ship_amt;
    IMPORT long order_num(void);
    long order_id;                              /* order number, from order_num() */
    long long_time;                                /* time of day, from time() */
    byte ipart;
    char is_ok[2];                              /* Are data OK? message buffer */
    char log_buf[80];                           /* buffer for logentry() string */
    stepcode step_rtn;

    /* Ask if order is OK. */
    tput(23, 2, "Is order OK? <y/n>  _ ");
    strcpy(is_ok, "y");                              /* Default is yes. */
    step_rtn = prompt(is_ok, "Q", 1, 1, MAND, 23, 22);

    if (step_rtn != STEPOK)
        return (step_rtn);
    else if (0 != strchr("NnO", is_ok[0]))
        return (STEPBACK);

    /* Write order data to standard output. Each line begins with */
    /*    two uppercase characters or numbers that indicate the   */
    /*    meaning of that data item.                              */
    order_id = order_num();
    sprintf(log_buf, "ORD %ld, SL %s, TL %ld", order_id, user, part_total);
    logentry(log_buf);                          /* Record order in log file as an audit */
                                                /*    trail for sales and commissions.  */
```

(continued)

ORDBUILD.C (continued)

```
printf("\nBEGIN ORDER %ld\n", order_id);
time(&long_time);                              /* Get time of day as a long. */
printf("TM %s", ctime(&long_time));                  /* Save time of day. */

printf("OF %s\nSL %s\nCN %s\nCO %s\n", office, user, cust_name, company);
printf("SN %s\nSC %s\nST %s\n", ship_name, ship_cmpy, ship_strt);
if (ship_strt2[0] != '\0')
    printf("S2 %s\n", ship_strt2);
printf("SY %s\nSS %s\nSZ %s\n", ship_city, ship_state, ship_zip);

if (bill_name[0] != '\0')              /* Save billing address if different. */
    {
    printf("BN %s\nBC %s\nBT %s\n", bill_name, bill_cmpy, bill_strt);
    if (bill_strt2[0] != '\0')
        printf("B2 %s\n", bill_strt2);
    printf("BY %s\nBS %s\nBZ %s\n", bill_city, bill_state, bill_zip);
    }

if (strchr("Yy1", is_resale[0]))                    /* Is order for resale? */
    printf("RS %s\n", resale_id);                   /* Yes; save resale_id. */

/* List each part, quantity, and price. */
for (ipart = 0; ipart <= last_part && quantities[ipart]; ++ipart)
    printf("PN %s\nQY %ld\nPR %ld\n", parts[ipart],
        quantities[ipart], prices[ipart]);
printf("TL %ld\nTX %ld\nSH %s\nSA %ld\nWT %d\n", part_total,
    tax_amt, ship_car, ship_amt, tot_weight);

if (adv_ref[0] != '\0')
    printf("AD %s\n", adv_ref);
printf("PA %s\n", pay_terms);
if (comment[0] != '\0')
    printf("CM %s\n", comment);
printf("END ORDER %ld\n", order_id);
return (STEPOK);
}
```

The Low Level

The four source files listed in this section hold the low-level application-specific functions that actually do the work managed by the middle-level functions.

get_addr ()

The *get_addr()* function prompts the user for the fields that make up a street address. It eliminates the need for duplicate address-prompting code in *id_cust()* (see *ordbuild.c*), which must prompt for both shipping and billing addresses.

GET_ADDR.C   ▶Page 175

```
/* SOURCE FILE: GET_ADDR.C */
/**********************************************************************/
/* get_addr() prompts for address data for order-entry programs. All data   */
/*    are returned to the caller by arguments 3-9 (yes, 9 is rather high).    */
/**********************************************************************/

#include <stddefs.h>
#include "projutil.h"
#include "ordentry.h"

stepcode get_addr(step_rtn, row, name, company,
    street, street2, city, state, zip)
stepcode step_rtn;                          /* step_rtn is passed in and returned. */
short row;                                          /* screen row to begin prompting */
char name[], company[], street[], street2[], city[], state[], zip[];

    {
    short step;
    enum prompts {NAME, COMPANY, STREET, STREET2, CITY, STATE, ZIP, ENDSTEPS};

    /* Begin at last prompt if screen backed into. */
    step = (step_rtn == STEPOK) ? 0 : (short)ENDSTEPS - 1;
    for (step_rtn = STEPOK; step_rtn != STEPCANC &&
        (step != (short)ENDSTEPS) && (step >= 0); )
        {
        switch (step)
            {
            case NAME:                                              /* Get name. */
                step_rtn = prompt(name, "L", 3, L_SHIP_NAME, MAND, row, 30);
                break;
            case COMPANY:                              /* Get company name. */
                step_rtn = prompt(company, "L", 3, L_SHIP_CMPY, OPT, row + 1, 30);
                break;
            case STREET:                      /* Get first line of street address. */
                step_rtn = prompt(street, "L", 3, L_SHIP_STRT, MAND, row + 2, 30);
                break;
            case STREET2:                      /* Get second line of street address. */
                step_rtn = prompt(street2, "L", 3, L_SHIP_STRT2, OPT, row + 3, 30);
                break;
            case CITY:                                              /* Get city. */
                step_rtn = prompt(city, "L", 2, L_SHIP_CITY, MAND, row + 4, 30);
                break;
            case STATE:                      /* Get state's two-letter abbreviation. */
                step_rtn = prompt(state, "A", L_SHIP_STATE,
                    L_SHIP_STATE, MAND, row + 4, 56);
                break;
            case ZIP:                                              /* Get zip code. */
                step_rtn = prompt(zip, "#", L_SHIP_ZIP,
                    L_SHIP_ZIP, MAND, row + 4, 65);
                break;
            }

        /* Determine next step based on return from last one. */
        if (step_rtn == STEPOK)                          /* Was last successful? */
            ++step;                                      /* Yes; go on to next step. */
        else if (step_rtn == STEPBACK)
            --step;                                      /* No; back up to last step. */
        }
    return (step_rtn);

    }
```

pnt_id_cust()

This "artistic" function paints the field names used to prompt the user for customer identification in an attractive and efficient format on the screen. Painting a screen is friendlier than just displaying the field names one by one as they are prompted for: It lets the user see exactly what data will be needed for the entire section before any individual inputs must be made, and therefore enhances productivity.

PNT_ID_C.C ▶Page 173

```
/* SOURCE FILE: PNT_ID_C.C */
/**********************************************************************/
/* pnt_id_cust() paints screen for order entry: identify customer. This  */
/*    function is called exclusively by id_cust() in ordbuild.c.         */
/**********************************************************************/

#include <stddefs.h>
#include "projutil.h"

void pnt_id_cust()
    {
    tput(4, 10, "Customer Name");
    tput(6, 10, "Company Name");
    tput(7, 10, "Phone Number");

    tput(9, 10, "Ship to Name");
    tput(10, 18, "Company");
    tput(11, 18, "Street");
    tput(12, 18, "2nd Street");
    tput(13, 18, "City");
    tput(13, 49, "State");
    tput(13, 60, "Zip");

    tput(15, 10, "Bill to Name");
    tput(16, 18, "Company");
    tput(17, 18, "Street");
    tput(18, 18, "2nd Street");
    tput(19, 18, "City");
    tput(19, 49, "State");
    tput(19, 60, "Zip");

    tput(21, 10, "Resale?");
    tput(21, 30, "Resale Permit Number");
    tput(23, 10, "Advertising Ref");
    }
```

pnt_ship_pay()

Like *pnt_id_cust()*, *pnt_ship_pay()* paints field names on a formatted prompt screen, this time to prompt for shipping and billing information.

PNT_SHIP.C   ▶Page 245

```
/* SOURCE FILE: PNT_SHIP.C */
/***************************************************************************/
/* pnt_ship_pay() paints the screen for order entry: ship, tax, pay. This  */
/*    function is called exclusively by ship_pay() in ordbuild.c.          */
/***************************************************************************/

#include <stddefs.h>
#include "projutil.h"

void pnt_ship_pay()
   {
   tput(4, 10, "Customer Name");
   tput(6, 10, "Company Name");
   tput(9, 10, "Shipping Weight");
   tput(11, 19, "Carrier");
   tput(11, 51, "Ship Charge");
   tput(11, 64, "$");
   tput(14, 10, "Sales Tax Percent");
   tput(17, 10, "Payment Terms Code");
   tput(18, 51, "Item Total");
   tput(18, 64, "$");
   tput(20, 51, "Order Total");
   tput(20, 64, "$");
   tput(22, 2, "Comment");
   }
```

Stub Functions: *stubs.c*

Top-down structured program development advocates designing and
coding high-level functions before the lower-level ones that they call. The
first versions of these lower-level functions can be dummies that merely
simulate the final versions, but still provide realistic enough behavior to
allow you to test and debug the calling functions. These lower-level dummies, commonly called *stubs,* are replaced later with fully operational
versions (we'll do this later in the book, as we discuss the new techniques
they require).

STUBS.C   ▶Pages 171, 178, 186

```
/* SOURCE FILE: STUBS.C */
/***************************************************************************/
/* Stubs are function prototypes called to test their callers.            */
/*    Here are inv_find(), pw_find(), order_num(), and logentry().        */
/***************************************************************************/

#include <stdio.h>
#include <stddefs.h>
#include "ordentry.h"
```

(continued)

STUBS.C (continued)

```
                                                      ▶Pages 178, 226, 280
/***********************************************************************/
/* inv_find() looks up a part's data in inventory and returns YES if the  */
/*    part is found, NO if it not found. Part description, price, and      */
/*    weight are passed back.                                              */
/***********************************************************************/

flag inv_find(part, part_desc, p_price, p_ship_wt)
char part[];                            /* part number to look up (pass in) */
char part_desc[];                         /* description of part (returned) */
money *p_price;                   /* pointer to unit price of part (returned) */
short *p_ship_wt;            /* pointer to shipping weight in ounces (returned) */

    {

    /* Return typical data to test inv_find()'s callers. */
    strcpy(part_desc, "Order-Entry Software Package");
    *p_price = 12345L;
    *p_ship_wt = 123;
    return (part[0] == 'S');                     /* YES if 'S' first, else NO */
    }
                                                      ▶Pages 171, 258
/***********************************************************************/
/* pw_find() looks up a user's name and password and returns YES if the user */
/*    is found, NO if not. If the user is found, office ID is also checked.   */
/*    User data contain indication of whether to ring bell.                  */
/***********************************************************************/

flag pw_find(office, user, password)
char office[];                    /* description of user's office (returned) */
char user[];              /* name, initials, or abbreviation of user to find */
char password[];                                   /* password to be looked up */

    {
    IMPORT bflag bell_ok;

    CDBG("pw_find 1 bell_ok", bell_ok);
    if (user[1] == 'S')                          /* OK to ring the bell? */
        bell_ok = NO;                            /* No. Silence the bell. */
    CDBG("pw_find 2 bell_ok", bell_ok);
    return (user[0] == 'S' && password[0] == 'S');
    }
                                                      ▶Pages 186, 260
/***********************************************************************/
/* order_num() returns the order number to use for the next order. The order */
/*    number is a counter that increases by one with each order.             */
/***********************************************************************/

long order_num()

    {
    return (10001L);
    }
                                                      ▶Pages 186, 259
/***********************************************************************/
/* logentry() appends message text to the end of the log file, typically for */
/*    audit, error detection, and security purposes.                         */
/***********************************************************************/

void logentry(msg)
    char msg[];
    {
    }
```

The Project Utility Functions

The project utility functions, which are general-purpose enough for use in many other applications, implement our program's communication with the user. They prompt for data, control input, validate input, and provide error messages. They are the "workhorses" of our application.

prompt()

The *prompt()* function prompts the user for string input, in a friendly but tightly controlled manner. The input may be either mandatory or optional, and you may supply a default value if you wish. This function is called to perform all user data inputs in the order-entry application; therefore, the user prompts are uniform and the user can learn the system more quickly.

PROMPT.C ▶Pages 168, 205

```
/* SOURCE FILE: PROMPT.C */
/******************************************************************************/
/* prompt() inputs text from standard input to the string "data".            */
/*    Input is matched against an optional match-string argument. Minimum and */
/*    maximum input lengths are checked. If Boolean (flag) argument mand      */
/*    is true, then "data" will not be allowed to remain null; an entry must  */
/*    be made. The parameter "data" is both passed in and returned to the     */
/*    caller. The value passed in is treated as a default to be used if input */
/*    is null. Data are input character-at-a-time, without automatic echo.    */
/* Return value: the outcome of prompt has synonym data type stepcode, which  */
/*    is used to indicate:                                                     */
/*       STEPOK     Step complete; go on to next step.                        */
/*       STEPBACK   Back up to closest previous step.                         */
/*       STEPCANC   Cancel order entry (quit).                                */
/*    C_BACK, C_NULL, and C_CANC are defined in projutil.h. The user can      */
/*       request to back up by entering C_BACK, to cancel by entering C_CANC, */
/*       or to erase data by entering C_NULL as any character in the reply.   */
/******************************************************************************/

#include <stdio.h>
#include <stddefs.h>
#include "projutil.h"

stepcode prompt(data, match_str, min_len, max_len, mand, row, col)
char data[];                    /* Default passed in, input data returned. */
char match_str[];                       /* match string to verify data against */
short min_len, max_len;             /* minimum and maximum input data lengths */
flag mand;                      /* If yes, data cannot be null on return.  */
short row, col;                         /* cursor location to begin input */
```

(continued)

PROMPT.C (continued)

```
    {
    IMPORT bflag bell_ok;                          /* global permission to ring bell */
    char buf[PRMTBSIZ];                                 /* prompt input buffer */
    short ichar;                                   /* input character counter */
    stepcode rtn = STEPOK;                                     /* return code */
    bflag more;                                        /* Expect more input? */

    /* Display prompt mask or default value, if any. */
    /* Copy default to buffer. Fill rest of buffer with prompt mask */
    /*    characters, to maximum length of field prompted for.      */
    strcpy(buf, data);
    for (ichar = strlen(buf); ichar < max_len; ++ichar)
        buf[ichar] = C_MASK;
    buf[ichar] = '\0';
    tput(row, col, buf);
    CUR_MV(row, col);

    /* Input each character. */
    strcpy(buf, data);                               /* Copy default value to buffer. */
    for (ichar = 0, more = YES; ichar < max_len && more; )
        {
        buf[ichar] = getch();                 /* Input a character (no auto echo). */
#if defined(DEBUG)
if (buf[ichar] < ' ')              /* DEBUG: Show all control characters input. */
    CDBG("prompt buf[ichar] = getch()", buf[ichar]);
#endif
        buf[ichar + 1] = '\0';
        switch (buf[ichar])
            {
            case C_CANC:                                      /* Cancel command. */
                rtn = STEPCANC, more = NO;
                break;
            case C_BACK:                            /* Back up to previous prompt. */
                rtn = STEPBACK, more = NO;
                break;
            case C_NULL:                    /* Force data to null, restart prompt. */
                IDBG("prompt C_NULL max_len", max_len);

                /* Fill buffer with mask characters to maximum length of field. */
                for (ichar = 0; ichar < max_len; ++ichar)
                    buf[ichar] = C_MASK;
                buf[ichar] = '\0';
                tput(row, col, buf);              /* Show prompt mask in buf. */
                ichar = 0;                        /* Restart at first character. */
                buf[ichar] = data[ichar] = '\0';                 /* Erase data. */
                CUR_MV(row, col);          /* Move cursor to beginning of mask. */
                break;
            case '\r':                                          /* end of line */
            case '\n':                                /* alternate end of line */
                if (ichar == 0 && data[0] != '\0')

                    /* Pass default back to caller. */
                    strcpy(buf, data), more = NO;
```

(continued)

```
            else if (ichar == 0 && data[0] == '\0' && mand)
                {                       /* mandatory entry, no default supplied */
                err_warn("Data must be entered:", "");
                CUR_MV(row, col);
                }

            /* Too few characters? Check, unless this is first */
            /*    character of reply and reply is optional.    */
            else if (ichar < min_len && !(ichar == 0 && !mand))
                {
                err_warn("Too few characters:", "");
                CUR_MV(row, col + ichar);                   /* Restore cursor. */
                }
            else
                buf[ichar] = '\0', more = NO;                /* end of input */
            break;
        case '\b':                              /* Backspace (BS) entered. */
            buf[ichar] = '\0';                  /* Delete backspace. */
            if (ichar > 0)
                {
                buf[--ichar] = '\0';            /* Wipe character before BS. */
                fputc('\b', stderr);            /* Fix display to match. */
                fputc(C_MASK, stderr);
                fputc(C_MASK, stderr);
                fprintf(stderr, "\b\b");
                }
            break;
        default:                     /* Check match and length; echo character. */

            /* Echo if character is legal; else ring bell. */
            buf[ichar + 1] = '\0';     /* Save character and increment ichar. */
            if (match(buf, match_str))
                putc(buf[ichar++], stderr);             /* Echo good character. */
            else if (bell_ok)              /* Bad character entered; ring bell. */
                putc('\7', stderr);
            if (ichar > max_len)
                more = NO;
            break;
        }
    }

/* Copy buf to data and erase rest of prompt mask (if any). */
if (rtn == STEPOK)
    strcpy(data, buf);
ichar = strlen(data);
CUR_MV(row, col + ichar);
for (; ichar < max_len; ++ichar)
    fputc(' ', stderr);                     /* Erase end of mask, using spaces. */
return (rtn);
}
```

nprompt() and *fprompt()*

The *nprompt()* and *fprompt()* functions are the numeric counterparts of the string-input function, *prompt(). nprompt()* asks the user for a *long* integer value, which is input first as a string through a call to

prompt( ), and then converted to binary format using the library function
atol( ). *fprompt( )* asks for a double-precision floating-point value and
uses the library function *atof( )* for the conversion.

NPROMPT.C
▶Pages 179, 211

```
/* SOURCE FILE: NPROMPT.C */
/***********************************************************************/
/* nprompt() inputs a long integer from standard input. Input is matched   */
/*   against an optional match-string argument. Minimum and maximum input  */
/*   values are checked. If the Boolean (flag) argument mand is true, then  */
/*   data will not be permitted to remain zero; data must be entered. The   */
/*   parameter *p_num is both passed in and returned to the caller. The     */
/*   value passed in is treated as a default to be used if input is null.   */
/* Return value: the outcome of nprompt() has synonym data type stepcode,   */
/*   which is used to indicate:                                             */
/*      STEPOK    Step complete; valid number obtained.                     */
/*      STEPBACK  Back up to the previous step.                             */
/*      STEPCANC  Cancel order entry (quit).                                */
/*   The user can request to back up by entering C_BACK, to cancel by       */
/*   entering C_CANC, or to set *p_num to zero by entering C_NULL as any    */
/*   character In reply.                                                    */
/***********************************************************************/

#include <stdio.h>
#include <stddefs.h>
#include "projutil.h"

stepcode nprompt(p_num, match_str, min_val, max_val, mand, row, col)
long *p_num;                    /* Default passed in, input data returned. */
char match_str[];                    /* match string to verify data against */
long min_val, max_val;               /* minimum and maximum input values */
flag mand;                      /* If yes, data cannot be zero on return. */
short row, col;                           /* cursor location to begin input */

    {
    /* With Microsoft C:  #include <stdlib.h> for next declaration. */
    long atol(char[]);          /* Library function atol() returns type long. */
    char buf[14];                                     /* prompt input buffer */
    bflag more = YES;                                 /* Prompt again? */
    long in_num;                /* ASCII input number converted to binary */
    short max_len = strlen(ltoa(max_val, buf, 10));
    short min_len = strlen(ltoa(min_val, buf, 10));
    stepcode rtn;                                     /* return code */

    /* Supply as default if p_num points to a non-zero long. */
    if (*p_num)                             /* Non-zero value passed in? */
        {
        ntput(row, col, *p_num, buf, max_len);          /* Display default. */
        }
    else                                            /* no default */
        buf[0] = '\0';
```

(continued)

NPROMPT.C (continued)

```
    /* Loop: Prompt for number in string form, until value    */
    /*    entered is in range, or cancel or back up requested. */
    do
        {
        rtn = prompt(buf, match_str, min_len, max_len, mand, row, col);
        if (rtn != STEPOK)
            more = NO;                      /* Done prompting (back up or cancel). */
        else                   /* Check whether input mandatory and reply in range. */
            {
            in_num = atol(buf);            /* Convert ASCII input to long integer. */
            SDBG("nprompt buf", buf);
            LDBG("nprompt in_num", in_num);

            /* If mandatory and number is zero, this is an error. */
            if (mand && in_num == 0)
                err_warn("Non-zero data mandatory:", "");

            /* Otherwise, verify in_num is inside specified range, provided */
            /*    prompt is mandatory or number entered is non-zero.        */
            else if ((in_num < min_val || in_num > max_val) &&
                (mand || in_num != 0))
                {
                sprintf(buf, "%ld to %ld", min_val, max_val);
                err_warn("Enter a number from:", buf);
                buf[0] = '\0';
                }
            else                           /* Got a good value; done prompting. */
                more = NO;
            }
        }
    while (more);

    if (rtn == STEPOK)                              /* Then echo, right justified. */
        {
        *p_num = in_num;                            /* Pass value back to caller. */

        /* Echo number right justified in screen field. */
        ntput(row, col, in_num, buf, max_len);
        }
    return (rtn);
    }
```

FPROMPT.C   ▶**Pages 182, 212**

```
/* SOURCE FILE: FPROMPT.C */
/**********************************************************************/
/* fprompt() inputs a double-precision floating-point number from standard  */
/*    input. It behaves the same as nprompt(), except that the arguments    */
/*    width and precision must be passed to fprompt() to indicate the width */
/*    of the field and the number of digits to prompt for on the right of the */
/*    decimal point.                                                        */
/**********************************************************************/

#include <stdio.h>
#include <stddefs.h>
#include "projutil.h"
```

(continued)

FPROMPT.C (continued)

```
stepcode fprompt(d_num, match_str, min_dval, max_dval,
    width, precision, mand, row, col)
double *d_num;                          /* Default passed in, input data returned. */
char match_str[];
double min_dval, max_dval;                  /* minimum and maximum input values */
short width, precision;                     /* field width and decimal places */
flag mand;                              /* If yes, data cannot be zero on return. */
short row, col;                             /* cursor location to begin input */

    {
    short dec, sign;                        /* dummy arguments to pass to fcvt() */
    double atof(char[]);        /* Library function atof() returns type double. */
    char buf[14], format[14];       /* prompt input buffer and format string */
    bflag more = YES;
    double in_dnum;                     /* ASCII input number converted to double */
    short max_len = width;
    short min_len = strlen(fcvt(min_dval, precision, &dec, &sign)) - precision;
    stepcode rtn;

    /* Supply as default if d_num points to a non-zero double. */
    if (*d_num != 0.0)                          /* Non-zero value passed in? */
        {
        ftput(row, col, *d_num, precision, buf, max_len);  /* Display default. */
        }
    else                                        /* no default */
        buf[0] = '\0';
    do
        {
        rtn = prompt(buf, match_str, min_len, max_len, mand, row, col);
        if (rtn != STEPOK)
            more = NO;
        else
            {
            in_dnum = atof(buf);                        /* Convert ASCII to double. */
            if (mand && in_dnum == 0.0)
                err_warn("Non-zero data mandatory:", "");
            else if ((in_dnum < min_dval || in_dnum > max_dval) &&
                (mand || in_dnum != 0.0))
                {

                /* Create string to pass to err_warn(). */
                sprintf(buf, "%.*f to %.*f", precision, min_dval,
                    precision, max_dval);
                err_warn("Enter a number from:", buf);
                buf[0] = '\0';
                CUR_MV(row, col);
                }
            else
                more = NO;
            }
        }
    while (more);

    if (rtn == STEPOK)                          /* Then echo, right justified. */
        {
        *d_num = in_dnum;                       /* Pass value back to caller. */
        ftput(row, col, *d_num, precision, buf, max_len);
        }
    return (rtn);
    }
```

tput()

The low-level terminal output routine *tput()* displays a string of text
at a specific cursor row and column.

TPUT.C   ▶Pages 173, 193

```
/* SOURCE FILE: TPUT.C */
/***********************************************************************/
/* tput() displays a string at a specified row and column.            */
/***********************************************************************/
#include <stdio.h>
#include <stddefs.h>

void tput(row, col, text)
short row, col;                                         /* cursor location */
char text[];                                            /* text to display */

    {
    CUR_MV(row, col);
    fputs(text, stderr);
    }
```

ntput() and ftput()

You may use the functions *ntput()* and *ftput()* as alternatives
to *printf()* for the output of a *long* or *double* value (respectively), right
justified in a designated field, at a specific cursor row and column on
the user's screen.

NTPUT.C   ▶Pages 178, 195

```
/* SOURCE FILE: NTPUT.C */
/***********************************************************************/
/* ntput() converts a long integer to ASCII and displays it right justified */
/*    in field of specified width. The left side is padded with blanks.     */
/***********************************************************************/

#include <stddefs.h>
#include "projutil.h"

void ntput(row, col, long_val, buf, field_len)
short row, col;                                         /* cursor location */
long long_val;                                      /* value to be displayed */
char buf[];
short field_len;                        /* length of field to right justify in */

    {
    ltoa(long_val, buf, 10);               /* Convert long to ASCII string. */
    strrjust(buf, field_len);                      /* Right justify field. */
    tput(row, col, buf);                     /* Display on screen for user. */
    }
```

FTPUT.C ▶Pages 179, 195

```
/* SOURCE FILE: FTPUT.C */
/*************************************************************************/
/* ftput() converts a double-precision floating-point number to ASCII and */
/*   displays it right justified in field of specified width, with       */
/*   specified decimal places.                                           */
/*************************************************************************/

#include <stddefs.h>
#include "projutil.h"

void ftput(row, col, double_val, dec_place, buf, field_len)
short row, col;
double double_val;                              /* value to be displayed */
short dec_place, field_len;         /* decimal places and length of field */
char buf[];

    {
    char *fcvt();   /* fcvt() returns a pointer to a temporary string buffer. */
    short dec, sign;    /* pointers to decimal and sign returned from fcvt() */
    short pos;                         /* position counter for "for" loop */

    /* Copy contents of temporary string buffer to buf. */
    strcpy(buf, fcvt(double_val, dec_place, &dec, &sign));

    /* Move digits on right of decimal point and '\0' */
    /*   one place to right and insert decimal point. */
    for (pos = strlen(buf); pos >= dec; --pos)
        buf[pos + 1] = buf[pos];
    buf[dec] = '.';
    strrjust(buf, field_len);
    tput(row, col, buf);
    }
```

beg_scrn()

The *beg_scrn()* function sets up a new screen by clearing the existing screen and displaying such headings as the user's name, the application name, and the screen title. This information is helpful to the user and also enhances system security.

BEG_SCRN.C ▶Pages 167, 172

```
/* SOURCE FILE: BEG_SCRN.C */
/*************************************************************************/
/* beg_scrn() clears the screen and displays screen heading strings. Four */
/*   headings may be shown: left, center, right, below. The first three   */
/*   headings appear on the top line, the last is centered on the next line. */
/*************************************************************************/

#include <stddefs.h>                       /* for CLR_SCRN (clear screen) */
#include <stdio.h>                     /* for stderr for screen control */
#include "projutil.h"                   /* for declarations of tput() */

#define SCRNWDTH 80                                    /* screen width */
```

(continued)

BEG_SCRN.C (continued)

```
void beg_scrn(left, center, right, below)
char left[], center[], right[], below[];               /* headings or null */

   {
   CLR_SCRN;
   tput(1, 1, left);
   tput(1, (SCRNWDTH - strlen(center)) / 2, center);   /* Center heading. */
   tput(1, 1 + SCRNWDTH - strlen(right), right);
   tput(2, (SCRNWDTH - strlen(below)) / 2, below);     /* Center heading. */
   }
```

match()

The *match()* function is called by *prompt()* to compare a string typed
by the user with a match pattern that represents all possible acceptable
inputs. This enables us to limit user input to specific kinds of data and also
helps the user catch typographical errors.

MATCH.C   ►Page 208

```
/* SOURCE FILE: MATCH.C */
/******************************************************************************/
/* match() verifies a data string, character by character, against a match   */
/*    string. If the match string is shorter than the data string, the       */
/*    last match-string character is used to verify the data string.         */
/*    The match string may be composed of these match characters:            */
/*                                                                            */
/*     A    A-Z                              (uppercase letters)              */
/*     #    0-9 only                         (numbers)                        */
/*     S    0-9 or + or -                    (signs or numbers)               */
/*     F    0-9 or .                         (floating-point numbers)         */
/*     L    a-z, A-Z, 0-9 or ;:.,/?*-$#()'!  (names, addresses)               */
/*          and non-leading spaces                                            */
/*     U    A-Z, 0-9 or ;:.,/?*-$#()'!       (uppercase names, addresses)     */
/*          and non-leading spaces                                            */
/*     P    0-9 or - or () or space          (phone numbers)                  */
/*     Q    one of "YylNn0"                  (question reply)                 */
/*     X    any printable character          (text)                          */
/*                                                                            */
/*     Any other character in the match string is ignored. Spaces are matched */
/*     by L, U, and P. Empty match string matches any data.                   */
/* Return value: YES = data string matches; NO = no match.                    */
/******************************************************************************/

#include <stddefs.h>
#include <ctype.h>                /* for isxxx() character-type macro definitions */

flag match(data_str, match_str)
char data_str[];                              /* source string to be verified */
char match_str[];                             /* match characters to match */
   {
   short ichar;                                    /* input character counter */
   char c_data;                                    /* character of data string */
   char c_match;                                   /* character of match string */
```

(continued)

MATCH.C (continued)

```c
/* Initialize a variable to a function return. */
short len_match = strlen(match_str);
bflag matches = YES;

for (ichar = 0; data_str[ichar] != '\0' && matches; ++ichar)
    {

    /* Determine match character. */
    if (ichar < len_match)                          /* Use next match character. */
        c_match = match_str[ichar];
    else if (len_match == 0)                                    /* null match_str */
        c_match = '\0';
    else                                   /* Use last character of match string. */
        c_match = match_str[len_match - 1];
    c_data = data_str[ichar];
    switch (c_match)                                    /* Check match with data. */
        {
        case 'A':                                                     /* A-Z */
            if (!isupper(c_data))
                matches = NO;
            break;
        case '#':                                                /* 0-9 only */
            if (!isdigit(c_data))
                matches = NO;
            break;
        case 'S':                                      /* 0-9 or + or - only */
            if (!isdigit(c_data) && !strchr("+-", c_data))
                matches = NO;
            break;
        case 'L':              /* a-z, A-Z, 0-9 or ;:.,/?*-$#()'! or space */
            if (!isalnum(c_data) && !strchr(";:.,/?*-$#()'! ",
                c_data))
                matches = NO;
            if (ichar == 0 && c_data == ' ')           /* no leading blanks */
                matches = NO;
            break;
        case 'U':                    /* A-Z, 0-9 or ;:.,/?*-$#()'! or space */
            if (!isupper(c_data) && !isdigit(c_data) &&
                !strchr(";:.,/?*-$#()'! ", c_data))
                matches = NO;
            if (ichar == 0 && c_data == ' ')           /* no leading blanks */
                matches = NO;
            break;
        case 'P':                                 /* 0-9 or - or () or space */
            if (!isdigit(c_data) && !strchr("-() ", c_data))
                matches = NO;
            break;
        case 'F':                                                /* 0-9 or . */
            if (!isdigit(c_data) && !strchr(".", c_data))
                matches = NO;
            break;
        case 'Q':                        /* YylNn0 as reply to yes/no question */
            if (!strchr("YylNn0", c_data))
                matches = NO;
            break;
        case 'X':                                /* Must be printable (' '-'~'). */
            if (!isprint(c_data))
                matches = NO;
            break;
        }
    }
return (matches);
}
```

strrjust()

The standard library lacks a function for right justifying text in a string of fixed length, so we need the project utility function *strrjust()* to accomplish this. The code for this function demonstrates conditionally compiled debugging techniques, using debug macros from *stddefs.h* and its own test-driver *main()* function that verifies *strrjust()*'s correctness and documents examples of its use. All the debug code here may be left in the source file without any execution overhead, provided the symbols *DEBUG* and *DBGMAIN* are not defined (thus the term *conditionally compiled*).

STRRJUST.C   ▶Page 195

```
/* SOURCE FILE: STRRJUST.C */
/***********************************************************************/
/* strrjust() takes a string and a length and right justifies the string in */
/*   a field of that length. If the string is longer than the field, no      */
/*   action is taken.                                                        */
/***********************************************************************/
#include <stdio.h>
#include <stddefs.h>

void strrjust(str, fld_len)
char str[];
short fld_len;

    {
    short end_char, ichar, move;

    SDBG("strrjust before str", str);
    IDBG("fld_len", fld_len);

    /* Find index of last non-space in str and back up from there  */
    /*   toward beginning; then fill left end of str with blanks.  */
    for (end_char = strlen(str) - 1;
        str[end_char] == ' ' && end_char > 0; --end_char)
        ;
    move = fld_len - end_char - 1;                          /* number of positions */
    IDBG("move", move);
    if (move > 0 && end_char >= 0)                          /* Need to move anything? */
        {

        /* Copy characters. */
        for (ichar = end_char; ichar >= 0; --ichar)
            str[ichar + move] = str[ichar];

        /* Fill left end with blanks. */
        for (ichar = move - 1; ichar >= 0; --ichar)
            str[ichar] = ' ';
        str[fld_len] = '\0';                               /* null terminator */
        }
    SDBG("strrjust str", str);
    }
```

(continued)

STRRJUST.C (continued)

```
#if defined(DBGMAIN)
#define TEST(cond, msg) printf((cond) ? "" : \
   "!!! TEST FAILED !!! %s\7\n", (msg))

/* Test driver main() for strrjust(). */
main()
   {
   char str[81];

   strcpy(str, "abc");
   strrjust(str, 5);
   TEST(0 == strcmp(str, "  abc"), "strjust #1");
   strcpy(str, "ABCDE");
   strrjust(str, 5);
   TEST(0 == strcmp(str, "ABCDE"), "strjust #2");
   strcpy(str, "");
   strrjust(str, 5);
   TEST(0 == strcmp(str, ""), "strjust #3");
   printf("strrjust tests complete\n");
   }
#endif
```

err_warn() and *err_exit()*

The functions *err_warn()* and *err_exit()* are a team. We employ
them to output diagnostic messages to the user. Use *err_warn()* for warn-
ings about errors that can be corrected and *err_exit()* for fatal errors after
which you want your program to terminate.

ERR_WARN.C   ▶Pages 170, 214

```
/* SOURCE FILE: ERR_WARN.C */
/********************************************************************************/
/* err_warn() displays a two-string diagnostic message on line 24, waits     */
/*    for the user to press ESC, and then erases the diagnostic message.     */
/********************************************************************************/

#include <stdio.h>
#include <stddefs.h>
#include "projutil.h"

#define ESC '\x1b'

void err_warn(first, second)
char first[], second[];                        /* two parts of diagnostic message */

   {
   IMPORT bflag bell_ok;
   short first_len = strlen(first);
   short second_len = strlen(second);
```

(continued)

ERR_WARN.C (continued)

```
    CUR_MV(24, 1);
    CLR_LINE;
    tput(24, 1, first);
    tput(24, 2 + first_len, second);
    tput(24, 3 + first_len + second_len,
        "_ (push ESC)\b\b\b\b\b\b\b\b\b\b\b");
    if (bell_ok)
        BELL;
    while (getch() != ESC)                          /* Loop until Escape entered. */
        if (bell_ok)
            BELL;
    CUR_MV(24, 1);
    CLR_LINE;
    }
```

►Page 214
```
/********************************************************************************/
/* err_exit() displays a diagnostic message through err_warn() and calls       */
/*   exit() to terminate execution. The two-part message is displayed on        */
/*   line 24. When the user presses ESC, the message is erased.                 */
/********************************************************************************/

void err_exit(first, second)
char first[], second[];                             /* two parts of diagnostic message */

    {
    char log_buf[512];

    strcpy(log_buf, first);
    strcat(log_buf, " ");
    strcat(log_buf, second);
    logentry(log_buf);                              /* Record the message in the log. */
    err_warn(first, second);                                  /* Display the message. */
    exit(FAIL);                                     /* Terminate program: FAIL status. */
    }
```

That concludes the source-code listings for the Software Vendor
Order-Entry Application. We'll spend the next few chapters discussing each
function in detail.

Top- and
Middle-Level Functions

11

Now that you have all the source listings in front of you, let's look at each part of the order-entry application in detail. The bulk of the code deals with the input of data about a customer and about the products being ordered. In the spirit of structured programming, we'll begin at a high level and work our way down to the low-level "workhorse" functions.

The User Interface

The user interface—the manner in which a program and its users communicate commands and data to one another—is at the heart of this highly interactive business application. It is the face our program shows to the human world.

The technology of the user interface has come a long way in a very short time. The earliest user/computer communication devices, such as teletypes, had keyboards and hard-copy output, but they were slow and cumbersome. Then came the CRT, with features like a directly addressable cursor, graphics symbols, and protected and highlighted fields. Today's interface options include light pens, touch screens, mice, track balls, and bit-mapped graphics displays. All of these innovations can decrease training time and increase user productivity.

The physical interface employed by our order-entry application consists of a simple monochrome CRT display and a standard PC keyboard. The CRT need be capable only of text display, cursor movement, screen erasure, and erasure from the cursor to the end of the line.

But the user interface is more than just hardware. It is also the invisible element—the software—that makes the application easy, efficient, and pleasant to use. Productivity is one way of measuring the quality of this side of an interface. Productivity in this case is defined as the number of transactions a user enters per hour, less the number of errors and the amount of effort involved in finding and correcting those errors. The users of our order-entry program are salespeople, not programmers, and they appreciate the ability to correct mistakes in an order quickly and easily, while they are entering it, rather than later. And they are more productive users if they do not need to retype the entire order just to correct a mistake in one line. Good defaults and abbreviations for frequently entered text also help the user by reducing keystrokes and chance of error.

The order-entry program incorporates most of these user-interface features, so we'll discuss them in detail as we work our way through the source code.

Top-Level Program Structure

The file *ordentry.c* holds the top-level function of the order-entry program, *main()*. This function controls the flow among prompt screens, each of which is implemented as a separate middle-level function called from *main()*. The screen called up for display may be the screen following the current screen or the one before it, depending upon the outcome of some of the entries in the current screen. (The structure of the *main()* function for our order-entry application was shown in Figure 10-1.)

The prompt-screen functions constitute the middle level of the order-entry application. They reside in the source file *ordbuild.c*. Each function "paints" the screen with field titles and messages that will be used to prompt the user for data. The middle-level functions contain many calls to low-level functions and are written to avoid device and environment dependencies (the code to handle such dependencies is hidden away in the low-level functions that they call).

Before I began to code the *main()* function, I had to make some decisions about how we would handle our data. Let's look at those decisions more closely before we begin analyzing the code itself.

Data Structures

There are only a few data structures in *main()*, and they are included in the first few lines of code. The defining declaration of *bell_ok* allocates memory to hold *bell_ok*'s value and sets the value initially to *YES*, to permit the bell to sound. Although *main()* itself doesn't use *bell_ok*, I chose to place the defining declaration at the start of the *main()* source file because *bell_ok* is *GLOBAL*. (In fact, the declaration could be in any single source file we choose, as long as it is outside the body of any function.)

```
#include <stddefs.h>
#include "projutil.h"

GLOBAL bflag bell_ok = YES;

main()
    {
    IMPORT stepcode id_user(void), id_cust(stepcode);
    IMPORT stepcode ord_itms(stepcode), ship_pay(stepcode);
    IMPORT stepcode wrt_ord(void);
    short step;
    stepcode step_rtn;
    enum prompts {ID_USER, ID_CUST, ORD_ITMS, SHIP_PAY, WRT_ORD,
        ENDSTEPS};
```

The three lines of *IMPORT*s declare the return and parameter types for the middle-level functions called by *main()*. Only two data types appear in these declarations: *void* and *stepcode*. The type *void* is standard and means "no data." A function declared to take a single parameter of type *void* is, practically speaking, declared to take no parameters. The type *stepcode* is a synonym data type we defined in the header file *projutil.h*; we'll discuss synonym data types next.

C A U T I O N

Many C compilers cannot check the number or types of arguments. These compilers usually ignore parameter declarations within function declarations, so the function declarations will compile without them and not create a portability problem.

Synonym Data Types

Sometimes the standard type declarations don't give us as much information about our data as we would like. C offers us the opportunity to correct this problem by creating *synonym* data types.

Programmer-defined synonym data types are absolutely equivalent to the underlying types they are declared to represent, so why use them? Readability, of course: They supply extra information for the reader of the program—information that clarifies the purpose or uses of the declared variables. Consider the synonym type *flag*, defined in our *stddefs.h* header file. Type *flag* is equivalent to type *int*, but since the word *flag* implies a Boolean true/false range of values, it gives a clearer, more accurate impression of the purpose of the variable. In this next example, *more_data*'s purpose would be pretty ambiguous with an *int* declaration:

```
#include <stddefs.h>                                     /*Needed for flag and YES. */

    /* ... */
flag more_data = YES;                                    /* Any data left? */

    /* ... */
while (more_data)                                        /* Loop for each item of data. */
```

More than one synonym type may be defined in a single *typedef* statement, as in this next example, where *byte* and *unchar* are both made synonyms of type *unsigned char*:

```
typedef unsigned char byte, unchar;
```

The *stepcode* type.   The type *stepcode* is designated as a synonym of type *char* by this *typedef* statement in the *projutil.h* header file:

```
typedef char stepcode;
```

The *stepcode* type is used in *main( )*'s declarations because it gives the reader more information than type *char*. (Type *char* merely designates a 1-byte value, an ASCII character.) A *stepcode* value is a number returned by a step in the prompting process, to describe the outcome of the prompt. The three possible return values defined in *projutil.h* are:

```
#define STEPOK 0
#define STEPBACK 1
#define STEPCANC 2
```

Although a *stepcode* declaration gives the reader more information than a *char* declaration, the program itself will behave the same in either case.

The *enum* type.   The last declaration in *main( )* that we need to discuss is the *enum* type *prompts*.

C's enumeration facility permits the declaration of a variable whose value must always be one of the constants in the declaration's enumeration list. In our programs, the *enum* type *prompts* creates a list of constants from 0 to 5, for use as case labels in a *switch* statement. The value of *ID_USER* is *0*, *ID_CUST* is *1*, and so on. The names in the enumeration list must be listed in the same order as they are normally executed. The *switch* command uses this list to control the call to the next step in the order-entry process, which may in fact be the previous step again, or a subsequent one, depending upon the *stepcode* return from the current step. (Uppercase is used for these named constants, as for *#define*d symbols, to avoid mistaking them for variables.)

The name following the keyword *enum* (in this case, *prompts*) is the enumeration type being defined. This new enumeration type is used to declare variables whose values are restricted to the list of enumerated constants in the type definition.

To assign a value other than *0* for the first *enum*-list identifier, or other than *1* plus the previous identifier's value to subsequent identifiers, use the = assignment operator and a constant expression after the identifier *within the list*. The value of the constant expression must be type *int,* and may be negative. The next name in the *enum*-list after this assignment will be 1 higher, unless it too is assigned

C A U T I O N

Many C compilers do not support the enumeration type, and restrictions on its use vary. Microsoft C does support enum-type variables, but does not allow arithmetic operations on them.

a different value. For example, the assignment you see embedded in the enumeration below causes the value of the constant *CAMEL* to be *100*, not *3*, and the value of *MULE* to be *101*:

```
enum shipper {POST, AIR, RAIL, CAMEL = 100, MULE};
enum shipper ship_via;                  /* Declare ship_via type shipper. */

ship_via = AIR;                         /* Assign legal value to ship_via. */
```

The Flow of Control at the Top

One of the interface requirements for our program is that the system permit the user to correct data in an earlier part of an order easily, without having to reenter all the data after the corrected field. To code for this capability without using the troublesome *goto* statement, we can use a *switch* statement that chooses the steps to perform. Let's look at how our *main()* handles this.

```
for (step = 0, step_rtn = STEPOK; step != (short)ENDSTEPS &&
    step_rtn != STEPCANC; )
    {
    switch (step)
        {
        case ID_USER:
            step_rtn = id_user();
            break;
        case ID_CUST:
            step_rtn = id_cust(step_rtn);
            break;
        case ORD_ITMS:
            step_rtn = ord_itms(step_rtn);
            break;
        case SHIP_PAY:
            step_rtn = ship_pay(step_rtn);
            break;
        case WRT_ORD:
            step_rtn = wrt_ord();
            break;
        }
    if (step_rtn == STEPOK)
        ++step;
    else if (step_rtn == STEPBACK && step > 0)
        --step;
    }
```

The body of the *main()* function is a loop. Each time the program passes through the loop, one step of the order-entry process is executed. A *short* counter variable named *step* is set and then used to select the next step to perform. The value of *step* is always one of the *enum*-type *prompts* values. The *if…else* at the bottom of the loop picks the step from the *prompts* enumeration to be executed next. The value of *step* is incremented after a step is completed successfully, or decremented if the user requests the program to back up to the previous step. Thus the *switch* statement gives a clean way for control to flow backward or forward, without using *goto*. This control structure makes it easy to add, remove, or reorder steps at a later time. (Remember that arithmetic operators such as increment and decrement are not permitted on enumerated variables, so we've declared the variable *step* as type *short*, rather than *enum*-type *prompts*.)

Middle-Level Program Structure

The source files *ordbuild.c* and *get_addr.c* hold the middle level of our order-entry application, the prompt screens. The middle level supplies the specifics of the prompt for each of the data fields and calls the low-level functions that actually input and output the data. Text is output at specific cursor locations on the screen, and inputs are made in a specific sequence and checked for validity.

The control-flow style used in *main()* is copied in some of these middle-level order-entry functions, to permit the user to move backward as well as forward through the individual fields of a screen, as well as between screens. For instance, if the user is being asked to input the first field of the third screen but instead gives the "back up" command (by typing ^R), the next prompt will be for the final field on the second screen.

The primary difference between top- and middle-level steps is the amount of work they do. A step in the *main()* function is all the interactions involved in inputting a whole prompt screen of order data. But in middle-level functions, a step is usually only the input of a single field of data. Figure 11-1 shows the functions included in the two middle-level source files.

FIGURE 11-1

Middle-level order-entry functions

FILE	FUNCTION NAME	PURPOSE
ordbuild.c	*id_user()*	Identify the user/salesperson.
	id_cust()	Identify the customer.
	ord_itms()	Input order items.
	ship_pay()	Arrange shipment and payment terms.
	wrt_ord()	Write order to standard output.
get_addr.c	*get_addr()*	Input an address for shipping or billing.

The *id_user()* Function

The *id_user()* function is responsible for application security. It is called every time an order is entered, to ensure that the user is really a bona fide company salesperson, and not a hacker trying to break into the system.

```
stepcode id_user()
    {
    IMPORT char user[];
    IMPORT char office[];
    IMPORT char scrn_title[];
    flag pw_find(char *, char *, char *);
    char password[L_PASSWORD + 1];
    stepcode step_rtn;
    short ichar;

    beg_scrn("", scrn_title, "", "SALESPERSON");
    tput(10, 20, "Office");
    tput(12, 20, "Salesperson");
    tput(14, 20, "Password");
    do
        {
        step_rtn = prompt(office, "L", 3, L_OFFICE, MAND, 10, 32);
        if (step_rtn == STEPBACK)
            err_warn("Office must be supplied:", "");
        }
    while (step_rtn == STEPBACK);
    if (step_rtn != STEPCANC)
        do
            {
            user[0] = '\0';
            step_rtn = prompt(user, "L", 2, L_USER, MAND, 12, 32);
            if (step_rtn == STEPBACK)
                err_warn("I must know who you are:", "");
            }
        while (step_rtn == STEPBACK);
    if (step_rtn != STEPCANC)
        {
        CUR_MV(14, 32);
        for (ichar = 0; ichar < L_PASSWORD &&
            (password[ichar] = getch()) >= ' '; ++ichar)
            ;
        if (password[ichar] >= ' ')
            ++ichar;
        password[ichar] = '\0';
        if (!pw_find(office, user, password))
            {
            err_warn("Access denied:", user);
            step_rtn = STEPCANC;
            }
        else
            {
            tput(17, 17,
                "Instructions for Commands Available at Prompts:");
            tput(19, 20, "^R = (control-R) Re-prompt for previous.");
            tput(20, 20, "^E = Erase data field, make it empty.");
            tput(21, 20, "^X = Exit and cancel order.");
            tput(23, 17,
                "Press ^X to exit, or another key to continue. _\b");
```

(continued)

```
            if (getch() == C_CANC)
                step_rtn = STEPCANC;
            }
        }
    return (step_rtn);
    }
```

We use a simpler style of prompting in *id_user()* than we did in the *main()* function: The user may move only *forward* through these prompt steps. If the user is unable to enter a valid name and password, *id_user()* displays the diagnostic message "Access denied: *user_name* _ (push ESC)" and returns the *stepcode STEPCANC*. The *main()* function then receives the instruction to cancel, and does so.

The processing in *id_user()* consists of the entry and subsequent validation of the user's name and password. If the user is known to the system, then brief instructions are displayed for entering orders.

Figure 11-2 lists the functions called by *id_user()*. All but *pw_find()* are useful general-purpose functions, so we'll talk about each in detail.

beg_scrn().   The function *beg_scrn()* expects four string arguments to be used to create the heading for a new screen. The first three arguments are displayed on the screen's top line, in the left, center, and right positions. The fourth argument is displayed on the second line of the screen, centered.

```
#define SCRNWDTH 80

void beg_scrn(left, center, right, below)
char left[], center[], right[], below[];

    {
    CLR_SCRN;
    tput(1, 1, left);
    tput(1, (SCRNWDTH - strlen(center)) / 2, center);
    tput(1, 1 + SCRNWDTH - strlen(right), right);
    tput(2, (SCRNWDTH - strlen(below)) / 2, below);
    }
```

FIGURE 11-2

The low-level functions called by id_user()

FUNCTION	ACTION
beg_scrn()	Begins a new screen, clears, and shows headings.
tput()	Displays a string at a specified cursor location.
prompt()	Inputs a string and validates match.
err_warn()	Displays diagnostic message for user.
pw_find()	Looks up user's name and password.
getch()	Inputs a character without echo (in Microsoft's C library).

The call to *beg_scrn()* in *id_user()* supplies no left or right headings
for the top line:

```
beg_scrn("", scrn_title, "", "SALESPERSON");
```

The subsequent three lines of *id_user()* call the terminal-output function
tput() (see Chapter 12) to display the prompt headings *Office, Salesperson,*
and *Password* in column 20 of lines 10, 12, and 14.

    prompt().   The next function, *prompt()*, is the heart of our application's
user interface.

```
stepcode prompt(data, match_str, min_len, max_len, mand, row, col)
char data[];
char match_str[];
short min_len, max_len;
flag mand;
short row, col;

    {
    IMPORT bflag bell_ok;
    char buf[PRMTBSIZ];
    short ichar;
    stepcode rtn = STEPOK;
    bflag more;

    strcpy(buf, data);
    for (ichar = strlen(buf); ichar < max_len; ++ichar)
        buf[ichar] = C_MASK;
    buf[ichar] = '\0';
    tput(row, col, buf);
    CUR_MV(row, col);
    strcpy(buf, data);
    for (ichar = 0, more = YES; ichar < max_len && more; )
        {
        buf[ichar] = getch();
#if defined(DEBUG)
if (buf[ichar] < ' ')
    CDBG("prompt buf[ichar] = getch()", buf[ichar]);
#endif
        buf[ichar + 1] = '\0';
        switch (buf[ichar])
            {
            case C_CANC:
                rtn = STEPCANC, more = NO;
                break;
            case C_BACK:
                rtn = STEPBACK, more = NO;
                break;
            case C_NULL:
                IDBG("prompt C_NULL max_len", max_len);
                for (ichar = 0; ichar < max_len; ++ichar)
                    buf[ichar] = C_MASK;
                buf[ichar] = '\0';
                tput(row, col, buf);
                ichar = 0;
                buf[ichar] = data[ichar] = '\0';
                CUR_MV(row, col);
                break;
```

(continued)

```
            case '\r':
            case '\n':
               if (ichar == 0 && data[0] != '\0')
                  strcpy(buf, data), more = NO;
               else if (ichar == 0 && data[0] == '\0' && mand)
                  {
                  err_warn("Data must be entered:", "");
                  CUR_MV(row, col);
                  }
               else if (ichar < min_len && !(ichar == 0 && !mand))
                  {
                  err_warn("Too few characters:", "");
                  CUR_MV(row, col + ichar);
                  }
               else
                  buf[ichar] = '\0', more = NO;
               break;
            case '\b':
               buf[ichar] = '\0';
               if (ichar > 0)
                  {
                  buf[--ichar] = '\0';
                  fputc('\b', stderr);
                  fputc(C_MASK, stderr);
                  fputc(C_MASK, stderr);
                  fprintf(stderr, "\b\b");
                  }
               break;
            default:
               buf[ichar + 1] = '\0';
               if (match(buf, match_str))
                  putc(buf[ichar++], stderr);
               else if (bell_ok)
                  putc('\7', stderr);
               if (ichar > max_len)
                  more = NO;
               break;
            }
         }
      if (rtn == STEPOK)
         strcpy(data, buf);
      ichar = strlen(data);
      CUR_MV(row, col + ichar);
      for (; ichar < max_len; ++ichar)
         fputc(' ', stderr);
      return (rtn);
      }
```

We call *prompt()* twice in *id_user()*, first for input of the office name and then for input of the user's name:

```
step_rtn = prompt(office, "L", 3, L_OFFICE, MAND, 10, 32);

   /* ... */
step_rtn = prompt(user, "L", 2, L_USER, MAND, 12, 32);
```

The *prompt()* function requires seven arguments: *reply_string, match_string, minimum_length, maximum_length, mandatory_flag, cursor_row,* and *cursor_column.* In both calls, the symbol *MAND* (defined in *projutil.h* as *1*), is passed to cause input to be mandatory. (The technique

of specifying an option by passing a *#defin*ed constant like *MAND,* rather
than an ordinary constant like *1,* makes your code much easier to understand.) The string *"L"*, a case option from *match.c* that permits the user to
type letters, numbers, punctuation, and non-leading spaces, is passed for
pattern matching of the input text.

Notice that once again both prompts are in the same column—this
time column 32. Since the human eye moves down columns more easily
than across lines of a screen, alignment of titles and fields into columns is
an important technique in designing the user interface. In our system, all
prompt titles are in column 20 and all input fields are in column 32, cour-
tesy of our *tput()* function.

err_warn().   The project utility function *err_warn()* issues diagnostic
messages to the user.

```
#define ESC '\x1b'

void err_warn(first, second)
char first[], second[];

    {
    IMPORT bflag bell_ok;
    short first_len = strlen(first);
    short second_len = strlen(second);

    CUR_MV(24, 1);
    CLR_LINE;
    tput(24, 1, first);
    tput(24, 2 + first_len, second);
    tput(24, 3 + first_len + second_len,
        "  (push ESC)\b\b\b\b\b\b\b\b\b\b\b\b");
    if (bell_ok)
        BELL;
    while (getch() != ESC)
        if (bell_ok)
            BELL;
    CUR_MV(24, 1);
    CLR_LINE;
    }
```

Like most diagnostic displays, *err_warn()* messages have two parts: a fixed
string and a variable string. For example, "Illegal account number" is a
typical fixed part and the actual incorrect account number is a typical variable part. Or "Can't open file" might be the fixed string and the name of
the invalid file the variable string. Both calls to *err_warn()* in *id_user()*
pass a null string for the variable string: That is, only the fixed diagnostic
message is displayed.

getch(). The next function called by *id_user()* is *getch()*. This Microsoft C library function is called to input a single character from the system console (normally the keyboard). The input character is not automatically echoed, so the user doesn't see what he or she types for *getch()*: The screen display is completely under the control of our program. For example, the user could type an *A* and our program could print * as an echo, if we wanted to acknowledge the input but keep it secret, as with a password. And in fact, that's one of the ways we're going to use *getch()*.

The *id_user()* function calls *getch()* repeatedly until the maximum length of *L_PASSWORD* is reached or a character with an ASCII value numerically lower than a space (32) is input. Each character input is saved as the next element in the character array *password*:

```
for (ichar = 0; ichar < L_PASSWORD &&
    (password[ichar] = getch()) >= ' '; ++ichar)
    ;
```

pw_find(). The last *id_user()* subfunction is *pw_find()*, the password finder. Three strings are passed to *pw_find()*: the office name, the user name, and the password entered by the user.

```
flag pw_find(office, user, password)
char office[];
char user[];
char password[];

    {
    IMPORT bflag bell_ok;

    CDBG("pw_find 1 bell_ok", bell_ok);
    if (user[1] == 'S')
       bell_ok = NO;
    CDBG("pw_find 2 bell_ok", bell_ok);
    return (user[0] == 'S' && password[0] == 'S');
    }
```

Right now, this function is a stub, but it will be replaced by a fully operational version after we learn more about accessing files.

The *id_cust()* Function

The *id_cust()* function is called by *main()* to prompt the user for customer identification information. This information includes such data as the customer's name, company, phone number, and shipping and billing addresses. In addition, we'd like to ask the customer how he or she heard about the company and its products, for advertising purposes. If the user is purchasing our products to resell them, we need to know that, too, for price and tax purposes.

```
stepcode id_cust(step_rtn)
   stepcode step_rtn;

   {
   IMPORT char office[], user[], cust_name[], company[], ship_name[],
      ship_cmpy[], ship_strt[], ship_strt2[], ship_city[], ship_state[],
      ship_zip[], bill_name[], bill_cmpy[], bill_strt[], bill_strt2[],
      bill_city[], bill_state[], bill_zip[], adv_ref[], is_resale[],
      resale_id[], scrn_title[];
   stepcode get_addr(stepcode, short, char[], char[], char[],
      char[], char[], char[], char[]);
   void pnt_id_cust(void);
   short step;
   enum prompts {NAME, COMPANY, PHONE, SHIP_ADDR, BILL_ADDR,
      RESALE, ADV_REF, ENDSTEPS};

   beg_scrn(user, scrn_title, office, "IDENTIFY");
   pnt_id_cust();
   tput(4, 30, cust_name);
   tput(6, 30, company);
   step = (step_rtn == STEPOK) ? 0 : (short)ENDSTEPS - 1;
   for (step_rtn = STEPOK; step_rtn != STEPCANC &&
      (step < (short)ENDSTEPS) && (step >= 0); )
      {
      switch (step)
         {
         case NAME:
            step_rtn = prompt(cust_name, "L", 3, L_CUST_NAME, MAND, 4, 30);
            break;
         case COMPANY:
            step_rtn = prompt(company, "L", 3, L_COMPANY, OPT, 6, 30);
            break;
         case PHONE:
            step_rtn = prompt(phone, "P", 7, L_PHONE, OPT, 7, 30);
            break;
         case SHIP_ADDR:
            if (ship_name[0] == '\0')
               {
               strcpy(ship_name, cust_name);
               strcpy(ship_cmpy, company);
               }
            step_rtn = get_addr(step_rtn, 9, ship_name, ship_cmpy, ship_strt,
               ship_strt2, ship_city, ship_state, ship_zip);
            break;
```

(continued)

```
        case BILL_ADDR:
            tput(15, 30, "Bill same address? <y/n>     ");
            step_rtn = prompt(bill_same, "Q", 1, L_BILL_SAME, MAND, 15, 56);
            CUR_MV(15, 30);
            CLR_LINE;
            if (step_rtn == STEPOK && strchr("NnO", bill_same[0]))
                step_rtn = get_addr(step_rtn, 15, bill_name, bill_cmpy,
                    bill_strt, bill_strt2, bill_city, bill_state, bill_zip);
            else if (step_rtn == STEPOK)
                bill_name[0] == '\0';
            break;
        case RESALE:
            step_rtn = prompt(is_resale, "Q", 1, L_IS_RESALE, MAND, 21, 25);
            if (step_rtn == STEPOK && strchr("Yy1", is_resale[0]))
                step_rtn = prompt(resale_id, "L", 3, L_RESALE_ID, OPT, 21, 53);
            break;
        case ADV_REF:
            step_rtn = prompt(adv_ref, "L", 1, L_ADV_REF, OPT, 23, 30);
            break;
        }
    if (step_rtn == STEPOK)
        ++step;
    else if (step_rtn == STEPBACK)
        --step;
    }
    return (step_rtn);
}
```

The customer identification screen has many fields, so the *id_cust()* function could become quite long. To avoid this problem, we just create a separate function called *pnt_id_cust()* to hold the numerous calls to *tput()* that paint the screen (see Chapter 12), and then call *pnt_id_cust()* from *id_cust()*.

```
void pnt_id_cust()
    {
    tput(4, 10, "Customer Name");
    tput(6, 10, "Company Name");
    tput(7, 10, "Phone Number");
    tput(9, 10, "Ship to Name");
    tput(10, 18, "Company");
    tput(11, 18, "Street");
    tput(12, 18, "2nd Street");
    tput(13, 18, "City");
    tput(13, 49, "State");
    tput(13, 60, "Zip");
    tput(15, 10, "Bill to Name");
    tput(16, 18, "Company");
    tput(17, 18, "Street");
    tput(18, 18, "2nd Street");
    tput(19, 18, "City");
    tput(19, 49, "State");
    tput(19, 60, "Zip");
    tput(21, 10, "Resale?");
    tput(21, 30, "Resale Permit Number");
    tput(23, 10, "Advertising Ref");
    }
```

Two noteworthy features in *id_cust()* are its single parameter *step_rtn* and the use of C's ternary conditional operator:

```
/* Begin at last prompt if screen backed into. */
step = (step_rtn == STEPOK) ? 0 : (short)ENDSTEPS - 1;
```

This statement sets the initial prompt step to be either the first field or the final field of this screen. If the user enters the *id_cust()* function from *id_user()* (the most typical way), *STEPOK* will be passed to the parameter *step_rtn*, making the value of *step 0* and thus setting the screen to begin at *NAME*. If the user backed into *id_cust()* from *ord_itms()* (the next screen), then *STEPBACK* will be passed to *step_rtn*, and *step* will begin at *(short) ENDSTEPS −1*, the last prompt step.

We use a *cast operator* here to force conversion of the value of *ENDSTEPS* to type *short*, in order to avoid a warning about performing arithmetic operations on an enumeration constant. The unary *cast* operator, which consists of a data type or synonym type within parentheses immediately preceding another expression, makes a new copy of an expression's value with a different data type than the original expression. (In some cases, such as an assignment, casts are optional, because the value on the right will automatically be converted to the type of the value on the left.) Let's look at an example of the use of *cast*.

If you wanted to obtain the square root of a *long* integer named *area*, you would probably use the library function *sqrt()*, which expects a type *double* argument. But your value is a *long*. What to do? One solution would be to pass a new variable named *dbl_area* that is type *double*:

```
dbl_area = area;
side = sqrt(dbl_area);
```

But a shorter, more readable approach would be to use a *cast* operator. To find the square root of the *long* integer *area*, you could cast its value to type *double* and then pass the copy of its value to *sqrt()*:

```
side = sqrt((double) area);
```

C A U T I O N

The unary cast *operator has high precedence. For safety, put the expression you want to apply the cast to in parentheses.*

get_addr().   All but two of the cases in *id_cust()* call for the input of a single field. The exceptions are *BILL_ADDR* and *SHIP_ADDR*, which call the function *get_addr()* to input billing and shipping addresses beginning at the row passed by the calling function.

```
stepcode get_addr(step_rtn, row, name, company,
    street, street2, city, state, zip)
stepcode step_rtn;
short row;
char name[], company[], street[], street2[], city[], state[], zip[];

    {
    short step;
    enum prompts {NAME, COMPANY, STREET, STREET2, CITY, STATE, ZIP, ENDSTEPS};

    step = (step_rtn == STEPOK) ? 0 : (short)ENDSTEPS - 1;
    for (step_rtn = STEPOK; step_rtn != STEPCANC &&
        (step != (short) ENDSTEPS) && (step >= 0); )
        {
        switch (step)
            {
            case NAME:
                step_rtn = prompt(name, "L", 3, L_SHIP_NAME, MAND, row, 30);
                break;
            case COMPANY:
                step_rtn = prompt(company, "L", 3, L_SHIP_CMPY, OPT, row + 1, 30);
                break;
            case STREET:
                step_rtn = prompt(street, "L", 3, L_SHIP_STRT, MAND, row + 2, 30);
                break;
            case STREET2:
                step_rtn = prompt(street2, "L", 3, L_SHIP_STRT2, OPT, row + 3, 30);
                break;
            case CITY:
                step_rtn = prompt(city, "L", 2, L_SHIP_CITY, MAND, row + 4, 30);
                break;
            case STATE:
                step_rtn = prompt(state, "A", L_SHIP_STATE,
                    L_SHIP_STATE, MAND, row + 4, 56);
                break;
            case ZIP:
                step_rtn = prompt(zip, "#", L_SHIP_ZIP,
                    L_SHIP_ZIP, MAND, row + 4, 65);
                break;
            }
        if (step_rtn == STEPOK)
            ++step;
        else if (step_rtn == STEPBACK)
            --step;
        }
    return (step_rtn);
    }
```

The *ord_itms()* Function

Now that we've identified the salesperson and customer, it's time
to find out which and how many of our products the customer is ordering.
The function *ord_itms()* is called by *main()* to prompt repeatedly for part
numbers and quantities for each item the customer wants to order. The
function behaves like a simplified spreadsheet in that it updates the display
of total price of the order with each input of a part number or quantity.
Changes to part numbers or quantities already entered will also cause
the function to update the total.

```
stepcode ord_itms(step_rtn)
stepcode step_rtn;

    {
    IMPORT char user[], office[], scrn_title[];
    IMPORT char parts[][L_PARTS + 1];
    IMPORT char part_descs[][L_PART_DESC + 1];
    IMPORT long quantities[];
    IMPORT short ship_weights[];
    IMPORT money prices[];
    IMPORT byte last_part;
    IMPORT money part_total;
    flag inv_find(char[], char[], money *, short *);
    short step;
    char dbuf[14];
    byte ipart, part_cnt;
    byte row;
    bflag part_found, more_items = YES;
    enum prompts {PART_NUM, QUANTITY, ENDSTEPS};

    beg_scrn(user, scrn_title, office, "ENTER ITEMS");
    tput(4, 10, "Customer Name");
    tput(4, 30, cust_name);
    tput(6, 10, "Company Name");
    tput(6, 30, company);
    tput(9, 10, "Part Number      Description");
    tput(9, 59, "Qty  Unit-Price");
    tput(22, 51, "Order Total");
    step = ipart = 0;
    for (step_rtn = STEPOK; step_rtn != STEPCANC &&
        ipart < MAX_ITEMS && ipart >= 0 && more_items; )
        {
        row = ipart + 11;
        switch (step)
            {
            case PART_NUM:
                do
                    {
                    step_rtn = prompt(parts[ipart], "L", 1, L_PARTS, OPT, row,
                    part_found = (step_rtn == STEPOK) && inv_find(parts[ipart],
                        part_descs[ipart], &prices[ipart], &ship_weights[ipart])
                    if (step_rtn == STEPOK && parts[ipart][0] == '\0')
                        more_items = NO;
```

(continued)

```
                        else if (!part_found && step_rtn == STEPOK)
                            err_warn("No such part:", parts[ipart]);
                        else if (part_found)
                            {
                            tput(row, 27, part_descs[ipart]);
                            tput(row, 64, "$");
                            ftput(row, 65, (double) prices[ipart] / 100.0, 2,
                                dbuf, L_PRICES);
                            if (!quantities[ipart])
                                quantities[ipart] = 1;
                            }
                        } while (step_rtn == STEPOK && !part_found && more_items);
                    break;
                case QUANTITY:
                    step_rtn = nprompt(&quantities[ipart],
                        "#", 0L, H_QUANTITY, MAND, row, 59);
                    break;
                }
            if (step_rtn == STEPOK)
                {
                if (ipart > last_part && ipart < MAX_ITEMS && quantities[ipart] > 0)
                    last_part = ipart;
                for (part_total = part_cnt = 0; part_cnt <= last_part; ++part_cnt)
                    part_total += prices[part_cnt] * quantities[part_cnt];
                tput(22, 64, "$");
                ftput(22, 65, (double) part_total / 100.0, 2, dbuf, L_PRICES);
                }
            if (step == (short)PART_NUM)
                {
                step = (short)QUANTITY;
                if (step_rtn == STEPBACK)
                    --ipart;
                }
            else
                {
                step = (short)PART_NUM;
                if (step_rtn == STEPOK)
                 ++ipart;
                }
            }
        return (step_rtn);
        }
```

The style of control flow used in *ord_itms( )* is a loop with two
prompt steps managed by a *switch* statement. The prompts are for a part
number and the quantity to order. Each part number the user inputs is
validated by the function *inv_find( )*. If the number is valid, *inv_find( )*
passes back the part's description, unit price, and shipping weight. The two
numbers are passed back through arguments, using the & (*address-of*)
operator:

```
part_found = (step_rtn == STEPOK) && inv_find(parts[ipart],
    part_descs[ipart], &prices[ipart], &ship_weights[ipart]);
```

inv_find().   There is more to the call to *inv_find( )* than first meets the eye. The function takes four arguments, and the first two arguments are *strings.* A quick look gives the impression that only a single character of the *part* and *part_desc* arrays is passed to *inv_find( )*, but that is not the case: Both *part* and *part_desc* are declared as two-dimensional arrays. The part-number string in row *ipart* of the *part* array will be passed to *inv_find( )*, and *inv_find( )* will fill the corresponding row of the *part_desc* array. (Arrays of more than one dimension will be covered in Chapter 15.)

```
flag inv_find(part, part_desc, p_price, p_ship_wt)
char part[];
char part_desc[];
money *p_price;
short *p_ship_wt;

    {
    strcpy(part_desc, "Order-Entry Software Package");
    *p_price = 12345L;
    *p_ship_wt = 123;
    return (part[0] == 'S');
    }
```

The *inv_find( )* stub will be replaced by a fully operational version later in the book.

ntput(), ftput(), and nprompt().   Three other order-entry functions are called either directly or indirectly by *ord_itms( )*: *ntput(), ftput(),* and *nprompt().* These functions are numeric versions of the string output and input functions *tput( )* and *prompt( )* from our project utility library. (The *ntput( )* function is not called by *ord_itms( )*; however, it *is* called by *nprompt( )*, so we'll discuss it here.)

```
void ntput(row, col, long_val, buf, field_len)
short row, col;
long long_val;
char buf[];
short field_len;

    {
    ltoa(long_val, buf, 10);
    strrjust(buf, field_len);
    tput(row, col, buf);
    }
```

We call *ntput( )* to display a *long* integer, right justified, with blank padding. The *ntput( )* function expects five arguments: the screen row (1 through 25), the screen column (1 through 80), the *long* integer to display, a pointer to a string it will use to return the ASCII representation of

the value, and the field width to use for justification and display. Here's
an example:

```
ntput(row, col, *p_num, buf, max_len);
```

The *ftput()* function is the double-precision floating-point equivalent
of *ntput()*.

```
void ftput(row, col, double_val, dec_place, buf, field_len)
short row, col;
double double_val;
short dec_place, field_len;
char buf[];

    {
    char *fcvt();
    int dec, sign;
    short pos;

    strcpy(buf, fcvt(double_val, dec_place, &dec, &sign));
    for (pos = strlen(buf); pos >= dec; --pos)
        buf[pos + 1] = buf[pos];
    buf[dec] = '.';
    strrjust(buf, field_len);
    tput(row, col, buf);
    }
```

In order to display the decimal point of a floating-point number in the
correct position, *ftput()* requires one additional argument: a *short* value
for the number of digits to appear to the right of the decimal.

```
ftput(row, col, f_money, 2, s_money, L_PRICES);
```

If the *double* value you pass to *ftput()* does not have enough precision,
ftput() will pad the field with zeros on the right.

We call the *nprompt()* function to prompt for a *long* integer, much
as we call *prompt()* to input a string. In this program, *ord_itms()* calls
nprompt() to get the quantity for the part being ordered. (The related
function for floating-point numbers, *fprompt()*, isn't called by *ord_itms()*,
so we'll discuss it a little later.)

```
stepcode nprompt(p_num, match_str, min_val, max_val, mand, row, col)
long *p_num;
char match_str[];
long min_val, max_val;
flag mand;
short row, col;

    {
    long atol(char[]);
    char buf[14];
    bflag more = YES;
    long in_num;
```

(continued)

```
    short max_len = strlen(ltoa(max_val, buf, 10));
    short min_len = strlen(ltoa(min_val, buf, 10));
    stepcode rtn;

if (*p_num)
    {
    ntput(row, col, *p_num, buf, max_len);
    }
else
    buf[0] = '\0';
do
    {
    rtn = prompt(buf, match_str, min_len, max_len, mand, row, col);
    if (rtn != STEPOK)
        more = NO;
    else
        {
        in_num = atol(buf);
        SDBG("nprompt buf", buf);
        LDBG("nprompt in_num", in_num);
        if (mand && in_num == 0)
            err_warn("Non-zero data mandatory:", "");
        else if ((in_num < min_val || in_num > max_val) &&
            (mand || in_num != 0))
            {
            sprintf(buf, "%ld to %ld", min_val, max_val);
            err_warn("Enter a number from:", buf);
            buf[0] = '\0';
            }
        else
            more = NO;
        }
    }
while (more);
if (rtn == STEPOK)
    {
    *p_num = in_num;
    ntput(row, col, in_num, buf, max_len);
    }
return (rtn);
}
```

The *nprompt( )* function expects seven arguments: *address_of_long, match_str, minimum_num, maximum_num, mandatory_flag, cursor_row,* and *cursor_column*. The return from *nprompt( )*, like that from *prompt( )*, is a value with our synonym type *stepcode*, to indicate whether data were entered (*STEPOK*) or not (*STEPBACK* or *STEPCANC*).

```
step_rtn = nprompt(&quantities[ipart], "#", 0L, H_QUANTITY, MAND, row, 59);
```

The & operator you see with *quantities[ipart]* in this example must be present in order for *nprompt( )* to assign a value to an element in the array (see Chapter 15).

The *ship_pay()* Function

Next, the user must enter the shipping carrier, sales tax, and payment terms. The *ship_pay()* function does those jobs by prompting for the remaining fields of the order after all part numbers and quantities have been input.

```
stepcode ship_pay(step_rtn)
   stepcode step_rtn;

   {
   IMPORT char office[], user[], cust_name[], company[],
      ship_car[], pay_terms[], comment[], scrn_title[];
   IMPORT money part_total, tax_amt, ship_amt;
   IMPORT double inp_ship_amt, tax_pcnt;
   IMPORT char is_resale[];
   IMPORT byte last_part;
   IMPORT short ship_weights[];
   IMPORT short tot_weight;
   short step;
   char dbuf[14];
   byte ipart;
   enum prompts {SHIP_CAR, SHIP_AMT, TAX, PAY_TERMS, COMMENT, ENDSTEPS};

   if (quantities[0] == 0 || parts[0][0] == '\0')
      {
      err_warn("Nothing ordered:", "");
      return (STEPBACK);
      }
   beg_scrn(user, scrn_title, office, "SHIP, TAX, PAY");
   pnt_ship_pay();
   tput(4, 30, cust_name);
   tput(6, 30, company);
   for (ipart = tot_weight = 0; ipart <= last_part; ++ipart)
      tot_weight += ship_weights[ipart];
   ntput(9, 30, (long) tot_weight, dbuf, 10);
   step = (step_rtn == STEPOK) ? 0 : (short)ENDSTEPS - 1;
   for (step_rtn = STEPOK; step_rtn != STEPCANC &&
      (step < (short)ENDSTEPS) && step >= 0; )
      {
      switch (step)
         {
         case SHIP_CAR:
            step_rtn = prompt(ship_car, "L", 1, L_SHIP_CAR, OPT, 11, 30);
            break;
         case SHIP_AMT:
            if (ship_car[0] != '\0')
               step_rtn = fprompt(&inp_ship_amt, "F", 0.20,
                  H_SHIP_AMT, 11, 2, OPT, 11, 65);
               ship_amt = (money) (inp_ship_amt * 100.0);
            break;
         case TAX:
            if (strchr("Yy1", is_resale[0]))
               tax_pcnt = 0.0;
            else
               step_rtn = fprompt(&tax_pcnt, "F", 0.0,
                  H_TAX_PCNT, 4, 2, OPT, 14, 30);
            if (step_rtn == STEPOK)
               tax_amt = (tax_pcnt * part_total) / 100;
```

(continued)

```
            tput(14, 64, "$");
            ftput(14, 65, (double) tax_amt / 100.0, 2, dbuf, L_TAX_AMT);
            ftput(18, 65, (double) part_total / 100.0, 2, dbuf, L_PRICES);
            ftput(20, 65, (double) (part_total + tax_amt + ship_amt) / 100.0,
                2, dbuf, L_PRICES);
            break;
        case PAY_TERMS:
            step_rtn = prompt(pay_terms, "L", 1, L_PAY_TERMS, MAND, 17, 30);
            break;
        case COMMENT:
            step_rtn = prompt(comment, "L", 1, L_COMMENT, OPT, 22, 11);
            break;
        }
    if (step_rtn == STEPOK)
        ++step;
    else if (step_rtn == STEPBACK)
        --step;
    }
return (step_rtn);
}
```

Processing in this module begins with a check to ascertain whether something has indeed been ordered: Obviously, it would be a waste of time to ask for shipping, tax, and payment information for an empty order. If nothing has been ordered, *ship_pay()* forces the user back to the last field in *ord_itms()* by returning *STEPBACK*. If something *has* been ordered, *ship_pay()* begins prompting for the shipping data.

The name of the shipping carrier is optional; however, if one is supplied, the shipping-charge entry becomes mandatory. The sales-tax percentage is prompted for only if this order is not for resale. (Goods for resale are not subject to sales tax, at least according to most tax laws at the time of this writing.)

fprompt().   The *ship_pay()* function calls *fprompt()* to input both tax percentage and shipping charge. Just as *ftput()* is the double-precision floating-point equivalent of *ntput()*, *fprompt()* is the alternative to *nprompt()*. Once again, the floating-point function requires additional arguments to handle the decimal point. These arguments specify the width and decimal precision of the number being input.

```
stepcode fprompt(d_num, match_str, min_dval, max_dval,
    width, precision, mand, row, col)
double *d_num;
char match_str[];
double min_dval, max_dval;
short width, precision;
```

(continued)

```
flag mand;
short row, col;

    {
    int dec, sign;
    double atof(char[]);
    char buf[14], format[14];
    bflag more = YES;
    double in_dnum;
    short max_len = width;
    short min_len = strlen(fcvt(min_dval, precision, &dec, &sign)) - precision;
    stepcode rtn;

    if (*d_num != 0.0)
        {
        ftput(row, col, *d_num, precision, buf, max_len);
        }
    else
        buf[0] = '\0';
    do
        {
        rtn = prompt(buf, match_str, min_len, max_len, mand, row, col);
        if (rtn != STEPOK)
            more = NO;
        else
            {
            in_dnum = atof(buf);
            if (mand && in_dnum == 0.0)
                err_warn("Non-zero data mandatory:", "");
            else if ((in_dnum < min_dval || in_dnum > max_dval) &&
                (mand || in_dnum != 0.0))
                {
                sprintf(buf, "%.*f to %.*f", precision, min_dval,
                    precision, max_dval);
                err_warn("Enter a number from:", buf);
                buf[0] = '\0';
                CUR_MV(row, col);
                }
            else
                more = NO;
            }
        }
    while (more);
    if (rtn == STEPOK)
        {
        *d_num = in_dnum;
        ftput(row, col, *d_num, precision, buf, max_len);
        }
    return (rtn);
    }
```

Saving the Entered Data: *wrt_ord()*

The order-entry program now holds all the data entered by the salesperson, in *SEMIGLOBAL* variables shared by the middle-level functions in the source file *ordbuild.c*. But if the program were to terminate right now, the order would be lost because the data are in electronic memory, which can be clobbered by the next program run or erased when the power is turned off. We must write the data to permanent storage before we exit the program. But before we decide how to do this, let's step back a minute and look at the larger picture.

```
stepcode wrt_ord()
    {
    IMPORT char office[], user[], cust_name[], company[], ship_name[],
        ship_cmpy[], ship_strt[], ship_strt2[], ship_city[], ship_state[],
        ship_zip[], bill_name[], bill_cmpy[], bill_strt[], bill_strt2[],
        bill_city[], bill_state[], bill_zip[], adv_ref[], resale_id[];
    IMPORT char is_resale[];
    IMPORT char parts[][L_PARTS + 1];
    IMPORT long quantities[];
    IMPORT money prices[];
    IMPORT byte last_part;
    IMPORT short tot_weight;
    IMPORT char ship_car[], pay_terms[], comment[];
    IMPORT money part_total, tax_amt, ship_amt;
    IMPORT long order_num(void);
    long order_id;
    long long_time;
    byte ipart;
    char is_ok[2];
    char log_buf[80];
    stepcode step_rtn;

    tput(23, 2, "Is order OK? <y/n>  _ ");
    strcpy(is_ok, "y");
    step_rtn = prompt(is_ok, "Q", 1, 1, MAND, 23, 22);
    if (step_rtn != STEPOK)
        return (step_rtn);
    else if (0 != strchr("NnO", is_ok[0]))
        return (STEPBACK);
    order_id = order_num();
    sprintf(log_buf, "ORD %ld, SL %s, TL %ld", order_id, user, part_total);
    logentry(log_buf);
    printf("\nBEGIN ORDER %ld\n", order_id);
    time(&long_time);
    printf("TM %s", ctime(&long_time));
    printf("OF %s\nSL %s\nCN %s\nCO %s\n", office, user, cust_name, company);
    printf("SN %s\nSC %s\nST %s\n", ship_name, ship_cmpy, ship_strt);
    if (ship_strt2[0] != '\0')
        printf("S2 %s\n", ship_strt2);
    printf("SY %s\nSS %s\nSZ %s\n", ship_city, ship_state, ship_zip);
    if (bill_name[0] != '\0')
        {
        printf("BN %s\nBC %s\nBT %s\n", bill_name, bill_cmpy, bill_strt);
        if (bill_strt2[0] != '\0')
            printf("B2 %s\n", bill_strt2);
        printf("BY %s\nBS %s\nBZ %s\n", bill_city, bill_state, bill_zip);
        }
    if (strchr("Yy1", is_resale[0]))
        printf("RS %s\n", resale_id);
    for (ipart = 0; ipart <= last_part && quantities[ipart]; ++ipart)
        printf("PN %s\nQY %ld\nPR %ld\n", parts[ipart],
            quantities[ipart], prices[ipart]);
    printf("TL %ld\nTX %ld\nSH %s\nSA %ld\nWT %d\n", part_total,
        tax_amt, ship_car, ship_amt, tot_weight);
    if (adv_ref[0] != '\0')
        printf("AD %s\n", adv_ref);
    printf("PA %s\n", pay_terms);
    if (comment[0] != '\0')
        printf("CM %s\n", comment);
    printf("END ORDER %ld\n", order_id);
    return (STEPOK);
    }
```

Storage format. We now have a completed order. Our goal is to forward that order to the company's central office, from which we ship all our products. The central office receives orders from several remote computers (via modem) and from floppy disks delivered overnight, so we want to choose a format that will work for both these media, as well as for new media we may add later.

We decide on ASCII rather than binary format for the data because ASCII has both portability and communication advantages. The portability advantage is simply that ASCII format is the same on all systems, whereas binary format is not. The communication advantage is that ASCII uses only 7 of the 8 bits in a byte, whereas binary uses all 8 bits, and the 7-bit data format can be handled by more communications software than machine-specific binary format.

There are 50 fields in our order (some of which may be empty). We'll output each field on its own line, each line beginning with a two-character code that identifies the kind of data it contains (*TM* for time, *OF* for office, and so on). This code is followed by a space and then the value of the associated data field. If the value is numeric, it is converted to an ASCII string by the library function *printf( )*.

The following segment of code from *wrt_ord( )* shows how *printf( )*'s format specifiers are used to output different data types in ASCII format. The variables *part_total*, *tax_amt*, and *ship_amt* are output using the *%ld* format specifier; *%s* is used for the string *ship_car*, and *%d* for the *short* integer *tot_weight*. The optional advertising reference ("How did you hear about us?") is included only if the salesperson got a response from the customer.

```
printf("TL %ld\nTX %ld\nSH %s\nSA %ld\nWT %d\n", part_total,
    tax_amt, ship_car, ship_amt, tot_weight);
if (adv_ref[0] != '\0')
    printf("AD %s\n", adv_ref);
```

This *printf( )* output is the first in the order-entry program to use the standard output file, *stdout*; all previous output has been directed to the user's screen, using the standard error output file, *stderr* (see Chapter 12).

We use *stdout* so that the command-line file-redirection commands >,
>>, and | will control only the order data, as in these examples from
wrt_ord()'s initial comment:

```
/*      ORDENTRY > SS841225.ORD          Creates new file;            */
/*                                        note date encoded in name.  */
/*      ORDENTRY >> NEWORDS.DAT           Appends data to existing file. */
/*      ORDENTRY | ORDSAVE | ORDPRINT    Serves as source for a pipeline. */
```

The order log.   It is good business practice to log every new order. The
function that performs this task for the order-entry application is named
logentry().

```
void logentry(msg)
   char msg[];

   {
   }
```

Here's how the process works: The call to *sprintf()* in *wrt_ord()* converts
its arguments to ASCII using the C format specifiers; the resulting string is
saved in *log_buf,* which is passed to *logentry()*. Then *logentry()* records
the string passed, by adding a new entry at the end of the log file. (The
logentry() function is a stub at this point, as is the *order_num()* function
called to obtain *order_id.*)

```
long order_num()
   {
   return (10001L);
   }
```

Time and date functions.   Getting the time and date for each order
may seem a confusing job at first because of the variety of time- and date-
associated functions in C's standard library, but we can limit ourselves to
only two of them.

The two library time functions we use are *time()* and *ctime()*.
The *time()* function saves the entry time (obtained from the system in
seconds elapsed since midnight January 1, 1970 GMT) in the *long* variable
whose address is passed to it. Then *ctime()* converts that *long* value to a
readable date-and-time format and returns the converted value to *printf()*
for output with the order:

```
time(&long_time);
printf("TM %s", ctime(&long_time));
```

The last word. It is good practice to inform the user when the program is about to save the order, and offer an opportunity to change data or cancel the transaction. This should be the very last step, after all data are entered but before the order is recorded. Consistently "asking before updating" makes a program easier and safer to use.

The code for this task simply asks the user a yes-or-no question and obtains a reply. The default value of the response variable *is_ok* (entered when the user simply presses Return) is set to '*y*'. In this call to the *prompt()* function, the match character is "*Q*". "*Q*" matches only responses acceptable to a yes-or-no question: '*Y*', '*y*', or '*1*' for yes; '*N*', '*n*', or '*0*' for no. If the user says that things are not OK, the program will back up to the shipping, tax, and pay terms screen. Otherwise, *wrt_ord()* sends the order to *stdout*.

Now that we've analyzed the mechanics of the top and middle levels of our order-entry application, let's move on to Chapter 12, where we'll take a closer look at the bottom-level functions that control screen output.

Painting the Screen

12

So far we've worked our way from the upper levels of the order-entry program downward, getting a top-down view. Now let's reverse our perspective for a while and see how things look from the bottom up. The techniques for outputting text to the user's screen will be the object of our bottom-up scrutiny.

Screen Management and Application Portability

Programmers writing for the family of MS-DOS-compatible personal computers have three choices for outputting text to the user's screen, listed here in order of decreasing portability and increasing speed:

- ▶ Standard C library I/O functions
- ▶ Calls to the operating system's ROM-BIOS
- ▶ Video RAM access for memory-mapped display

As you can see, the fastest display technique is unfortunately the least portable (you probably would have guessed that anyway).

Standard Library I/O Functions

Our first option is to use output functions from the C compiler's standard library. The standard error file, *stderr*, is the library file normally directed to the user's display. However, if command-line output redirection is not applied, output from the standard output file *stdout* will also appear

on the screen. The standard I/O functions *printf()*, *puts()*, and *putchar()*
output only to *stdout*, but *fprintf()*, *fputs()*, and *fputc()* may be used
to output to *stdout*, *stderr*, or any other file. All of these functions actually output by calling the low-level library function *write()*.

Strings of ordinary printable ASCII characters sent to the screen by
the standard I/O functions are displayed as you would expect: What you
send is what you see. However, special strings of ASCII characters known as
escape sequences are interpreted as screen-control commands: They move
the cursor, erase a line or the entire screen, and control highlighting. These
escape sequences all begin with the escape character '\33' (or the hexadecimal or decimal equivalent '\x1b' or 27, respectively).

In our order-entry application, the header file *stddefs.h* gives us
control of the screen through macros that output escape sequences for
various screen-control commands. One of these is the *CUR_MV* macro,
which outputs a cursor-movement command to the *stderr* file. For example,
CUR_MV(8, 15) moves the cursor to line 8, column 15 by sending the string
"\33[8;15H" to the screen, and *CUR_UP(1)* moves the cursor up a line by
sending the string "\33[1A".

```
#define CUR_MV(row, col) fprintf(stderr, "\33[%d;%dH", row, col)
#define CUR_UP(num) fprintf(stderr, "\33[%dA", num)
#define CUR_DN(num) fprintf(stderr, "\33[%dB", num)
#define CUR_RT(num) fprintf(stderr, "\33[%dC", num)
#define CUR_LT(num) fprintf(stderr, "\33[%dD", num)
#define CUR_SKIP fputs("\n", stderr)
#define CUR_SAVE fputs("\33[s", stderr)
#define CUR_REST fputs("\33[u", stderr)
#define CLR_SCRN fputs("\33[2J", stderr)
#define CLR_LINE fputs("\33[K", stderr)
#define CLR_EOS(r, c) {byte i_; CUR_MV(r,c); \
    for (i_ = r; i_ <= 25; ++i_) CLR_LINE, CUR_DN(1); CUR_MV(r,c); }
#define BELL fputc('\7', stderr)
```

I have not included the five commands used to control highlighting in
stddefs.h, since highlighting is hard on the eyes and in any case is not portable to some types of display. If you want to use highlighting, you will
need to add the following macros:

```
#define HLT_OFF fputs("\33[0m", stderr)          /* normal mode */
#define HLT_BOLD fputs("\33[1m", stderr)          /* bold display */
#define HLT_UNDR fputs("\33[4m", stderr)          /* underscored display */
#define HLT_BLNK fputs("\33[5m", stderr)          /* blinking display */
#define HLT_RVRS fputs("\33[7m", stderr)          /* reverse video display */
```

On some systems, MS-DOS requires that the *CONFIG.SYS* file on the boot disk contain the statement *DEVICE = ANSI.SYS*. To determine whether or not this is the case for your system, compile and execute this short C program:

```
/* Test screen commands: Clear screen and say "Hi" in center. */
#include <stdio.h>
#include <stddefs.h>

main()
    {
    CLR_SCRN;
    CUR_MV(12, 40);
    puts("Hi");
    }
```

If the program outputs something like *[2J[12;40HHi* instead of *Hi*, add *DEVICE = ANSI.SYS* to your *CONFIG.SYS* file, reboot the system, and run the program again. This time it should execute properly.

(The escape sequences used for display commands in the *stddefs.h* macros are by no means universal. They work on MS-DOS systems, but not for most CRT terminals. If portability to multiuser systems is required, you will have to deal with the tremendous variety of escape sequences used by different CRTs. In that case, you might want to consider using the UNIX operating system, with its *termcap* database of hundreds of encoded descriptions for terminal control. The functions necessary to access and use *termcap* data are supplied with UNIX. A higher-level UNIX package called *curses* is also available for more advanced screen-control functions.)

Except in unusual circumstances, C's standard-library I/O functions are the best choice for screen output. Their portability is excellent and they offer a wide range of display features. However, you should at least be aware of the alternatives, so we'll take a minute to discuss each of them.

ROM-BIOS

The IBM PC-compatible class of personal computers comes with a ROM (read-only memory) chip that holds functions used by the operating system to perform basic input/output services (BIOS) for itself and for your programs. These service programs are known as *firmware* because they can be changed only by replacing the existing ROM chip with one that is programmed differently.

NUMBER	ROM SERVICE
0	Set video mode (text/graphics, color/monochrome, resolution).
1	Set cursor size.
6	Scroll up.
7	Scroll down.
15	Read current video mode.

FIGURE 12-1

Commonly used ROM-BIOS services

Calls to C's standard-library I/O functions for screen output actually execute code that interfaces with the ROM-BIOS routines, so the only reason to call ROM-BIOS directly would be the need to use a feature not supported by the library. Figure 12-1 lists a few of the ROM input/output services (notice that the services are numbered).

In order to call a ROM-BIOS routine, you must use either assembly language or one of the C library's three DOS interface functions: *bdos,* *intdos,* and *intdosx.* (These particular functions are specific to Microsoft's C library, but other C vendors supply similar DOS interface functions for various operating systems.) C programs that make use of these DOS interface functions will not be portable to other operating systems because of software incompatibilities, but when maximum display performance is needed, portability concerns sometimes have to go out the window!

Video RAM Access for Direct Display

Memory mapping is a display technique that ties what is displayed on the screen directly to the contents of a specific block of memory. To change what is displayed, you must change the specific bytes of memory to which the display is mapped. In effect, the screen is a slave of that special area of memory. The IBM PC and PC-compatible microcomputers all have memory-mapped displays, as does the Apple II.

The reason for storing directly into video memory is, quite simply, speed: It is obviously much faster to store a byte directly than to ask a C library output function to ask a ROM-BIOS routine to store that same byte. You go right to the heart of things when you play with video RAM, and such breakneck speed can be important in selected applications such as animation and special effects.

The thought of accessing video memory directly sends tingles up the spines of many application programmers. Just think of it: direct control of hardware that you can watch! So why should something that sounds like so much fun be regarded as bad programming practice? Well, mainly because memory-mapping schemes vary greatly among systems. Code that directly manipulates screen memory is portable to only a very small class of "clone" systems, and converting code from one display scheme to another can be very time-consuming. In addition, future upgrades in display hardware may render your programs inoperative because they depend on the now-obsolete memory-mapping scheme. However, it *is* possible to manipulate screen memory directly using C's pointers. We'll discuss this in detail in Chapter 14.

To summarize the bottom-level view of screen output: You call *printf("Hi")* to say *Hi*; *printf()* calls the low-level library function *write()*; *write()* calls ROM-BIOS for screen output; ROM-BIOS saves *Hi* in screen memory; and finally you see *Hi* on your monitor.

Displaying Information for the User

Now let's move up one level and talk about how we want our order-entry application to display information to the user. We need to look more closely at the library functions *ltoa()* and *sprintf()* and the order-entry functions *tput()*, *strrjust()*, *ntput()*, and *ftput()*, all of which are associated with screen output of character strings and numeric values.

Displaying a String of Text

The *tput()* function moves the cursor to a designated position on the screen and then prints a string of text. More specifically, the *CUR_MV* macro moves the cursor and then *fputs()* prints the text on the screen.

```
void tput(row, col, text)
short row, col;
char text[];

    {
    CUR_MV(row, col);
    fputs(text, stderr);
    }
```

To call *tput()*, you must supply three arguments: a row, a column, and the text to display, like this:

```
tput(12, 20, "Salesperson")
```

Displaying a Number

Lists of integers are almost always displayed and printed right justified, with spaces for padding on the left. Floating-point numbers, on the other hand, are right aligned on the decimal point and then padded on the left with spaces and on the right with zeros to a specified number of decimal places. In C, we can use formatted output to display numbers in a much more flexible way than we have seen so far, by storing the field width and precision in variables. For instance, to display the *long* integer *quantities[ipart]* on line 14, column 65, in a field whose width is calculated to be the *short* variable *max_len,* you would just enter the following commands:

```
CUR_MV(14, 65);
fprintf(stderr, "%*ld", max_len, quantities[ipart]);
```

The * in the format specifier means that the width of the field is passed as an argument. Since *max_len* is calculated to be the length of the largest allowable value of *quantities* (999), the preceding statement produces the same output as:

```
fprintf(stderr, "%3ld", quantities[ipart]);
```

Both forms of *fprintf()* print the value of *quantities[ipart]* right justified in a field three characters wide.

When formatting floating-point numbers for output, you must also consider the number of decimal places to be displayed. In the following example, the *double* variable *inp_shp_amt* is displayed in a field *width* number of characters wide and with *precision* digits to the right of the decimal point:

```
fprintf(stderr, "%*.*f", width, precision, inp_ship_amt);
```

We can simplify things considerably for our order-entry application by writing a few new functions that consolidate several of these standard operations. First we'll create a function *ntput()* that produces the same output as the two steps in the first example with just one simple call:

```
ntput(14, 65, quantities[ipart], buf, max_len);
```

and then we'll create a companion function *ftput()* to do the same for *double* variables:

```
ftput(14, 65, inp_ship_amt, precision, buf, width);
```

In both of these examples, *buf* is a string containing the formatted number to be returned by *ntput()* or *ftput()*. We'll use the order-entry function *strrjust()* to right justify the string in *buf* for the appropriate field width.

```
void strrjust(str, fld_len)
char str[];
short fld_len;

    {
    short end_char, ichar, move;

    SDBG("strrjust before str", str);
    IDBG("fld_len", fld_len);
    for (end_char = strlen(str) - 1;
        str[end_char] == ' ' && end_char > 0; --end_char)
        ;
    move = fld_len - end_char - 1;
    IDBG("move", move);
    if (move > 0 && end_char >= 0)
        {
        for (ichar = end_char; ichar >= 0; --ichar)
            str[ichar + move] = str[ichar];
        for (ichar = move - 1; ichar >= 0; --ichar)
            str[ichar] = ' ';
        str[fld_len] = '\0';
        }
    SDBG("strrjust str", str);
    }
```

The data we'll be outputting with these new functions are in the computer's internal binary format, not in human-readable ASCII format, so we'll need to call library functions to convert the binary values to their ASCII representations. We'll use *ltoa()* to convert the *long* values, in whatever *radix* (also known as *modulo* or *base*) we choose, from 2 to 36. We'll use *fcvt()* to convert the floating-point numbers (*fcvt()* does not use a radix).

```
void ntput(row, col, long_val, buf, field_len)
short row, col;
long long_val;
char buf[];
short field_len;
```

(continued)

```
{
ltoa(long_val, buf, 10);
strrjust(buf, field_len);
tput(row, col, buf);
}
```

Since *fcvt()* does essentially the same task as *ltoa()*, you would expect it to operate in much the same manner; however, that is not the case. The *fcvt()* function has a couple of quirks you need to be aware of. First, you do not pass a string to *fcvt()*. Instead, it creates its own temporary string and returns its address. Since this string is temporary, you must call *strcpy()* to copy its contents to your own string after you call *fcvt()*, or you will lose it at the next *fcvt()* call.

```
void ftput(row, col, double_val, dec_place, buf, field_len)
short row, col;
double double_val;
short dec_place, field_len;
char buf[];

{
char *fcvt();
int dec, sign;
short pos;

strcpy(buf, fcvt(double_val, dec_place, &dec, &sign));
for (pos = strlen(buf); pos >= dec; --pos)
    buf[pos + 1] = buf[pos];
buf[dec] = '.';
strrjust(buf, field_len);
tput(row, col, buf);
}
```

Second, *fcvt()* does not put a decimal point in the string it creates. Instead, you must pass it the address of a *short* variable whose value, on return, will be the element of the string where the decimal point belongs. It is up to you to actually *insert* the decimal point. (This allows for international variations in the character that represents the decimal point.) The actual call to *fcvt()* from *ftput()* looks like this:

```
strcpy(buf, fcvt(double_val, dec_place, &dec, &sign));
```

Notice that *fcvt()* is also passed another address, *&sign*. The *short* variable *sign* will be set to zero if the sign of the *double* value is positive or to a non-zero value if it is negative.

To insert the decimal point into the proper position in the string, we'll use the following loop:

```
for (pos = strlen(buf); pos >= dec; --pos)
    buf[pos + 1] = buf[pos];
buf[dec] = '.';
```

Now, like *printf()*, the library function *sprintf()* performs formatted output conversions, but without producing any output. The data produced for output are saved in a string that is passed as *sprintf()*'s first argument, so this next call to *sprintf()* produces the same results as the two calls to *ltoa()* and *strrjust()* in the preceding *ntput()* example:

```
sprintf(buf, "%*ld", field_len, long_val);
```

In this example, the value of the *long* variable *long_val* is converted to a string of ASCII characters and placed in *buf,* right justified in a field *field_len* characters wide.

If we can do the same job with one function call, why would we want to use *ntput()* instead of *sprintf()*? Quite simply, because *sprintf()* consumes about 5,000 bytes of object code, so replacing it with the smaller *ntput()* saves both disk space and program memory.

C O M M E N T

The object code for printf(), fprintf(), *and* sprintf() *is large, but if your program never actually* calls *these functions, then their object code won't be linked into your program at all.*

Designing the Screen

Now that we've created the necessary low-level screen-output tools, let's see how they're used to create a whole screen.

We use the expression *painting a screen* to describe the process by which our program displays the names and values of data fields in an attractive, readable, and efficient format. In the case of our order-entry prompt screens, that means placing fields in the order they are needed, with no extraneous data to confuse or distract the user, and aligning the field titles and the input fields themselves in columns (scanning down a column is the easiest motion for the human eye).

Uniformity among the visible features of a program and among the styles of user interface is very important to user productivity. A good place to begin addressing these concerns is at the top of the prompt screen. The heading of the screen should show the name of the user (most users will hesitate to use another's name and password, knowing that a passerby could easily notice), the office identification, the name of the program in use, and the portion of the program currently executing. The order-entry function *id_cust()* calls *beg_scrn()* (see Chapter 11) to clear the screen and display these headings. It passes *beg_scrn()* the arguments *user,* *scrn_title, office,* and *"IDENTIFY"*. Only the last argument, which is a description of the part of the order-entry process currently executing, changes in subsequent calls made by other order-entry functions.

Armed with this knowledge of how to manage screen output and paint entire screens, let's move on to management of the user's input through prompts and error messages.

Prompting for Data

13

The job of obtaining data from the user is the most important task of our order-entry program. In this chapter, we'll look at the standard library functions used for prompting, as well as some custom functions that perform more strictly controlled prompting. First, let's talk about some of the elements that make prompts "friendlier." Then we'll look at the way our order-entry application handles prompting for data.

Friendly Prompting

We want our software to be easy for new users to learn to use. We also want experienced users, who know the software very well, to be able to work as productively as possible. These two goals can sometimes pull programmers in opposite directions, but it doesn't have to be that way. Here are some suggestions that meet both goals without difficulty.

Menus and Help Screens

Menus that give detailed lists of commands and plenty of on-line help messages where needed will help a new user feel at home and become productive sooner. But to experienced users, menus and messages they already know by heart are just clutter that distracts them and slows them down.

One solution is to provide at least two modes of operation and make them user-selectable. In novice mode, the user sees full instructions on order entry and on how to obtain additional help. In expert mode, the more experienced user sees only brief explanations and receives no help messages. If an application is so complex that two user levels are insufficient, it is easy to add more.

On-line help messages should always be presented within the program that they explain, right at the step where they are needed, and should make it clear what the user must do next.

Defaults and Abbreviations

Good defaults are helpful to both the novice and the experienced user. They permit the user to just press Return to enter frequently given responses. User-defined abbreviations for responses are also a helpful feature. We don't use abbreviations in our order-entry software because we don't expect to have many common responses that aren't already included as defaults, but this may not be the case in your next application.

Screen Controls and Uniformity

The amount of effort required to correct a typing error after the user has entered subsequent data items can most definitely separate friendly from unfriendly software. What if the customer changes something on the order, or the salesperson misunderstands a word and discovers the mistake a few steps later? What about typographical errors? It's important that we plan our screen controls so the user can back up, rather than having to start over again from the beginning.

All software users appreciate uniform prompting and option conventions. There is security and efficiency in knowing what to expect. For instance, in our order-entry application, the user always has the same four options at data-entry prompts: type some data; type ^R to back up and retype the response to a previous prompt; type ^E to erase the field; or type ^X to cancel the order.

The computer's "bell" can also be used to make software friendlier. For example, many data-entry operators don't read the screens as they type. They are busy looking at pieces of paper that contain the information they are to enter, and it seriously affects their efficiency to keep looking back and forth between paper and monitor. This makes it important for programs to include a means of attracting the operator's attention when necessary. Ringing the bell is an easy and inoffensive solution.

Prompt Messages

A prompt message is text your program displays to inform the user that some kind of response is required. The message should make it very clear just what that requirement is. For instance, if you are asking the user to choose among several actions, list *all* the options clearly, omitting no possibilities.

Each prompt message is followed by the field on the screen that is to contain the user's response. It is helpful to mark this field by filling it with a repeated character such as the underscore, to create a *prompt mask*. Always move the cursor to the first character of the prompt mask before beginning the user's input. If your program has provided a default response, the prompt mask should display that default value. If a response is mandatory and there is no default reply, the user *must* enter data.

In this next example of a screen display, adapted from the *id_cust()* function in *ordbuild.c*, you see two prompts for names. The name of the customer making the order is input first. Then the default value for the ship-to name is set to the customer's name, since in our business the order is usually shipped directly to the customer:

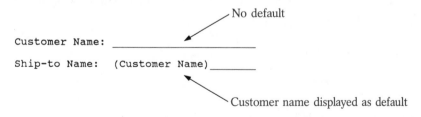

This kind of friendly default often saves the user a considerable number of keystrokes.

Input Control

User productivity (quantity) is a major concern in planning prompts, but correctness of the data entered (quality) is equally important. There are a number of ways we can use prompting to prevent or detect user errors:

▶ Each character of input may be matched against a list of acceptable characters.

▶ A character string may be compared with a match-pattern string that defines which characters are acceptable in each position of the input.

▶ A check may be made for a reasonable response and a message such as "Are you sure? <y/n>" or "Please reenter the last item" displayed if the program finds the user's entry "unreasonable." (One way to set up a reasonableness check is to require that all item quantities above a certain number, such as 100, be entered twice.)

▶ More complex diagnostics may be used to actually explain errors to the user and describe remedial actions to be taken.

We'll spend the rest of this chapter looking at these techniques individually, using some of our order-entry functions as examples.

Input Using Standard Library Functions

Data read from the standard input file may come from a user typing at a keyboard or, if *stdin* is redirected from a saved file, from a modem or other device. Filter tool programs (see Chapter 6) usually obtain their input through these standard input functions:

FUNCTION	INPUT
getchar()	Character
gets()	Line
scanf()	Formatted

There are a couple of things we need to discuss before we begin talking about these functions individually. First, buffering input by line makes it possible for the user to correct typing errors before the program sees them, since the characters of the input line are not handed over to the program until the user has typed the entire line and pressed Return. This means that, even when the program is calling for single-character input using *getchar( ),* it appears to input complete lines at a time, rather than individual characters.

Second, remember that standard input can be redirected from the command line so that data are obtained from a disk file. When this is done, end-of-file checking becomes important. When input is not redirected, the user at the keyboard can easily give the standard input functions an end-of-file signal simply by typing ^Z alone on a line (UNIX and some other systems use ^D instead).

Character-at-a-time: *getchar( )*

The macro *getchar( )* is defined in the header file *stdio.h.* The returned character is an integer. If a program attempts to read past the end of the file, the value of *stdio.h*'s defined symbol *EOF* is returned. The value of *EOF* in our environment is −1, but use *EOF,* not −1, for end-of-file checking, so that your code will operate correctly on other systems where the value of *EOF* may not be −1.

This next filter program copies its standard input to standard output one character at a time:

```
/* Copy standard input to output using getchar() and putchar(). */
#include <stdio.h>

main()
    {
    int input;

    input = getchar();
    while (input != EOF)                              /* end-of-file checking */
        {
        putchar(input);
        input = getchar();
        }
    }
```

When this copy program is executed interactively, without redirections, it produces this kind of dialogue:

```
Hello there!
Hello there!
Bye!
Bye!
^Z
```

But why does the program echo after each line, rather than after each character? The answer, of course, is that input is buffered a line at a time. The program *would* echo after each character if no input buffering were performed and the program obtained each character immediately after it was typed. (Some operating systems, such as UNIX, permit the C programmer to turn off input buffering and actually input one character at a time with calls to *getchar()*. MS-DOS systems, however, use a separate function, *getch()*, to perform unbuffered input.)

This next filter program counts lines and characters in its standard input file. Notice how we avoid using two separate calls to *getchar()* by embedding the call in the loop test *(input = getchar()) != EOF*:

```
/* Count the number of lines and characters in stdin(). */
#include <stdio.h>

main()
    {
    int input;                          /* input returned from getchar() */
    long chars, lines;                  /* counters for lines and characters */

    for (lines = chars = 0; (input = getchar()) != EOF; ++chars)
        if (input == '\n')                              /* End of a line? */
            ++lines;                    /* Yes. Increment count of lines. */
    printf("%ld lines, %ld characters\n", lines, chars);
    }
```

An important point to remember when working with *getchar()* is that it automatically sends your program the newline character \n at the end of each line it inputs. That's how our program was able to count the lines.

Line-at-a-time: *gets()*

The standard input function *gets()* is called to obtain an entire line of character input from the standard input file. The newline character \n is stripped off the end of the line and replaced with the null character \0, making the line a null-terminated string. The value *0* is returned by *gets()* if the program tries to read beyond the end of the standard input file.

To copy a file a line at a time using *gets()*, try this small program:

```
/* Copy file from stdin to stdout one line at a time. */
#include <stdio.h>

main()
    {
    char line[BUFSIZ];          /* BUFSIZ is defined in stdio.h as the size */
                                /*    of the stdin buffer, typically 512.    */

    /* Loop: For each line of input, Output the same line. */
    while (gets(line))
        puts(line);
    }
```

If the user types an input line longer than the dimension of *line* in the preceding program, *gets()* will go ahead and store characters beyond the end of the line, possibly clobbering other data. Any time a program stores array data in locations beyond the end (or before the beginning) of the declared dimension of the array, it is using storage designated for other purposes. The result can be anything from lost data to a hung system that needs rebooting. The only protection we have against this is to write our own functions with built-in input controls.

Formatted Input: *scanf()*

You have already seen the details of inputting data using *scanf()* (Chapters 2 and 3). However, formatted input with this function *is not safe.* Here's why: Arbitrary numbers of spaces, newline characters, and tab characters may be typed by the user and completely ignored by *scanf()* if it is trying to input a number. Since there is no way to prevent the user from typing unacceptable characters, such as a letter in the middle of a number, such errors must be dealt with *after* the user has finished typing the entire entry. Once again, we just don't have enough control over the type of input with *scanf()*, so we need to develop some alternatives of our own.

Input of Text Under Strict Control

Given the problems connected with *gets()* and *scanf()*, we naturally prefer to write our own input functions for the order-entry application. I've named the text-input function *prompt()* and placed it in the order-entry source file *prompt.c.*

```
stepcode prompt(data, match_str, min_len, max_len, mand, row, col)
char data[];
char match_str[];
short min_len, max_len;
flag mand;
short row, col;

    {
    IMPORT bflag bell_ok;
    char buf[PRMTBSIZ];
    short ichar;
    stepcode rtn = STEPOK;
    bflag more;
```

(continued)

```
    strcpy(buf, data);
    for (ichar = strlen(buf); ichar < max_len; ++ichar)
        buf[ichar] = C_MASK;
    buf[ichar] = '\0';
    tput(row, col, buf);
    CUR_MV(row, col);
    strcpy(buf, data);
    for (ichar = 0, more = YES; ichar < max_len && more; )
        {
        buf[ichar] = getch();
#if defined(DEBUG)
if (buf[ichar] < ' ')
    CDBG("prompt buf[ichar] = getch()", buf[ichar]);
#endif
        buf[ichar + 1] = '\0';
        switch (buf[ichar])
            {
            case C_CANC:
                rtn = STEPCANC, more = NO;
                break;
            case C_BACK:
                rtn = STEPBACK, more = NO;
                break;
            case C_NULL:
                IDBG("prompt C_NULL max_len", max_len);
                for (ichar = 0; ichar < max_len; ++ichar)
                    buf[ichar] = C_MASK;
                buf[ichar] = '\0';
                tput(row, col, buf);
                ichar = 0;
                buf[ichar] = data[ichar] = '\0';
                CUR_MV(row, col);
                break;
            case '\r':
            case '\n':
                if (ichar == 0 && data[0] != '\0')
                    strcpy(buf, data), more = NO;
                else if (ichar == 0 && data[0] == '\0' && mand)
                    {
                    err_warn("Data must be entered:", "");
                    CUR_MV(row, col);
                    }
                else if (ichar < min_len && !(ichar == 0 && !mand))
                    {
                    err_warn("Too few characters:", "");
                    CUR_MV(row, col + ichar);
                    }
                else
                    buf[ichar] = '\0', more = NO;
                break;
            case '\b':
                buf[ichar] = '\0';
                if (ichar > 0)
                    {
                    buf[--ichar] = '\0';
                    fputc('\b', stderr);
                    fputc(C_MASK, stderr);
                    fputc(C_MASK, stderr);
                    fprintf(stderr, "\b\b");
                    }
                break;
```

(continued)

```
            default:
                buf[ichar + 1] = '\0';
                if (match(buf, match_str))
                    putc(buf[ichar++], stderr);
                else if (bell_ok)
                    putc('\7', stderr);
                if (ichar > max_len)
                    more = NO;
                break;
        }
    }
    if (rtn == STEPOK)
        strcpy(data, buf);
    ichar = strlen(data);
    CUR_MV(row, col + ichar);
    for (; ichar < max_len; ++ichar)
        fputc(' ', stderr);
    return (rtn);
}
```

The goal of the *prompt()* function is to control the type of text data the user is allowed to input in response to a prompt message. Only valid characters are echoed as they are typed. If the user types an invalid character, such as *W* in response to a yes-or-no question, nothing is displayed, the bell rings, and the cursor remains where it is. Also, if the user tries to press Return before the expected number of characters have been entered, *err_warn()*, a diagnostic project utility function, alerts the user that more characters are required, and allows another try.

Here is a pseudocode outline of the processing to be done by our order-entry *prompt()* function:

Build and display prompt mask, using defaults where available.

Loop once for each character of response that is input.

Switch: Depending upon input character, do one of the following:

Cancel (^X) or back-up (^R) command? If yes, then done.

Erase (^E) command? If yes, print spaces to erase the field's old value, then display new mask.

Newline (\r or \n)? If yes, check for mandatory and null, then check length.

Backspace (\b)? If yes, delete previous character.

Default: Check match pattern and save character if OK.

Erase any leftover prompt mask characters after user's data.

Notice the declaration and comment for the character array named
data, which is the first parameter for *prompt()*:

```
stepcode prompt(data, match_str, min_len, max_len, mand, row, col)
char data[];                    /* Default is passed in, input data are returned. */
char match_str[];                               /* match string to verify data against */
short min_len, max_len;                 /* minimum and maximum input data lengths */
flag mand;                              /* If yes, data cannot be null on return. */
short row, col;                                 /* cursor location to begin input */
  {
```

The *data* parameter does two jobs: It passes a default to *prompt()* and it
also passes the user's reply back to the function that called *prompt()*. You
must *always* assign a value to the argument passed to *data* before calling
prompt(); if you don't want to provide a default, just pass an empty string.

Character-Type and Match-Pattern Checking

The second parameter for *prompt()* is *match_str,* a match-pattern
string that is passed to the order-entry *match()* function (the sole contents
of the source file *match.c*). This function verifies a data string passed by
prompt(), character by character, against a specified match string. The
return value is *1* if the data match the pattern, *0* if a character in the
data does not match the pattern.

```
flag match(data_str, match_str)
char data_str[];
char match_str[];

  {
  short ichar;
  char c_data;
  char c_match;
  short len_match = strlen(match_str);
  bflag matches = YES;

  for (ichar = 0; data_str[ichar] != '\0' && matches; ++ichar)
     {
     if (ichar < len_match)
        c_match = match_str[ichar];
     else if (len_match == 0)
        c_match = '\0';
     else
        c_match = match_str[len_match - 1];
     c_data = data_str[ichar];
     switch (c_match)
        {
        case 'A':
           if (!isupper(c_data))
              matches = NO;
           break;
        case '#':
           if (!isdigit(c_data))
              matches = NO;
           break;
```

(continued)

```
            case 'S':
                if (!isdigit(c_data) && !strchr("+-", c_data))
                    matches = NO;
                break;
            case 'L':
                if (!isalnum(c_data) && !strchr(";:.,/?*-$#()'! ",
                    c_data))
                    matches = NO;
                if (ichar == 0 && c_data == ' ')
                    matches = NO;
                break;
            case 'U':
                if (!isupper(c_data) && !isdigit(c_data) &&
                    !strchr(";:.,/?*-$#()'! ", c_data))
                    matches = NO;
                if (ichar == 0 && c_data == ' ')
                    matches = NO;
                break;
            case 'P':
                if (!isdigit(c_data) && !strchr("-() ", c_data))
                    matches = NO;
                break;
            case 'F':
                if (!isdigit(c_data) && !strchr(".", c_data))
                    matches = NO;
                break;
            case 'Q':
                if (!strchr("Yy1Nn0", c_data))
                    matches = NO;
                break;
            case 'X':
                if (!isprint(c_data))
                    matches = NO;
                break;
        }
    }
    return (matches);
}
```

Figure 13-1 shows those match characters used with the prompts in the order-entry application. Notice that none of the match characters listed permits the user to enter leading spaces, although non-leading spaces are

MATCH CHARACTER	DATA ALLOWED	USE
#	0–9 only	Numbers
F	0–9 or .	Tax and dollar amounts
L	a–z, A–Z, 0–9 or ;:.,/?*– $#()'! and non-leading spaces	Names, addresses
U	A–Z, 0–9 or ;:.,/?*– $#()'! and non-leading spaces	Uppercase names, addresses
P	0–9 or – or ()	Phone numbers
Q	Y y 1 N n 0 (one only)	Yes/no question responses

FIGURE 13-1 ▍ *Match characters for order-entry prompts*

MACRO	RETURN VALUE
isupper(c)	1 if *c* is an uppercase letter, else 0
isdigit(c)	1 if *c* is a numeric digit 0 through 9, else 0
isalnum(c)	1 if *c* is a letter or number, else 0
isprint(c)	1 if *c* is a printable ASCII character, else 0

FIGURE 13-2

Macros from ctype.h *used in the order-entry application*

accepted by *L* and *U* (something *scanf()* can't control). The other match characters included in *match.c* are for general use. Feel free to add new ones of your own, to suit your own applications.

Nearly all C compilers come with a header file named *ctype.h,* which contains macros for classifying a character by type. Figure 13-2 shows the *ctype* macros we use in our order-entry *match()* function.

This next code segment for the *L* match character uses both the macro *isalnum()* and the library string function *strchr()* (called *index()* in some other C libraries). The *strchr()* function searches within the string passed as its first argument (;:.,/?*-$#()'!") for the character passed as its second argument (*c_data*), and returns *0* if the character is not found.

```
case 'L':  /* a-z, A-Z, 0-9 or ;:.,/?*-$#()'! or space */
   if (!isalnum(c_data) && !strchr(";:.,/?*-$#()'! ",
      c_data))
      matches = NO;
   if (ichar == 0 && c_data == ' ')                /* no leading blanks */
      matches = NO;
```

The *match()* function performs one iteration of the loop for each character in the data string being tested. The character is compared against a match character from within a large *switch* statement that holds case actions for several match characters, all similar to the one in the preceding example. The loop ends when all of the characters have been checked or a non-matching character is found.

Input of Numbers Under Strict Control

The *#* and *S* match characters offer us some interesting possibilities for controlling numeric input. (The string *"#"* will match a string of digits; the string *"S#"* will match a string of digits that begins with a plus or minus sign.)

The kinds of numbers that we want to input in our order-entry application are money, quantities, and percentages. (We don't consider phone numbers and zip codes numeric input because we keep them in string form and do not perform arithmetic on them.) Let's talk about money first—the bottom line, right?

```
stepcode nprompt(p_num, match_str, min_val, max_val, mand, row, col)
long *p_num;
char match_str[];
long min_val, max_val;
flag mand;
short row, col;

    {
    long atol(char[]);
    char buf[14];
    bflag more = YES;
    long in_num;
    short max_len = strlen(ltoa(max_val, buf, 10));
    short min_len = strlen(ltoa(min_val, buf, 10));
    stepcode rtn;

    if (*p_num)
        {
        ntput(row, col, *p_num, buf, max_len);
        }
    else
        buf[0] = '\0';
    do
        {
        rtn = prompt(buf, match_str, min_len, max_len, mand, row, col);
        if (rtn != STEPOK)
            more = NO;
        else
            {
            in_num = atol(buf);
            SDBG("nprompt buf", buf);
            LDBG("nprompt in_num", in_num);
            if (mand && in_num == 0)
                err_warn("Non-zero data mandatory:", "");
            else if ((in_num < min_val || in_num > max_val) &&
                (mand || in_num != 0))
                {
                sprintf(buf, "%ld to %ld", min_val, max_val);
                err_warn("Enter a number from:", buf);
                buf[0] = '\0';
                }
            else
                more = NO;
            }
        }
    while (more);
    if (rtn == STEPOK)
        {
        *p_num = in_num;
        ntput(row, col, in_num, buf, max_len);
        }
    return (rtn);
    }
```

The data type you use to hold amounts of money depends, quite simply, upon the size of the largest possible amount to be handled and whether or not decimal values are expected. (Remember to allow for the effects of arithmetic operations such as addition and multiplication.) In the order-entry application, we will use *long* variables to hold amounts of money in cents (giving us a range of ±$21,474,836.47), since *float* and *double* can cause rounding errors that drop or add pennies and drive accountants crazy. However, we will convert money values to *double* before *displaying* them, so that they will appear on the screen (or printer) in familiar decimal format.

```
stepcode fprompt(d_num, match_str, min_dval, max_dval,
    width, precision, mand, row, col)
double *d_num;
char match_str[];
double min_dval, max_dval;
short width, precision;
flag mand;
short row, col;

    {
    int dec, sign;
    double atof(char[]);
    char buf[14];
    bflag more = YES;
    double in_dnum;
    short max_len = width;
    short min_len = strlen(fcvt(min_dval, precision, &dec, &sign)) - precision;
    stepcode rtn;

    if (*d_num != 0)
        {
        ftput(row, col, *d_num, precision, buf, max_len);
        }
    else
        buf[0] = '\0';
    do
        {
        rtn = prompt(buf, match_str, min_len, max_len, mand, row, col);
        if (rtn != STEPOK)
            more = NO;
        else
            {
            in_dnum = atof(buf);
            if (mand && in_dnum == 0)
                err_warn("Non-zero data mandatory:", "");
            else if ((in_dnum < min_dval || in_dnum > max_dval) &&
                (mand || in_dnum != 0))
                {
                sprintf(buf, "%.*f to %.*f", precision, min_dval,
                    precision, max_dval);
                err_warn("Enter a number from:", buf);
                buf[0] = '\0';
```

(continued)

```
            CUR_MV(row, col);
            }
        else
            more = NO;
        }
    }
while (more);
if (rtn == STEPOK)
    {
    *d_num = (double) in_dnum;
    ftput(row, col, *d_num, precision, buf, max_len);
    }
return (rtn);
}
```

The *nprompt()* and *fprompt()* functions begin by obtaining a numeric value and converting it to a string to be passed to *prompt()* as a default response. The *prompt()* function is called to input a string of digits, which is then converted from ASCII to either *long* or *double* by the library functions *atol()* and *atof()*, respectively. If the number is within the acceptable range of values, it is right justified and echoed by *ntput()* or *ftput()*. (We echo numbers right justified to align columns of numbers on the decimal point.)

The functions *atol()* and *atof()* are from a very small family of library functions used to convert ASCII strings of digits to binary numbers:

FUNCTION	ACTION
atof()	ASCII to *double*
atoi()	ASCII to *int*
atol()	ASCII to *long*

Diagnostic Messages

Even with all these safeguards, there will be times when the user will enter something unacceptable. The most helpful thing we as programmers can do at such times is provide a diagnostic message explaining the problem. For example, in *nprompt()* and *fprompt()* we would alert the user about a zero at a mandatory prompt or a value too high or too low for the range of the prompt field. These messages are sent to the user by the order-entry function *err_warn()*. (The diagnostic-message functions *err_warn()* and *err_exit()* are part of the project utility library.)

```
#define ESC '\x1b'

void err_warn(first, second)
char first[], second[];

   {
   IMPORT bflag bell_ok;
   short first_len = strlen(first);
   short second_len = strlen(second);

   CUR_MV(24, 1);
   CLR_LINE;
   tput(24, 1, first);
   tput(24, 2 + first_len, second);
   tput(24, 3 + first_len + second_len,
      "_ (push ESC)\b\b\b\b\b\b\b\b\b\b\b\b");
   if (bell_ok)
      BELL;
   while (getch() != ESC)
      if (bell_ok)
         BELL;
   CUR_MV(24, 1);
   CLR_LINE;
   }

void err_exit(first, second)
char first[], second[];

   {
   char log_buf[512];

   strcpy(log_buf, first);
   strcat(log_buf, " ");
   strcat(log_buf, second);
   logentry(log_buf);
   err_warn(first, second);
   exit(FAIL);
   }
```

A uniform format for error-message displays is helpful to the user: It makes it obvious what is happening whenever that type of message appears. Both of our application's error-message functions take two string arguments, and since *err_exit()* actually calls *err_warn()* to display the warning message, we need to change only one function to modify the message format. The *err_warn()* function does not return a value, and *err_exit()* never returns at all, because it calls the library function *exit()*, which terminates program execution and returns control to the operating system. Which to use? Well, call *err_warn()* for warning messages to the user about things that can be fixed, and call *err_exit()* for serious or fatal error conditions that require that the program be terminated.

You'll notice two calls to *logentry()* in the *err_exit()* source code. These are used to preserve the serious warning messages in the log file, so that we can trace the actions that led to the disaster and help the user avoid them in the future.

One last thing before we leave the subject of prompting. You may have noticed the declaration *long* ∗*p_num;* in the code for *nprompt()*. The ∗ operator is used before the variable *p_num* to refer to the *long* integer whose *address* the variable holds. Such variables are called *pointer variables,* and we'll spend the next few chapters learning how, when, and why to use them.

Section IV presents a pragmatic discussion of some of the features that give C greater power and flexibility than other high-level languages. Chapter 14 deals with pointers, a low-level C data type that holds the address of another variable or value in memory. Chapter 15 explores multi-dimensional arrays, including pointer arrays that pass command-line arguments to a C program's *main()* function. Chapter 16 discusses the declaration and manipulation of structures, C's most powerful and flexible data type.

SECTION IV

Pointers: Variations on Data Access

14

We've talked about the fact that C has features for system programmers usually not available in higher-level languages—features powerful enough to allow the C programmer to write operating systems or hardware interfaces (machine-level programming). Now that you know enough C to produce entire applications, we'll begin looking at some of these special features, to see how they can help streamline our programs and extend their capabilities.

Let's begin with the *pointer* data type, which holds the *address* of a variable in memory, rather than the value of the variable. Pointers make it easy for system programmers to perform operations that used to require tedious assembly-language routines. Moreover, the close relationship between expressions using pointers and the underlying CPU instructions they compile to makes for very efficient programs.

Your first exposure to pointers was in Chapter 2, where the *address-of* operator (&) appeared in our discussion about inputting numbers with the library function *scanf()*:

```
scanf("%ld", &long_to_be_input);
```

Then you heard about them again in Chapter 3, when we discussed one-dimensional arrays. Now, at last, we'll look at pointers in detail, but first I want to explain my approach to the topic.

Rather than overwhelm you with the full depth of this subject in one dose, I'll introduce pointers a little at a time. In this chapter, you will learn as much about pointers as you need to know in order to use them for their most important application: returning more that one value from a function to its caller. Then in Chapter 15, I'll expand on the use of pointers for string manipulation. I've saved such advanced pointer topics as dynamic allocation of memory and linked lists until Chapter 19, when we will have covered some other advanced techniques involved in those applications.

Declaring Pointers

A pointer variable has two important attributes: the *data type* it is *declared* to point to and the *address* it is *assigned* to point to. We'll begin by seeing how to declare pointer variables.

The syntax used to declare a variable as a pointer to any data type is like the syntax of an ordinary declaration, except that an asterisk (*) is placed before the name of the variable being declared. Let's look at some examples.

The following statements declare the variables *p_long, p_short,* and *p_char* as pointers to types *long, short,* and *char,* respectively:

```
long  *p_long;          /* p_long is type pointer to long.  */
short *p_short;         /* p_short is type pointer to short. */
char  *p_char;          /* p_char is type pointer to char.  */
```

Every variable declared in a program consumes memory to hold its value: 1 byte for type *char,* 2 bytes for *short,* and 4 bytes for *long.* Pointers are no exception: They consume the same amount of storage as an *int* variable, namely 2 bytes on 16-bit systems and 4 bytes on 32-bit systems. Thus, the declarations in the preceding example use a total of either 6 or 12 bytes of memory, depending upon the system. The important point to remember here is that at this stage, no memory has been allocated for any *long, short,* or *char* variables—only for the three *pointer* variables. Also, since the pointers in our example have not been initialized, their values are undefined and they cannot safely be used. Let's take care of that problem right now.

Initializing Pointers

Like other data types, *pointers* may contain an initializer in their declarations. The syntax of the initializing declaration uses the & and ∗ operators, like this:

```
long long_val;
long *p_long = &long_val;
```

The unary & operator may be used only on lvalues (Chapter 3). You will recall that the compiler is free to assign any available location in memory to hold an lvalue; you have no control over this allocation. Let's suppose the compiler has allocated 1 byte at location 1006 to the *char* variable *char_val*. The following pointer declaration obtains that address and assigns it to the pointer *p_char*:

```
char *p_char = &char_val;   /* Assign address of char_val to pointer p_char. */
```

The variable *p_char* is now said to be "pointing to" *char_val*, like this:

You can see that the value of *p_char* is the address of *char_val*, not the contents ('*S*'). Diagrams like this can be very helpful, both in learning about pointers and in designing *pointer* data structures.

A double-quoted string constant also may be used to initialize a *pointer to type char* variable, just as it is used to initialize a *static,*

SEMIGLOBAL, or *GLOBAL* array of characters. The following diagram illustrates the difference in how the initializer is stored in memory in these two cases:

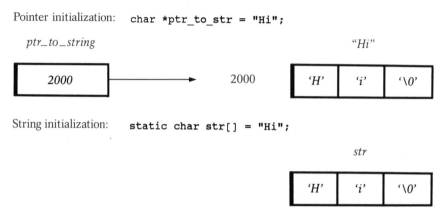

Pointer initialization: `char *ptr_to_str = "Hi";`

ptr_to_string   *"Hi"*

String initialization: `static char str[] = "Hi";`

In this example, the initialization of *ptr_to_string* simply assigns an address value to that pointer, whereas the initialization of the string *str* actually copies the bytes of the initializer into the bytes of the character string. In C, the string constant *"Hi"* can act either as the address of a string or as a constant array of characters.

Assignment to Pointers

Initializers are only one way to assign values to pointers. We can also use assignment expressions to assign values to pointer variables *after* they have been declared.

We've already seen the & operator used to obtain the address of a scalar or an element of an array (Chapters 2 and 3). Well, we can also assign the resulting *pointer expression* to a variable that has been declared to point to the data type of that scalar or element, as in this example:

```
long long_val, *p_long;
char buffer[80], *p_buffer;

p_long = &long_val;                    /* p_long now points to long_val. */
p_buffer = &buffer[2];         /* p_buffer points to 3rd byte of buffer. */
```

The value of a pointer may even be assigned to another *pointer* of the same type, like this:

```
double discount;
double *p_discount = &discount, *p_perc_off;          /* Declare pointers. */

p_perc_off = p_discount;                         /* Assign a pointer to a pointer. */
```

Now both *pointers to type double, p_discount* and *p_perc_off,* point to the same location: the address of *discount.*

Once again, we need to keep in mind a couple of DON'Ts:

▶ Don't assign a pointer declared for one data type to a pointer variable that has been declared for a different data type. Your CPU's memory alignment requirements may cause the address you are assigning to be rounded to a boundary suitable for the data type pointed to (for example, an address divisible by 4 for type *long* data), and the pointer variable might therefore receive an address other than the one you intended.

▶ Don't assign a pointer value to a non-pointer variable. It's senseless, it makes your code confusing to read, and it can also cause alignment problems. (It will also generate a warning message from the compiler!)

Accessing Data Indirectly

Let's look more closely at how we go about accessing the data a pointer is pointing to, so that we can begin to use pointers in real programs.

The familiar *PEEK* and *POKE* functions from BASIC permit you to examine and change a specific byte in memory if you know the address of that byte. C has an analogous and more powerful feature known as indirection. The unary *indirection operator* (*) is used on a pointer to obtain or alter the value it points to, so the expression *p_var could be read as "the contents of the location p_var points to." The operator is called *indirection* because it uses the pointer's value (an address) to obtain the value of the variable the pointer points to, rather than using the direct route, the variable itself.

Let's look at some examples of indirection. Observe how the pointer *p_credit_code* is used to indirectly examine and modify the value of *credit_code* in this next program:

```
/* View and change a variable through a pointer to it. */
main()
    {
    char credit_code = 'B', old_credit_code;
    char *p_credit_code = &credit_code;

    old_credit_code = *p_credit_code;                    /* PEEK at credit code. */
    *p_credit_code = 'A';                                /* POKE new credit code. */
    printf("Credit Code is now %c. Credit Code formerly was %c.\n",
        credit_code, old_credit_code);
    }
```

Notice that the line of output from *printf()* reflects the changes made to *credit_code* through the pointer variable *p_credit_code*:

```
Credit Code is now A. Credit Code formerly was B.
```

Once a pointer is assigned the address of a variable, all indirect references using that pointer (**p_credit_code*, in our example) refer to the variable itself, not to a copy of the variable's value, so the original value of *credit_code* stored in memory ('B') is actually *replaced* with the new value ('A'). Now you can understand why C requires that pointers be declared to point to a specific data type: The data type that a pointer is declared to point to and that of the expression made up of the unary indirection operator (*) acting on that pointer variable will always be the same.

Here's another example, using the same pointer in a conditional application (since *A* has the lowest ASCII value of the alphabet, we have to decrement, not increment, to raise the credit rating):

```
if (*p_credit_code > 'A')         /* If not at top credit level, raise credit */
    --(*p_credit_code);           /*    code one grade. (A has lowest ASCII    */
                                  /*    value of the alphabet.)                */
```

Remember: What is decremented in this example is the contents of the *char* variable, *not* the pointer address. (The parentheses in the second line are for readability only. They have no effect, because unary operators like -- and * group from right to left.)

Now to see what we can actually *do* with pointers. We'll just take a quick peek here, and then devote the next few chapters to the details.

Passing Pointer Arguments

The value of a pointer variable is an expression and therefore may be passed as an argument to a function—a fact that explains how *array* arguments are passed to functions. Let's look at how this works.

Arrays and pointers are very closely related in C. In fact, whenever you use the name of an array in any expression, the value of the array name is taken to be the starting address of the array, which is in effect a pointer to its zeroth element. Thus, if *str* is an array of characters and *p_str* is a *pointer to type char*, these two statements are equivalent:

```
p_str = str;
p_str = &str[0];
```

Here's another example of this equivalence. The following three calls to the library function *strcpy()* all cause the text *"This is it."* to be assigned to *str*.

```
char str[80];
char *p_str = str;                     /* Same as:  char *p_str = &str[0]; */

strcpy(str, "This is it.");
strcpy(&str[0], "This is it.");
strcpy(p_str, "This is it.");
```

Returning Pointer Values

Functions can also *return* a pointer value. Library string functions often take advantage of this capability by returning a pointer to one of their arguments, which is then passed to other library functions, to be used in constructing larger, more complex expressions. For example, in this next statement *strcpy()* returns the starting address of the string it copies to, which is its first argument. This means that you can copy *"This is it."* to *str* and then print *str*, all with one statement:

```
printf("str = %s\n", strcpy(str, "This is it."));
```

Here's what actually happens in this example-
ple: The starting address of *str* is passed to
strcpy(), which copies the message *"This is it."*
to *str* and returns *str*'s starting address to the
calling function. This value is then passed to
printf() as the starting address of the string it
should print. Pointers allowed us to get a lot
of mileage out of that one line of code!

C A U T I O N

*You can easily write tricky, hard-to-
read, hard-to-debug code using pointers, so good style and readability are
especially important here.*

Returning More Than One Value

Regardless of the number of arguments passed to a function, C's
return-value mechanism permits the function to *return* only a single value.
Scalar (non-array) arguments to a C subfunction are passed as copies of
their individual values. Changes the subfunction makes to its *copy* of a
passed value have no effect on the original value owned and passed
by the caller.

But there are times when we need to be able to return more than one
value from a function. For example, we might need to keep a tally of the
function's main activity, like the library function *scanf()*, which returns a
count of the number of legal values that were input, as well as the values
themselves. How can we handle such a situation? Well, fortunately, C's
pointer data type provides a neat solution to the problem. We'll use an
example from our order-entry application to see how a subfunction can
actually save a value in a calling function's variable if the calling function
passes the *address* of its variable, rather than the value itself.

The function *inv_find()* from the *stubs.c* source file is passed a part
number to find. If it is successful, it passes back a description, price, and
shipping weight, as well as a verification that a valid part was found in the
inventory list:

```
flag inv_find(part, part_desc, p_price, p_ship_wt)
char part[];                          /* part number to look up (pass in) */
char part_desc[];                        /* description of part (returned) */
money *p_price;                /* pointer to unit price of part (returned) */
short *p_ship_wt;              /* pointer shipping weight in ounces (rtn'd) */
```

(continued)

```
{
    /* Return typical data to test inv_find()'s callers. */
    strcpy(part_desc, "Order-Entry Software Package");
    *p_price = 12345L;
    *p_ship_wt = 123;
    return (part[0] == 'S');                    /* YES if 'S' first, else NO */
}
```

The four lines relevant to this discussion are the declarations and initializations of the pointers *p_price* and *p_ship_wt*. The variable *p_price* is declared as *pointer to type money* (that is, *pointer to type long*). It is used to pass the "typical" price *12345L* back to the calling function. The *pointer to type short, p_ship_wt*, is used to pass *123* back to the *short* integer whose address was passed to *inv_find()* in the following expression from *ord_itms()*:

```
part_found = (step_rtn == STEPOK) && inv_find(parts[ipart], part_descs[ipart],
    &prices[ipart], &ship_weights[ipart]);
```

The third *argument* to *inv_find()*, *&prices[ipart]*, is the address of a *long* integer in the array *prices,* an expression of type *pointer to long,* and the third *parameter* of *inv_find()*, *p_price*, is declared as type *pointer to long* (since *money* is defined in *ordentry.h* as *long*). Thus argument and associated parameter are both of the same type. This is true for all of *inv_find()*'s other arguments as well.

The declaration of the argument and return types for *inv_find()* in the function *ord_itms()* reads:

```
flag inv_find(char[], char[], money *, short *);
```

This prototype declaration permits the compiler to verify that you have passed the right number of arguments of the right data types to *inv_find()*, and that you have used *inv_find()*'s return value correctly.

Now here's what happens when the program is executed. The address of a *long, prices[ipart]*, is passed to the third parameter, *p_price*. Then *p_price* is used in the statement **p_price = 12345L;* to assign *12345L* back to the *long* whose address was passed, namely *prices[ipart]*. The following diagram of memory just after the *∗p_price = 12345L;* statement assigns *12345L* to *prices[ipart]* may make this clearer:

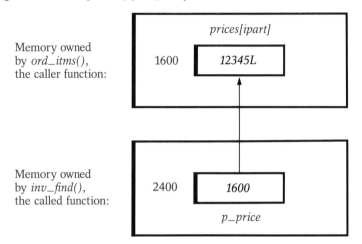

Memory owned by *ord_itms()*, the caller function:

prices[ipart]

1600   12345L

Memory owned by *inv_find()*, the called function:

2400   1600

p_price

So that's how the interaction between the calling function that passes an address argument and the called function's pointer parameter enables the called function to assign data back to the calling function's variable. Actually, you've already used this technique with one-dimensional arrays, perhaps without realizing it.

Now let's look at some more powerful applications of the array and pointer constructs: multidimensional arrays and arrays of pointers.

15

Advanced Arrays

C's implementation of arrays is far more flexible than the examples you've seen so far. For instance, you can declare arrays of as many dimensions as you like (although more than two or three dimensions are hard for most of us to visualize), and you can create arrays of pointers to data.

When would you use such advanced arrays? Well, here's one very practical example from the business world.

Suppose you open a small business to sell custom software. You decide to hire a salesperson to take care of marketing, so that you can concentrate on application development. After a year, you want to get a picture of how the business is going and whether there are any seasonal fluctuations in sales. To help you analyze the monthly sales record, you could use a one-dimensional array of 12 *long* integers, each of which is one month's total sales (if you use a *#defined* constant for the dimension in the array's declaration, your code will be more flexible):

```
#define MONTHS 12

/* ... */
long sales_total[MONTHS];
```

But as your business grows and you hire new salespeople, you'll probably want to *compare* their sales records. Now there are two dimensions to your analysis, so you'll need an array with a row for each salesperson and a column for each month. Your modified array declaration will look like this:

```
#define SALESPEOPLE 4
#define MONTHS 12

/* ... */
long sales_total[SALESPEOPLE][MONTHS];
```

As business continues to increase and data accumulate, you can continue to add new dimensions to your array, to broaden your sales analysis. For instance, if you also want to analyze sales for each product over a period of years, your declaration might become:

```
#define SALESPEOPLE 4
#define YEARS 5
#define MONTHS 12
#define PRODUCTS 3

/* ... */
long sales_total[SALESPEOPLE][YEARS][MONTHS][PRODUCTS];
```

What we've actually been doing in these examples is using multidimensional arrays as in-memory databases, to store and access tables of numbers and characters.

Declaring Multidimensional Arrays

You probably noticed that the array declarations from our scenario look a little different from those you are used to. C does not use a comma-separated list of indices, as many other languages do, to declare the dimensions of an array or to access one of its elements. Instead, C requires that you supply a pair of square brackets (*[]*) for each dimension. Let's look at some examples.

The following code segment declares the identifier *matrix* to be a two-row, three-column array of *short* integers and assigns the numbers 0 through 5 to its elements:

```
short matrix[2][3], row, col;

for (row = 0; row < 2; ++row)              /* Loop through each row */
   for (col = 0; col < 3; ++col)           /*    and each column.   */
      matrix[row][col] = row * 3 + col;    /* Assign this value. */
```

This is how the data for *matrix* would be stored:

	Column 0	Column 1	Column 2
Row 0	*0*	*1*	*2*
Row 1	*3*	*4*	*5*

The diagram shows that *matrix [1][2]* (read as *matrix sub one sub two*) is equal to *5*. (Remember that the first row and column have index 0, not 1.)

Now suppose we want to display the elements of *matrix* in an actual matrix format. This next code segment does that for us:

```
for (row = 0; row < 2; ++row)                    /* Loop through each row. */
   {
   for (col = 0; col < 3; ++col)                     /* For each column, */
      printf("%d  ", matrix[row][col]);              /*    print element. */
   putchar('\n');                                /* Skip line after printing row. */
   }
```

The output from our routine will look like this:

```
0   1   2
3   4   5
```

Like their one-dimensional counterparts, multidimensional arrays with *auto* storage class may not be initialized. However, in this next example, *matrix* has *static* storage class, so the same values could be assigned by an initializer:

```
static short matrix[2][3] = {0, 1, 2,
                             3, 4, 5};
```

Notice that, as with one-dimensional arrays, the elements of a row can be grouped in curly braces. And here too, if you supply fewer initializers than elements, the remaining elements are automatically initialized to zero.

The syntax for declaring explicitly initialized *static* or *extern* multidimensional arrays allows us to omit the size of the first dimension. In that case, the number of initializers will determine the size of the array. But empty brackets *must* be included in the declaration, to mark the place of the omitted dimension:

```
static short matrix[][3]  = {0, 1, 2,
                             3, 4, 5};
```

There are two other instances where empty brackets are permitted in array declarations. One is when you *IMPORT* an array that was declared with *SEMIGLOBAL* or *GLOBAL* storage class:

```
SEMIGLOBAL short matrix[][3] = {0, 1, 2,              /* outside all functions */
                                3, 4, 5);
/* ... */
IMPORT short matrix[][3];                             /* within a function body */
```

and the other is when you declare an array parameter within a function, as in this next program to sum each row of a two-dimensional array of *short* integers. (C does require us to decide how many elements are in each row: that is, how many columns our array will have. We'll use three columns for this example.)

```
#define NCOLS 3

/* Sum rows of an n-row, 3-column array of short integers. */
main()
    {
    static short matrix[][NCOLS] = {0, 1, 2,
                                    3, 4, 5);
    short nrows = 2;

    show_sums(matrix, nrows);
    }

show_sums(matrix, nrows)
short matrix[][NCOLS];                       /* array of rows to sum */
short nrows;                                 /* number of rows to sum */

    {
    short irow, icol, sum;

    for (irow = 0; irow < nrows; ++irow)
        {
        for (sum = icol = 0; icol < NCOLS; ++icol)
            sum += matrix[irow][icol];
        printf("Sum of row %d is %d.\n", irow, sum);
        }
    }
```

This two-function program outputs these two lines of text:

```
Sum of row 0 is 3.
Sum of row 1 is 12.
```

The row of a two-dimensional (2D) array of any data type is actually a one-dimensional array and therefore may be used in any expression where a one-dimensional array would be legal. (The fact that 2D arrays are actually stored in memory as 1D row arrays explains why it is impossible to treat a *column* of a 2D array as an array.) This ability to manipulate array cross-sections greatly increases the flexibility of string arrays in C programs. In this chapter, we'll see how to use this technique to create a list of salespeople by storing one name in each row of the array.

Multidimensional Arrays of Characters

Our last version of the *pw_find()* function from *stubs.c* merely checked to be sure that the first letters of the user name and password were equal to '*S*'. Now that we know how to work with multidimensional arrays, we can modify *pw_find()* so that it will search a list of names for the complete user name to validate, and then compare the password entered by the user with the correct password for that name. Here's how it's done:

```
static char user_names[][20] = {"Dan", "Mary", "Greg", ""};
static char passwords[][10] = {"tuna", "piano", "fish"};
short iname;

for (iname = 0; iname < 20 && user_names[iname][0]; ++iname)
   if (0 == strcmp(user, user_names[iname]))                  /* Name found? */
      return (0 == strcmp(password, passwords[iname]));
return (NO);
```

The array *user_names* in this example has four rows, each 20 bytes wide. The empty brackets set the number of initializers to the number of rows—in this case four. Each row's initializer has fewer than 20 bytes; any unused bytes in the row are filled with null characters. The last row, *user_names[3]*, is completely filled with null characters, to mark the end of the list. During program execution, the *for* loop test checks the first byte of each name for the null character, to see if the final name has been reached.

Both calls to *strcmp()* in *pw_find()* pass two strings: the string to check and a row from one of the 2D arrays to compare it with. The second call to *strcmp()* (within the *return* statement) compares the password entered with the password for the user whose name is known from the first call. Then *pw_find()* compares the return from *strcmp()* with *0* (remember, *strcmp()* returns a negative value if the first string sorts lower in the ASCII scale than the second, a positive value if it sorts higher, and zero if they are identical), and returns either *1* (true) or *0* (false).

The order-entry application uses two other 2D arrays of characters, *parts* and *part_descs,* for holding part numbers and part descriptions, respectively. Their declarations in *ordbuild.c* read:

```
SEMIGLOBAL char parts[MAX_ITEMS][L_PARTS + 1] = {""};
SEMIGLOBAL char part_descs[MAX_ITEMS][L_PART_DESC + 1] = {""};
```

The function *ord_itms()* (also in *ordbuild.c*) calls the function *inv_find()* to pass rows of these arrays, like this:

```
part_found = (step_rtn == STEPOK) && inv_find(parts[ipart],
    part_descs[ipart], &prices[ipart], &ship_weights[ipart]);
```

Arrays of Pointers

Now let's look at a different kind of array: the *array of pointers.* This structure gives C programmers another means of storing a collection of strings under a single name. Since each row in a conventional 2D rectangular array of characters has enough storage allocated to it to hold the longest string and all rows must be the same length, this construct wastes space if the strings in each row do not completely fill the row. When a set of strings is pointed to by the elements of an array of pointers, however, we don't have this problem. Let's see how this new approach works.

Pointers to Strings

We've already modified *pw_find()* to work with two-dimensional arrays of characters. Now we're going to modify it again, this time declaring *user_names* and *passwords* as arrays of *pointers to type char.* Here is the new body for *pw_find()*:

```
static char *user_names[] = {"Dan", "Mary", "Greg", NULL};
static char *passwords[] = {"tuna", "piano", "fish"};
short iname;

for (iname = 0; iname < 20 && user_names[iname] != NULL; ++iname)
   if (0 == strcmp(user, user_names[iname]))                /* Name found? */
       return (0 == strcmp(password, passwords[iname]));
return (NO);
```

Notice that although the declarations have been modified, the two calls to *strcmp()* use the same arguments in both versions. The difference is that now *user_names* is a one-dimensional array of *pointers,* whereas before it was a two-dimensional array of characters, and the expression *user_names[iname]* now has the data type *pointer to type char*. Let's look at a diagram of the new *user_names* data structure:

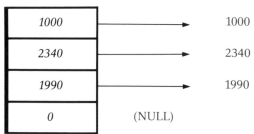

`char *user_names[];`

Strings pointed to by *user_names*

You'll have noticed that the last initializer for *user_names* is now *NULL*, rather than empty quotation marks. The symbol *NULL* is defined in the library header file *stdio.h* as the integer 0, and is often used to mark the end of an array of pointers, so that the number of elements need not be saved in a separate variable. It is perfectly safe to end a list of pointers with *NULL* because the compiler ensures that no variable or string constant in your program is assigned *NULL* as its address.

You've already seen how you can change the value of a string in a 2D character array by using the library functions *strcpy()* and *strncpy()* (Chapter 14), or by using the assignment operator on one character at a time (Chapter 3). But this isn't always the best way to change a string pointed to from an array of pointers. Let's look at an example.

The strings pointed to by elements of *user_names* in the following line of code may not be changed because they are constants:

> C A U T I O N
>
> *Do not confuse the NULL pointer with the null character. Both are used by convention to end an array and both have the numeric value zero, but the NULL pointer 0 is an integer used to end an array of pointers, whereas the null character '\0' is a single byte used to end an array of characters.*

```
static char *user_names[] = {"Dan", "Mary", "Greg", NULL};
```

As things stand, if you want to make the second element of *user_names* point to *"Marie"* instead of *"Mary"*, you don't copy the *"ie"* from *"Marie"* over the *'y'* in *"Mary"*; instead, you assign a new value to *user_names[1]*, like this:

```
user_names[1] = "Marie";
```

Had the elements of *user_names* been made to *point to* string variables instead, we could have assigned back into those strings through the individual elements of *user_names*.

In most cases, you would still replace the pointer to a string with a pointer to a different string, rather than change the string itself. However, when you *do* need to obtain a character from the middle of a string pointed to from an array, you can use the one-dimensional array of *pointers to type char* as though it were in a two-dimensional (rectangular) array of characters. For example, to get the '*r*' in *"Marie"*, you use the following type *char* expression, not an array or string expression:

```
user_names[1][2]
```

If you need to use the address of a character from within *user_names* in a larger expression, the syntax should by now be no surprise. The next two code fragments test for *"ie"* after the '*r*' in *"Marie"*:

```
if (0 == strcmp(&user_names[1][3], "ie"))
```

or

```
if (0 == strcmp(strchr(user_names[1], 'r'), "rie"))
```

Now that you understand the basics of the *array of pointers* data structure, let's look at a common application: obtaining command-line arguments passed to *main()*.

Command-Line Arguments

The command line is the line of text you type to direct the operating system to execute your compiled, linked C program. (The command line also may come from a DOS batch file or UNIX shell script, rather than from keyboard input.) The first word on the command line is the name of the executable file (for DOS, omit the *.EXE* extension). Any additional strings of text on the command line, except file-redirection commands, are gathered and passed as arguments to *main()*. Thus command-line arguments are simply strings passed from the command line to your *main()* function. (Your *main()* function may choose to ignore these arguments if they aren't appropriate to the environment, thus helping to preserve the portability of your programs.)

The processing of the command line, before it is passed to *main()*, involves placing the words that are separated by white space (spaces and tab characters) into individual strings. (This process of character checking and string isolating is known as *parsing* the command line for its arguments.) The new data structure that is built and passed is actually an array of *pointers to type char.* (If you want to pass an argument that contains white space, you must surround that argument with double quotes.) Let's see how we can use this new structure to obtain command-line arguments.

Declaring command-line parameters. The changes you must make to your *main()* to obtain command-line data are minor, and no additional compiler options need be specified. The declaration of the parameters for *main()* is no different than for any other function: *main()*'s parameters, and *only* its parameters, must be declared before its opening curly brace. A typical declaration would look like this:

```
main(ac, av)                        /* Begin the main function. */
unsigned ac;                        /* ac is the argument count. */
char *av[];                         /* av is the argument vector, a */
    {                               /*    pointer to the arguments.  */
```

The data passed to *main()* are in string form and so may be copied and compared using the standard-library string functions. For example, if you want to allow the first argument to *main()* to be the switch '*-s*', to instruct your program to copy the second argument to the string variable *arg*, you would just code:

```
if (ac > 2 && 0 == strcmp(av[1], "-s"))    /* Test first argument. */
    strcpy(arg, av[2]);                    /* Copy second argument. */
```

Obtaining numeric data. Let's take these concepts one step further and use them in a real program that uses numeric data from the command line. The example we'll use is a reindenting program that changes the number of spaces used for each level of indentation from some previous number to a new one. This program can be used to reformat C source files that are indented with spaces (but not with tab characters).

Numbers you get from the command line will be in string form and must be converted to internal binary format before they may be used for counting purposes. The library functions *sscanf()* (for *scanf()* strings) and

atoi() (ASCII to integer) both can do this for us. We'll use *atoi()* because it is
simpler and smaller than *sscanf()*, so we can save some space and end up
with less code. Here is the source file *rein.c*:

```
/******************************************************************************/
/* REIN reindents C programs, converting from one number of spaces per      */
/*   indent to another. REIN is a filter. The following call converts from 5 */
/*   spaces per indent to 3:                                                 */
/*      REIN 5 3 <OLDPGM.C >NEWPGM.C                                         */
/******************************************************************************/

#include <stdio.h>

main(ac, av)                                   /* main() is passed two parameters. */
unsigned ac;                  /* command line argument count; 1 if no arguments */
char *av[];                   /* array of pointers to strings from command line */

    {
    char buf[BUFSIZ];
    short old_indent, new_indent, indent, new_spc;

    if (ac != 3)
       err_exit("Usage: REIN #_old_indent #_new_indent\n", "");

    old_indent = atoi(av[1]);                      /* Convert command-line numbers */
    new_indent = atoi(av[2]);                      /*   from string to binary.    */
    if (old_indent < 1 || new_indent < 1)
       err_exit("REIN: Pass two numbers, both > 0", "");
    while (gets(buf))                                   /* Loop for each input line. */
       {

       /* Count leading spaces. */
       for (indent = 0; buf[indent] == ' '; ++indent)
          ;
       new_spc = indent * new_indent / old_indent;
       while (new_spc--)                                /* Print new leading spaces. */
          putchar(' ');
       puts(&buf[indent]);                     /* Print rest of line after spaces. */
       }
    }
```

To use this program to reindent the source file *oldpgm.c* from five
spaces per level to three and direct the output to the file *newpgm.c,* just
enter this command line:

```
A>REIN 5 3 <OLDPGM.C >NEWPGM.C
```

The diagram on the next page illustrates the way the data will be passed
to the reindenting program's *main()* function.

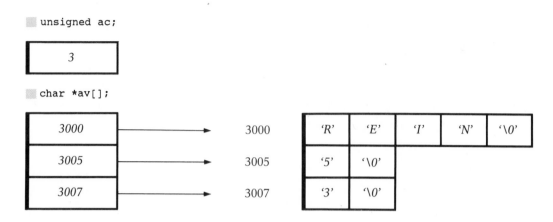

```
unsigned ac;
```

3

```
char *av[];
```

Variations in command-line mechanisms.   Some C environments do differ
in their handling of command-line arguments. For instance, the name of the
program is not always passed as the first vector argument, *av[0]*. And some
of us use *argc,* instead of *ac,* for the argument count, and *argv,* instead of *av,*
for the argument-vector array. Except for readability, it makes absolutely
no difference what you name *ac* and *av*: It is their data types that are important to the compiler.

Many, but not all, C compilers pass a third argument called the
environment vector (Microsoft's C under MS-DOS and C under UNIX both
support environment variables and pass an environment pointer as the third
argument to the *main()* function). The argument strings passed are the
definitions for operating-system environment variables—data that come
from outside your program.

Environment variables are maintained by the operating system from
the time they are created in *AUTOEXEC.BAT* onward: They are not erased
at the termination of a program. These variables actually represent another
source of input data for your program. The programs that comprise the
Microsoft compiler use environment variables to hold file-directory paths.

We've already discussed use of the MS-DOS *SET* command to assign
a value to an environment variable (Chapter 8). The C library function

putenv( ) also can be used to do this, and you can call the library function *getenv( )* to find out an environment variable's present value (or to find out if that variable exists at all). See your compiler manual for the proper use of these functions.

Environment data take the same structure as the command-line argument vector: an *array of pointers to type char*. To include the environment vector, just declare the parameters to *main( )* like this:

```
main(ac, av, ev)
unsigned ac;
char *av[];
char *ev[];

   {
```

The multidimensionial array and array-of-pointers structures we studied in this chapter permit you to build large lists of data in memory, provided all the elements in any array are of the same data type. Powerful as these constructs are, they still impose some limitations on data management, so C has also provided for structures that allow you to combine data elements of *different* types. We'll discuss those next.

Structures: The Unifying Data Type

16

C's *structure* data type allows us to combine scalar and array data of many different data types under a single name. In addition, C allows us to simplify management of structures with large numbers of elements by organizing them into substructures, much as we organize files into directories. Let's see how structures can be used to manipulate complex combinations of data in an understandable fashion.

First of all, just what are structures? Are they like records in a file, with fields of different types of data? Well, yes and no. Structures do resemble records, but they are actually better suited to in-memory data manipulation than to holding data being read from or written to files by library functions. The reasons for this distinction will become clearer as we go along.

In order to learn how to create and use structures, we'll write a screen-painting function that combines a cursor location (row and column numbers) with the text of a message to be displayed beginning at that location, and then declare, initialize, and pass an array of such messages.

Declaring Structures

As you can see from the following example, there are usually two steps to declaring a structure:

```
struct term_msg                    /* Declare structure tag term_msg. */
    {
    short row, col;                          /* screen location */
    char *msg;                              /* message to display */
    };
```

The first step declares the *structure tag*, which is simply a name that can be used as a new data type. This step in the declaration process consumes no program memory and is optional. Its sole purpose is to give meaning to the tag. Once a structure tag is declared, you may use it again and again, whenever you want to declare a structure of that type.

The *tag declaration* defines the actual structure by declaring the elements, or *members*, of the structure inside a set of braces. Notice the position of the structuretag *outside* the opening brace that marks the declaration of the members of the structure, and the required semicolon following the closing brace of the declaration.

C   O   M   M   E   N   T

It is good style to always declare a structure tag, even though it is optional. It contributes greatly to the clarity of your source code.

From now on, we can use the tag *term_msg* (for terminal message) to declare structures exactly as though *struct term_msg* were a new data type, as in this example of a structure named *form*:

```
struct term_msg form;
```

Structure-tag declarations used in more than one source file should be placed in a header file that is *#include*d everywhere the structure type is used. This makes it possible for functions in many different source files to use the declarations without making additional copies of them, and also significantly reduces the effort involved in adding a new member to a structure.

Accessing Members of Structures

The *dot operator* (.) is used to access members of a structure. The name of the structure is the left operand and the name of the member of that structure is the right operand. The dot operator is a primary operator: None has higher precedence. Both for style and to remind us of their precedence, we don't use spaces around primary operators:

```
form.row += 2;
form.col = 18;
form.msg = "Street";
```

Assignment to Structures

Structure declarations may have initializers, provided the structures are not declared as *auto* storage class. The syntax is the same as for array initializers, and here again, if fewer initializers are provided than there are structure members, the remaining members are automatically initialized to zero.

The following example is a *static* version of our structure *form,* declared with an initializer:

```
static struct term_msg form = {4, 10, "Customer Name"};
```

Memory would typically be allocated to the members of the *form* structure from left to right, like this:

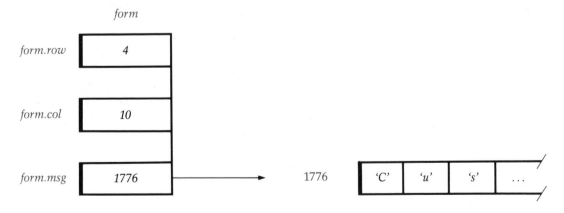

As you can see from the diagram, the alignment needs of the members of a structure may not necessarily leave them adjacent to one another in memory.

    The Microsoft C compiler also permits us to assign an entire structure to another. For example, we could declare two instances of our *form* structure, initialize one, and assign the values of its members to the uninitialized version, like this:

> C O M M E N T
>
> *This feature is new and comes by way of ANSI; however, its use limits the portability of your code to only those compilers that support structure assignment.*

```
static struct term_msg form_one = {6, 10, "Company Name"};
struct term_msg form_buf;

form_buf = form_one;                /* structure assignment, equivalent to: */
                                    /*    form_buf.row = form_one.row;      */
                                    /*    form_buf.col = form_one.col;      */
                                    /*    form_buf.msg = form_one.msg;      */
```

Nesting Structures

    As I mentioned earlier, a member of a structure can itself be a structure, making it possible for us to simplify large or complex structures by grouping related members into substructures that can then be declared within other structures.

    Let's change our *term_msg* structure to include such a nested structure for the cursor row and column locations, just to see how this construct works:

```
struct cur_loc    /* Declare structure tag cur_loc for cursor row and column. */
    {
    short row, col;                                     /* screen location */
    };

struct term_msg                   /* Declare structure tag term_msg for display. */
    {
    struct cur_loc cursor;
    char *msg;                                          /* message to display */
    };
```

If we now were to write a program containing the structure declaration *struct term_msg hello;* we could make assignments to its members using the member-name syntax shown on the next page.

```
hello.cursor.row = 12;
hello.cursor.col = 30;
hello.msg = "WELCOME TO THE PROGRAM!";
```

It looks like our *term_msg* structure is becoming useful enough
to be placed in a header file! But let's wait a bit: There's more.

Arrays of Structures

The usefulness of the *term_msg* structure is still somewhat limited
in its present form. However, if we used an *array* of *term_msg* structures,
we could paint an entire screen. Here's how it's done.

As with ordinary arrays, *static* or *external* arrays of structures can be
dimensioned by their initializers: That is, if they are declared with empty
brackets, they simply take their dimensions from the number of initializers.
The following example from the source file *pnt_ship.c* shows a declaration
for some of the field titles painted on the screen by the order-entry function *pnt_ship_pay()*:

```
static struct term_msg form_names[] =
    {
    4, 10, "Customer Name",
    6, 10, "Company Name",
    9, 10, "Shipping Weight",

    /* ... */
    0, 0, NULL
    };
```

The *0* row and column numbers plus the *NULL* pointer mark the end of
the list of messages in the *field_names* array of *term_msg* structures.

To access specific members in the elements of an array of structures,
we use a slightly different form of array subscript:

```
form_names[imsg].row
form_names[imsg].msg
```

The square brackets used to obtain the structure array element with index
imsg are applied directly to *field_names,* because it is the *structure* that is

declared as an array, not its members. Therefore, the entire structure is repeated in memory for each array element:

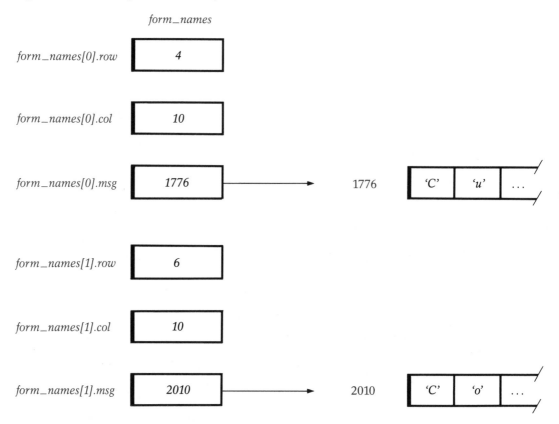

Structures as Arguments

Another new ANSI feature supported by Microsoft C is the ability to pass structure arguments to a function. Normally, when you pass a structure argument, a complete copy of that structure is made (you would need to use a copy of a structure if you wanted to make temporary changes to the values of its members without altering the original structure). However, if a copy is not needed, you may pass just the address of the structure instead.

To see how this works, let's look closely at the completed *scrn_pnt()* function, which does not return a value and takes an array of *term_msg* structures as its single argument:

```
struct term_msg                          /* Declare structure tag term_msg. */
   {
   short row, col;                                      /* screen location */
   char *msg;                                        /* message to display */
   };
/* Paint the screen with an array of field names. */
void scrn_pnt(form)
struct term_msg form[];
   {
   void s_tput(struct term_msg *);          /* structure version of tput() */
   short imsg;
   for (imsg = 0; form.msg != NULL; ++imsg)
      s_tput(&form[imsg]); /* Pass structure address to function listed next.*/

/* The structure version of tput() prints a message on the */
/*   screen by calling the order-entry function tput().     */
void s_tput(p_form)
struct term_msg *p_form;      /* p_form is a pointer to a term_msg structure. */
   {
   tput(p_form->row, p_form->col, p_form->msg);
   }
```

The processing performed by *scrn_pnt()* consists of looping to obtain each *term_msg,* until one with a *NULL* pointer is encountered. Each *term_msg* in *form* is passed to the function *s_tput(),* which is declared right after *scrn_pnt().* The *primary structure operator* (–>) used with *tput()* in *s_tput()* allows the program to directly access a member whose address is known, without using the structure name with the dot operator.

The arrow operator (a minus sign immediately followed by a greater-than symbol) is provided as a *convenience:* Its job can also be done (if less elegantly) by the dot and indirection (*) operators. Thus, the following two expressions are equivalent:

```
p_form->row        ◄─────────►        (*p_form).row
```

The values being passed to *tput()* are the row, column, and message in the *term_msg* structure pointed to by *p_form.*

That about winds up our discussion of C's special data types. In the next section, we'll look at the compiler library's I/O functions and the role of structures in manipulating data in files, and then we'll move on to the C tools formerly available primarily to assembly-language programmers.

Section V deals with the C compiler's library functions for input and output control. (These are quite standard from one C compiler to another.) By combining library functions with one another, C programmers can implement a wide range of file-access options and data formats. Chapter 17 deals with normal buffered access and stream file functions. Chapter 18 discusses direct access to data files, including both the use of variable-length ASCII records and low-level unbuffered file access.

SECTION V

Stream File Input and Output

17

We've already seen that the C language lacks functions for performing file input and output—that in fact, it has no built-in functions at all. These features must be obtained from a vendor-supplied library such as the standard library that comes with your C compiler. This library contains functions for file access, math, string manipulation, dynamic memory allocation, searching and sorting, process control, and much more. The library is not built into the compiler, so you do not *have* to use its functions (you may write your own similar functions or purchase additional libraries), but you should at least become familiar with the kinds of file accesses made possible by standard library functions, if only to avoid reinventing the wheel.

You may have heard experienced C programmers refer to files as streams and wondered about that. Are they talking about streams of bytes? Well, yes, sort of. Data saved in C files are treated as large arrays of bytes. The concept of records and fields is not built into the structure of a C file: Your *program* superimposes the structure you desire. A series of records made up of fields of data is only one possibility.

The standard library provides low-level file-access functions that you may work with directly or use to implement higher-level file schemes. File-access methods like indexes and binary trees, as well as a variety of database-management systems, are currently available to supplement the standard library. These vendor libraries enhance your programming capabilities, but may become a portability problem, depending upon the number of environments the vendor intends to support.

Normal Buffered Access

Buffered access is a technique that increases the efficiency of file input and output by reducing the *number* of inputs and outputs: that is, by making each access handle more data. A buffer is an area of memory—an array used as an intermediate holding place for file data. Buffers are normally 512 bytes, the value of the symbol BUFSIZ in the header file *stdio.h.*

Here is how input buffering works. You call a function to input a character from a file. However, instead of reading just one character, the function inputs enough characters to fill the entire buffer. Then the first character in the buffer is handed to your program. The next time you ask to input a byte, no actual input is performed; instead the next character from the buffer is handed to your program. This loop repeats until the buffer is emptied. Then when you ask for another character, the buffer is completely refreshed (filled again) with new file data. I've used input of a single character only as an example. You may have asked to input a whole line or some other amount of data, depending upon the exact function called to do the input: The principle is still the same. All input functions eventually call the low-level library function *read()*.

Buffering of output is similar to buffering of input. Your program outputs bytes and the bytes are held in the output buffer, instead of being written directly to the device receiving the file. Each output from your program adds data to the output buffer, until it becomes full and is automatically flushed (written to the file) or you *force* a flush with *fflush()*, *flushall()*, *fclose()*, or *fcloseall()*.

Opening a File

The buffering of data going to and from a file is accomplished using a *FILE* type structure. The *FILE* structure is defined in the header file *stdio.h*, which must be *#include*d in your program in order to open a file for buffered access. The *FILE* structure is allocated and initialized by a call to the library function *fopen()*. The structure contains a buffer, its associated pointers and counters, and a flag that indicates the kind of access permitted on the file being opened (read, write, or both).

The function *fopen()* itself expects two string arguments: the name of the file to open and the mode of access. The return value from *fopen()* is a pointer to a *FILE* structure, or *NULL* if the file could not be opened. The following code segment opens a file named *ordernum.dat*, or else calls *err_exit()*:

```
#include <stdio.h>

FILE *p_file;
static char file_name[] = "ORDERNUM.DAT";

p_file = fopen(file_name, "r");                    /* Open file for reading. */
if (p_file == NULL)
    err_exit("No file:", file_name);
```

Actually, you will often want to obtain the name of the file to open as a command-line argument, for greater program flexibility. The call to *fopen()* to open a file whose name is passed as the first command-line argument may be made in an embedded assignment expression, like this:

```
if (NULL == (p_file = fopen(av[1], "r")))
    err_exit("No file:", av[1]);
```

You may use drive names and directory path names in a command-line file name (don't forget to use " \\" to make a single backslash in a string constant), like this:

```
"B:\\DIRNAME\\FILENAME.EXT"
```

Be aware, though, that file names that include drive names and directory paths can lead to portability difficulties. The UNIX and XENIX operating systems use a regular slash (/) in directory paths, rather than the backslash used by MS-DOS, and UNIX and XENIX directory paths point to a specific device, so these systems do not recognize drive names. A better approach is to use MS-DOS environment variables to supply drive-name and the directory-path text to be used as prefixes to a file name. These environment variables have UNIX and XENIX counterparts, so your program will remain more portable.

The *fopen()* function expects a *mode* as its second argument. A mode is a string of one to three characters that defines how the file will be accessed. The first letter may be any one of the following:

MODE	ACTION
r	Read mode; file positioned at start for input
w	Write mode; file positioned at start for output (existing data overwritten)
a	Append mode; file positioned at end for output of new data to follow existing data

Both output modes, write and append, will create a new file if the file does not already exist.

XENIX and recent versions of UNIX have added the + as a second mode character, designating these update modes:

MODE	ACTION
r+	Update mode; both read and write permitted
w+	Write update mode; empty file created for write and read access
a+	Append update mode; both read and write permitted, with all writes forced to end of file

However, for maximum portability, it is best to restrict your mode to
r, w, or *a* alone, since reads and writes may not follow each other freely
in update mode; they must have an *fseek()* or *rewind()* function call
between them.

The last mode option character, *t* for text or *b* for binary, is specific
to MS-DOS and a few other non-UNIX operating systems that distinguish
between text and binary files. The difference between opening a file for
text mode and opening a file for binary mode is in how the end of a line is
handled. In text mode, input of the string "\r\n" sends your program only
'\n', and output of the string '\n' by your program actually sends "\r\n".
(You may know "\r\n" as CR/LF, or carriage return/linefeed.) In binary
mode, no translations are made; all characters are treated the same.

There are two other ways to control *fopen()*'s selection of text or
binary mode: The external *int* variable *_fmode* may be *IMPORT*ed and set
to *O_BINARY* (from *fcntl.h*), or *binmode.obj* may be linked with your object files to make binary mode the default.

The three standard I/O files, *stdin, stdout,* and *stderr,* are *automatically* opened for your program. (These names are actually pointers
to *FILE* structures declared in *stdio.h*.)

Once all the necessary files are open, we need to learn how to move
data in and out of them.

File I/O Library Functions

ASCII data are portable to many different systems, whereas binary
data, because of variations in byte ordering and data format, usually need
to be converted to suit each CPU's specific requirements. In this chapter,
we'll concentrate on saving data in the more portable ASCII text format,
to become familiar with file I/O in C. Then in Chapter 18, we'll discuss
the more restrictive binary file formats.

FUNCTION	ACTION
int fprintf(p_file, fmt, arg1, arg2, ...)	Converts *arg1, arg2, ...* according to the format string *fmt* and outputs the resulting ASCII text to the file *p_file*. Returns the number of characters printed.
int fscanf(p_file, fmt, p_arg1, p_arg2, ...)	Inputs text from *p_file*, converts it according to the format string *fmt*, and stores the results where *p_arg1, p_arg2, ...* point. Returns the number of values converted and assigned, or the integer defined as *EOF* if the program attempts to read beyond the end of the file.
char *fgets(string, n, p_file)	Inputs a line (including the '\n') of up to n−1 bytes from *p_file* and appends a '\0'. If the input line is longer than n−1 bytes, the next call to *fgets()* will get the rest of the line. Returns the zero pointer, *NULL*, if the program attempts to read beyond the end of the file.
int fputs(string, p_file)	Copies *string* to *p_file*. Microsoft C returns the last character output, or 0 if the string is empty. (Other versions of *fputs()* don't return anything, so avoid using the return if portability counts.)
int getc(p_file) *int fgetc(p_file)*	Macro *getc()* and related function *fgetc()* both input a character from *p_file*. Both return the character input as an *int*, or *EOF*.
int putc(c, p_file) *int fputc(c, p_file)*	Macro *putc()* and related function *fputc()* both output a character to *p_file*. Both return the character output.
int fclose(p_file)	Closes the file associated with *p_file*. Completes any output, flushing all buffered data first. Returns 0, or *EOF* if error.

FIGURE 17-1 | *Standard-library file-input and output functions*

The standard library's file input and output functions are actually a family of functions with uniform, easy-to-remember names. The functions used to access stream files that have been opened with *fopen()* strongly resemble the character, line, and formatted I/O functions *printf()*, *scanf()*, *puts()*, *gets()*, *putchar()*, and *getchar()*. Figure 17-1 shows the file versions of these familiar input and output functions.

Stream-File Functions in Use

Now that we've learned how to access text files, we can complete the order-entry functions stored in *stubs.c*. The three functions we need to rewrite are:

FUNCTION	ACTION
pw_find( )	Reads and scans for records sequentially. Each record is a text line of fields delimited by '|'.
logentry( )	Appends diagnostic messages to the log file, which holds lines of text with no special format.
order_num( )	Updates an order-number counter by reading the old value, adding 1, and writing over the old value.

Delimiting Records

Earlier, I said that a C file is not made up of records, and that each file should be thought of as a stream of bytes. The first file operations we discussed used the standard input and output files to interact with the user, so we didn't have to think much about how things were organized for storage and retrieval, but now we need to take the time to discuss the management of that stream of bytes in detail.

Each order in our order-entry file may be regarded as a record made up of a group of lines of data. Each output line *within* the record may be regarded as a field that begins with a two-character label identifying the kind of data saved on the rest of that line. The kind of record we are using is a variable-length line of ASCII characters that ends with a *newline* ('\n') delimiter; fields are separated by a vertical-bar ('|') delimiter. (It is important that the field itself never contain the delimiter, to prevent its being treated as two fields.) The '\n' delimiter already exists within C, but you must create the '|' delimiter yourself, using *#define*:

```
#define DELIM '|'
```

(As an enhancement, you may choose to allow fields to be further divided into subfields delimited by a different delimiter, such as '^'.)

The benefits of using files made up of delimited records or labeled lines of ASCII text are threefold:

▶ All records and fields can be of variable length, thus saving storage space.

▶ Every record need not contain the same number of fields, and no memory is allocated to trailing empty fields.

▶ All data files are portable, because they are ASCII text.

Reading and Scanning Sequentially

Now let's rewrite the stub *pw_find( )* so that it reads a file named *passfile* to validate our user's identification. (Be sure to remove *pw_find( )* from *stubs.c* now, and place it in its own source file.) The file holds lines of text, each considered a record. Each record has three or four fields, separated by the symbol *DELIM*, which is defined in *pw_find.c* as a '|':

```
/* SOURCE FILE: PW_FIND.C */
/**************************************************************************/
/* pw_find() looks up a user's name and password and returns YES if the user */
/*    is found, NO if not. If the user is found, office ID is also checked.  */
/**************************************************************************/

#include <stdio.h>
#include <stddefs.h>
#include "ordentry.h"

#define DELIM '|'                       /* delimiter to separate fields of a record */
flag pw_find(office, user, password)
char office[];                          /* description of user's office (returned) */
char user[];                     /* name, initials, or abbreviation of user to find */
char password[];                                       /* password to be looked up */

    {
    IMPORT bflag bell_ok;

    /* Use static so file will be opened only in the first call to pw_find(). */
    static FILE *p_passfile = NULL;
    char rec[L_OFFICE + L_USER + L_PASSWORD + 6];
    char find_rec[L_OFFICE + L_USER + L_PASSWORD + 4];
    short len_find;
    flag found = NO;                                /* Have not found the user yet. */

    /* Open passfile if it isn't already open from a previous call. */
    if (!p_passfile && !(p_passfile = fopen("PASSFILE.DAT", "r")))
        err_exit("No file:", "passfile.dat");
    len_find = sprintf(find_rec, "%s%c%s%c%s", office,
        DELIM, user, DELIM, password);      /* first three fields to search for */

    /* Loop for each record until user found, or EOF. */
    while (!found && fgets(rec, sizeof rec, p_passfile))
        if (0 == strncmp(rec, find_rec, len_find))
            found = YES;
    if (found && rec[len_find] != '\n')                 /* Fourth field in record? */
        bell_ok = NO;                                   /* Yes; turn off bells. */
    return (found);
    }
```

The string *find_rec* is set to the first three fields we want. Then record lines are input one by one until the end of the file is reached or the user is found. Such a sequential pass through a file is an acceptable way to search for a record if the file is fairly short.

Appending Error Messages to a Log

Users are rarely able to give a complete error report when something goes wrong with their entries, which can present difficulties for the programmer maintaining the software. To avoid this problem, we can append all error messages to a permanent log file, so that our programmers need no longer depend upon the users for accurate error reports. (The same function can also be used to provide an audit trail, to verify commissions, and for other similiar activities.)

We'll expand the *logentry()* stub to perform these record-keeping tasks, and store the completed function in its own source file, *logentry.c*:

```
/* SOURCE FILE: LOGENTRY.C */
/*******************************************************************************/
/* logentry() appends message text to the end of the log file, typically for */
/*    audit, error detection, and security purposes.                         */
/*******************************************************************************/

#include <stdio.h>

void logentry(msg)
   char msg[];

   {
   static FILE *p_logfile = NULL;
   long long_time;

   /* Open logfile, if it isn't already open. */
   if (!p_logfile && !(p_logfile = fopen("LOGFILE.DAT", "a")))
      {
      /* We can't call err_exit() because it tries to update log. */
      err_warn("No file:", "logfile.dat");
      abort();
      }
   time(&long_time);
   fprintf(p_logfile, "%s %s\n", ctime(&long_time), msg);
   }
```

The *a* option of the last *fopen()* call requests append mode, which means that *logfile.dat* can continue to grow indefinitely. To prevent it from consuming too much disk space, you should periodically print an archival hard copy and delete the file.

Updating a Counter

The file *ordernum.dat* is actually just one line with a single number on it: the last order number used in our order-entry application. This order number is read and incremented by *order_num()*, saved in the file, and then returned to the calling function. Let's look at the rewritten code:

```
/* SOURCE FILE: ORDERNUM.C */
/********************************************************************/
/* order_num() returns the order number to use for the next order. The order */
/*    number is a counter that increases by one with each order. It is      */
/*    stored in the file ordernum.dat.                                      */
/********************************************************************/

#include <stdio.h>

#define FRSTONUM 10001
#define LASTONUM 99999

long order_num()
    {
    static FILE *p_ordernum = NULL;
    long order_cnt;

    /* Open ordernum, if it isn't already open.*/
    if (!p_ordernum &&                        /* Is this the first call to pw_find()? */
      !(p_ordernum = fopen("ORDERNUM.DAT", "r+")))
        err_exit("No file:", "ordernum.dat");
    rewind(p_ordernum);            /* before switching from writing to reading. */
    fscanf(p_ordernum, "%ld", &order_cnt);               /* Input old number. */
    rewind(p_ordernum);            /* before switching from reading to writing. */
    if (order_cnt >= LASTONUM)                        /* Highest order number? */
        order_cnt = FRSTONUM;                        /* Yes; start over again. */
    else
        ++order_cnt;                                 /* Increment order number. */
    fprintf(p_ordernum, "%ld\n", order_cnt);           /* Save new number. */
    return (order_cnt);
    }
```

Note the calls to *rewind()* following *fscanf()* and *fprintf()*. These calls are required by *fopen()*'s update mode, to switch between reading and writing to the data file.

File-Related Operations

The standard library also contains file functions that don't read and write data, but are used in conjunction with the I/O functions we've just discussed to handle such operations as run-time diagnostic messages, break-key control, and file and directory control. Let's take a very quick look at the most useful of these.

Run-Time Errors

Many library functions return a value to let you know an error has occurred, without informing you of the *type* of error. Fortunately, the global *int* variable *errno* is set by some of these functions to record the type of error that has occurred. So when debugging or troubleshooting, you should first check the function's return value to see if there was an error. Then, if there was, you can *IMPORT errno* and examine its value. A simpler approach, however, is to call the library function *perror()*, which checks *errno* for you and prints the appropriate error message, if any, to *stderr.* You can also pass *perror()* a string to print with the error message, to identify the program and the circumstances of the error. Since *perror()* does not write to our log file, a separate call to *logentry()* to record the error is also a good idea:

```
IMPORT int errno;
char log_buf[81];

if (!(p_ordernum = fopen("ORDERNUM.DAT", "r+")))
    {
    perror("order_num() can't open ordernum.dat");
    sprintf(log_buf, "order_num() fopen() error: %d", errno);
    logentry(log_buf);
    }
```

The combination of *perror()* and *errno*'s value will help you to identify errors from a variety of library functions, but these next three functions handle only I/O errors associated with open stream files whose file pointers are passed to them:

FUNCTION	ACTION
int ferror(p_file)	Returns 0 if no read or write errors found.
int feof(p_file)	Returns 0 if end of file not yet reached.
void clearerr(p_file)	Clears the file's error indication.

Disarming the Break Key

You can improve data integrity by disabling the action of the break key during such noninterruptible operations as a series of file updates that must run to completion. To do this, you first need to *#include* the header file *signal.h* in your program. Then call the *signal()* function, like this:

```
#include <signal.h>

/* ... */
signal(SIGINT, SIG_IGN);                                    /* Turn break key off. */

/* ...critical processing ... */
signal(SIGINT, SIG_DFL);                                    /* Turn break key back on. */
```

File and Directory Control

The Microsoft C, UNIX, and XENIX standard libraries also supply functions for three important file-management tasks that many other C compilers do not address:

FUNCTION	ACTION
mktemp()	Makes up a unique name to use for a temporary file.
unlink()	Deletes a file.
rename()	Renames a file.

Since the grouping of files into directories is being implemented in more and more operating systems as an organizing tool, they also supply the following functions for directory management:

FUNCTION	ACTION
chdir()	Changes directory to a new directory.
getcwd()	Gets the name of the current working directory.
mkdir()	Makes a new empty directory.
rmdir()	Removes an *empty* directory.

Since most of these functions will be at least generally familiar to you, we won't spend any more time on them here. See your compiler's standard library manual for details.

Now that you are comfortable with the concepts and standard library functions related to sequential processing of stream files, let's move on to *direct* access of file data.

Direct Access and Keyed Record Retrieval

18

To purchase a file-access method or database-management system or to implement one, that is the question: to buy, to build, or to work with stream functions and their fixed style of output. In this chapter, we'll look at one possibility: using combinations of the standard library functions to access records by matching a *key field* that identifies the record. This approach is often used for business programs.

The low-level, flexible file structure generated by the standard library functions makes it possible for the programmer to use these functions to create a variety of other file structures for accessing and managing data. The two we'll discuss in this chapter are variable-length ASCII text records and fixed-length binary records.

The records we are about to examine are text lines with fields separated by the '|' delimiter, as discussed in Chapter 17. Here are a couple of typical lines from *passfile.dat*:

```
San Diego|Steve|tuna
Hoboken|Bob|sturgeon|n
```

The first field is an office name, the second a user name, and the third a password. The optional fourth field seen in the second record is used to set the global variable *bell_ok,* which controls use of the bell in functions like *err_warn( )* and *prompt( )* (the standard library functions do not use *bell_ok*).

Record String Manipulation

The library function *sprintf()* makes record construction easy
(*sprintf()* does formatted output conversion and places the result in a
string, rather than printing it). We used an example of this in the rewritten version of *pw_find()* in Chapter 17:

```
#define DELIM '|'                       /* delimiter to separate fields of a record */

    /* ... */
  len_find = sprintf(find_rec, "%s%c%s%c%s", office,
      DELIM, user, DELIM, password);    /* first three fields to search for */
```

However, the standard library does not have a function for *extracting*
a field from a record string. The closest it comes is the function *strchr()*
(sometimes called *index* by other vendors), which searches a string for a
single character, so we'll have to write our own field-extractor function.
We'll call the function *strfld()*, and for now we'll code it like this:

```
#define DELIM '|'                       /* delimiter to separate fields of a record */

/**************************************************************************/
/* strfld() copies a field from a record to a separate string and returns   */
/*    the starting address of the target, to_str.                           */
/**************************************************************************/
char *strfld(to_str, from_rec, fld_num);
char to_str[];                          /* target string to copy field to */
char from_rec[];                        /* record string to copy field from */
short fld_num;                          /* field number to copy */

    {
    short ifrom, ito;                   /* indices into from_rec and to_str */

    /* Skip over (fld_num - 1) delimiters to the field to copy. */
    for (ifrom = 0; --fld_num && from_rec[ifrom] != '\0';)
        {
        while (from_rec[ifrom] != '\0' && from_rec[ifrom] != DELIM)
            ++ifrom;
        if (from_rec[ifrom] == DELIM)
            ++ifrom;
        }

    /* Copy field from from_rec to to_str. */
    for (ito = 0; from_rec[ifrom] != '\0' && from_rec[ifrom] != '\n'
        && from_rec[ifrom] != DELIM; ++ifrom, ++ito)
        to_str[ito] = from_rec[ifrom];          /* Copy a character to to_str. */
    to_str[ito] = '\0';
    return (&to_str[0]);
    }
```

We'll refine this function further in Chapter 21, when we discuss incre-
menting pointer variables stored in registers to speed access to array data.

Variations on Direct Access

Ultimately all direct accesses to disk files made through standard library functions are by byte number. If we think of the file as a large array of bytes, the byte number is, in effect, the *index* of the byte within the file.

Direct Access by Byte Number

The standard library functions *fseek()* and *ftell()* are used as a team for direct access of a stream file by byte number. As stream data are read or written, the system keeps a byte count that indicates the present position in the file. You can obtain the value of this index by calling the library function *ftell()* and passing it a pointer to the open *FILE* structure. As your program continues to read and write to this stream, the byte number naturally changes. If you want the program to jump to the location returned earlier by *ftell()*, or to any other byte in the file, you call the library function *fseek()*. The next input or output to the open file will begin at the *fseek()*ed byte. Here is the syntax for these two functions, with details of their behavior:

FUNCTION	ACTION
long ftell(stream)	Returns the current byte number (file-pointer position) in the stream, a pointer to a *FILE* structure for an open file. Return is a *long* integer and the first byte of the file is always zero.
int fseek(stream, offset, origin)	Moves the file-pointer position in the stream to the byte specified by the offset (*long* integer) and origin arguments. The origin may take these values:
	0 Offset is the number of bytes to move the file pointer beyond the beginning of the file.
	1 Offset is the number of bytes to move the pointer relative to the present byte number.
	2 Offset is the number of bytes to move the pointer relative to the end of the file.

The current pointer position in a file is not always what you might expect it to be, especially in a file opened for text, rather than binary, mode. This is because the text-mode byte number is thrown off by the

translations between '\r\n' and '\n' on both input and output. So don't
rely upon your own estimation of location in a file opened as a text
file; instead, let *ftell()* be your guide.

Direct Access Through an Index

In a file that uses keys, a specific field (typically, the first field of
each record) is designated as the key field that identifies the record it is part
of. A key value may be used in a program to obtain a specific record by
matching the value to the record's key field.

We'll use a data file consisting of a series of text lines made up of
delimited fields to demonstrate the use of keys. Our goal is to read one
specific line from anywhere in the data file without first having to read all
the lines preceding it (the definition of direct access). The index and data
in our file represent the inventory for our software business:

invntory.ndx	*invntory.dat*
S1|0	S1|System One: Integrated Business Pkg|69500|230
6GL|52	6GL|Sixth-Generation Language|99500|190
DBMS|92	DBMS|Database-Management System|59500|200

Each index record in *invntory.ndx* has two fields: a key and a file offset.
The file offset is passed to *fseek()* to locate and read the *invntory.dat* record (line) for the part identified by the key (the first field of our database).

The index file for the *invntory.dat* data file was built with a program
called *bldindex,* which combines our custom *strfld()* function and several
library functions to do its job. This program loops through a data file, calling *ftell()* to obtain the byte numbers for the keys by inputting each line
of the data file and extracting its key field. Each key field and offset
returned from *ftell()* is written to output as a line of text with two fields,
separated by the '|' delimiter. Here is *bldindex.c*:

```
/* SOURCE FILE: BLDINDEX.C */
/**********************************************************************************/
/* bldindex() constructs an index file for direct access to a data file.        */
/*    Each output line has two fields: key and offset. The output is written    */
/*    to stdout, so it can be redirected.                                       */
/*    The function takes one or two command-line arguments:                     */
/*        BLDINDEX datafile [key_field_number]                                  */
/**********************************************************************************/
```

(continued)

```
#include <stdio.h>
#include <stddefs.h>
#define DELIM '|'

main(ac, av)
unsigned ac;
char *av[];

    {
    IMPORT char *strfld(char[], char[], short), *strchr();
    char buf[BUFSIZ];                           /* buffer for data record */
    char key[BUFSIZ];                           /* key field of data record */
    FILE *p_infile;                                 /* input file stream */
    long file_pos;                          /* return from ftell(): offset */
    short key_field_num = 1;                /* field number that holds key */
    char *end_pos;                              /* end-of-record position */

    if (ac < 2 || ac > 3)
        err_exit("Use: BLDINDEX datafile [key_field_number]", "");
    if (NULL == (p_infile = fopen(av[1], "r")))
        err_exit("Can't open file: ", av[1]);
    if (ac >= 3)                        /* Key field command-line argument? */
        key_field_num = atoi(av[2]);               /* Yes; get field number. */

    /* Loop for each record (line) of input file. */
    file_pos = ftell(p_infile);
    while (fgets(buf, BUFSIZ, p_infile))
        if ((end_pos = strchr(buf, '\n')))          /* Is there a newline symbol? */
            {
            *end_pos = '\0';                               /* Strip it. */
            strfld(key, buf, key_field_num);
            if (key[0] != '\0')                         /* Is there any key? */
                printf("%s%c%ld\n", key, DELIM, file_pos);
            file_pos = ftell(p_infile);
            }
    }
```

The *bldindex* program also permits us to create more than one index file for a single data file, with each of the index files using a different key field. However, keep in mind that adding, changing, or deleting information in a data file will usually cause some of the offsets in its index file to become incorrect, and the problem can be greatly compounded when the data file has more than one index. (Fixed-length fields simplify things somewhat, since the offsets may not change when the file is updated, but this is a trade-off on space.)

Access to data-file information through an index can be facilitated by a function that searches the index for the key and, if found, reads and passes back the associated data-file record. Such a function, which we'll call *get_rec()*, could begin like this:

```
flag get_rec(rec, key, pf_data, pf_index)
char rec[];                                    /* record to pass back to caller */
char key[];                                            /* key for record to read */
FILE *pf_data, *pf_index;                      /* data and index file pointers */

{
/* Look up key in index file to obtain offset of record in data file. */
/*    Then call fseek() for data file, using offset. Read data file    */
/*    record into rec and return 1 if OK.                              */
```

As I stated earlier, there are no easy answers to the direct-access question. Variable-length ASCII text files are just one approach. Let's look at another possibility, using a binary file format.

Binary File Format

Numeric data in binary format are more compact and therefore faster to access than the same data in ASCII. For instance, a 4-digit number takes up 2 bytes in a *short* integer but 4 bytes as ASCII text, and a 10-digit *long* integer needs only 4 bytes in binary format, versus 10 bytes as a string of digits. And numeric data read from an ASCII text file must first be converted to binary before you can perform arithmetic on the values, whereas numeric data read from a binary file are ready for use in arithmetic

> C A U T I O N
>
> *Modification of data files with a text editor can be very hazardous to the data they contain, and therefore should be done very carefully.*

expressions, without conversion. However, when you must choose between ASCII and binary data formats, keep in mind that although binary data formats offer better performance and use less space, they are unfortunately less portable. Also, data in a text file are human-readable and can easily be modified with a text editor, whereas data in binary format often contain bytes with unprintable bit patterns and must be converted to ASCII before they can be viewed or edited.

Data in binary format *can* be accessed using some of the standard stream functions we have seen so far. Alternatively, the standard library has a pair of functions, *fread()* and *fwrite()*, that are specifically intended for buffered input and output of binary data. But right now we are going to pursue a different avenue: *unbuffered* access to binary data.

Low-Level Unbuffered Access Functions

Input buffering improves program performance when a file's records are read one after another, in sequential order, since the record is often waiting in the buffer before you ask for it. However, buffering of input can *impair* performance if access to the file is fairly random, since the program must still read the entire buffer, even though it needs only one record from it. So when random access is the dominant mode for your program, consider using unbuffered input and output.

> **C A U T I O N**
>
> *All of the stream functions we've discussed are implemented using calls to the low-level unbuffered functions. In order to avoid bugs, never mix the two types of functions for the same open file.*

The standard library's functions for unbuffered input and output allow you to read and write blocks of data of any size. (Strangely enough, you may even choose to use the unbuffered routines because you desire to work *with* buffers, if the buffers are larger than the standard 512 bytes.) The data structures used by the standard library's low-level unbuffered file functions are simpler than their stream-file counterparts. Instead of using a *FILE* structure holding a buffer, the unbuffered functions use a single integer, known in UNIX circles as a *file handle* or *file descriptor number.* These file handles are assigned by calling either *open()* or *creat().* The first three file handles in a program are always assigned to the standard files, as in our *stddefs.h* header file:

```
/* File handles (descriptor numbers) for standard files, to be */
/*    used with the low-level I/O functions read() and write(). */
#define STDIN 0
#define STDOUT 1
#define STDERR 2
```

Here is a summary of the low-level library functions for unbuffered input and output:

FUNCTION	ACTION
int open(pathname, oflag[, pmode])	Opens file for type of access described by *oflag*. Returns a file handle to use to access that file, or −1 to indicate an error. Third argument is used only if a new file is requested. Specific values of *oflag* and *pmode* are portable among MS-DOS, XENIX, and recent UNIX versions of C (less so to UNIX System III and earlier).
int close(handle)	Closes the file opened to the handle named.
int creat(pathname, pmode)	Creates a new file or, if file exists, deletes its data. Then opens the file for type of access described by *pmode* (read, write, or both).
int read(handle, buffer, count) *int write(handle, buffer, count)*	Work as a team and are used by all other input and output functions. *read()* inputs a maximum of *count* bytes into *buffer*. Returns the number of bytes input. *write()* outputs *count* bytes of data from *buffer* to the file associated with *handle*. Returns the number of bytes output.
long lseek(handle, offset, origin) *long tell(handle)*	Work as a team, much like the stream team *fseek()* and *ftell()*. Provide direct access by byte number to a file opened for low-level access. *lseek()* returns the file-pointer location *after* the seek is made on the file opened to *handle*. *tell()* returns the present file-pointer location for *handle*'s file.

Structures and Record-Oriented Access

Structures (see Chapter 16) can be used to hold the binary data from a record in a file. Structures work best with fixed-length fields (especially for arrays of characters). We'll use our inventory data file again to learn how we can use structures to read and write fixed-length records of binary data, and how to update data in place.

We'll create a program called *invmaint* to build and maintain the inventory-file data. We'll use the low-level unbuffered functions *read()* and *write()* for all file accesses, including standard file/user interactions, and we'll change the part-numbering scheme so that each part in the inventory is assigned an integer as its part number. Since each new part gets the next higher unused part number, this eliminates the need to store part numbers: The position of the record in the file *is* actually the part number.

```c
/* SOURCE FILE:  INVMAINT.C */
/****************************************************************************/
/* Inventory file maintenance: lists and adds parts to inventory.         */
/****************************************************************************/

#include <stdio.h>
#include <fcntl.h>
#include <sys\types.h>
#include <sys\stat.h>
#include <io.h>
#include <stddefs.h>

/* Macros PROMPT and ERR_EXIT use read() and write() to perform user I/O */
#define PROMPT(msg, mlen, ans, alen) write(STDOUT, msg, mlen), \
ans[read(STDIN, ans, alen) - 1] = '\0'
#define ERR_EXIT(s1) write(STDERR, s1, strlen(s1)), \
write(STDERR, "\7\n", 2), exit(FAIL)

main()
    {
    IMPORT long atol(char[]);
    int fh_inv;                          /* invntory.dat file handle */
    long part_num;                           /* integer part number */
    char cmd;                          /* command to add or list part */
    char reply[81];                /* user input buffer to hold replies */
    char buf[20];              /* buffer for binary-to-ASCII conversions */
    struct s_inv_rec              /* Declare structure type; define tag. */
        {
        long price;                 /* price to charge for part, in cents */
        short weight;                    /* shipping weight, in ounces */
        char desc[31];                        /* description of part */
        };
    struct s_inv_rec inv_rec;             /* Declare record struct inv_rec. */

    /* Open inventory file invntory.dat for reading and writing. Create */
    /*   the file if it does not exist, and open it in binary mode.    */
    if (-1 == (fh_inv = open("INVNTORY.DAT", O_RDWR | O_CREAT | O_BINARY)))
        ERR_EXIT("No file: invntory.dat");

    while (1)              /* Infinite loop; exit is in loop body. */

        {

        /* Prompt for command: Add or List? <a/l> */
        PROMPT("\nInventory Maint: Add or List? <a/l> ", 37, reply, 80);
        cmd = reply[0];

        /* No cmd, so we're done. */
        if (cmd != 'a' && cmd != 'l')
            close(fh_inv), exit(SUCCEED);
```

(continued)

```
/* Prompt for part number to add or list. */
PROMPT("\nPart #: ", 9, reply, 80);
part_num = atol(reply);                     /* Convert from ASCII to binary. */

/* Position file pointer at start of record for part. */
lseek(fh_inv, (long) part_num * sizeof inv_rec, 0);

if (cmd == 'a')                                         /* Add a part. */
    {

    /* Prompt for part_desc, price, and ship_weight. */
    PROMPT("\nDesc: ", 7, inv_rec.desc, 30);
    PROMPT("\nPrice: ", 8, reply, 80);
    inv_rec.price = atol(reply);            /* ASCII to binary */
    PROMPT("\nWeight (oz.): ", 14, reply, 80);
    inv_rec.weight = atoi(reply);           /* ASCII to binary */

    /* Output record from structure inv_rec. */
    write(fh_inv, &inv_rec, sizeof inv_rec);
    }
else if (cmd == 'l')                        /* Read record and list part. */
    {

    /* Got whole record? Then list part_desc, price, and ship_weight. */
    if (read(fh_inv, &inv_rec, sizeof inv_rec) == sizeof inv_rec)
        {
        write(STDOUT, "\nDesc: ", 7);
        write(STDOUT, inv_rec.desc, strlen(inv_rec.desc));
        write(STDOUT, "\nPrice: ", 8);
        ltoa(inv_rec.price, buf, 10);           /* Convert price and output. */
        write(STDOUT, buf, strlen(buf));
        write(STDOUT, "\nWeight: ", 9);
        itoa(inv_rec.weight, buf, 10);          /* Convert weight and output. */
        write(STDOUT, buf, strlen(buf));
        write(STDOUT, "\n\n", 2);               /* Skip two lines. */
        }
    }
}
}
```

Now that you're pretty familiar with the standard library's file I/O functions (both their virtues and their limitations), let's descend a step farther, into the realm of bits and bytes. In Section VI, we'll look at tools available primarily to assembly-language programmers—until C.

And now, the advanced C topics: Section VI gives you information about tools formerly available primarily to assembly-language programmers. Chapter 19 covers dynamic allocation of memory, with emphasis on the linked list that can grow and shrink as the program executes. Chapter 20 discusses C's easy-to-read bitwise operators that give the C programmer access to and control over every bit of each byte of data. Chapter 21 presents advanced options for handling array data, discusses sophisticated coding and library techniques for optimizing program performance, and takes a hard look at the pros and cons of various kinds of performance tuning.

SECTION VI

Efficient Use of Memory

The amount of installed memory varies from system to system, and you'll always want to take advantage of all the memory you have available: Your programs will perform better, and your users will love you for it. But how can you ensure that your programs will adapt themselves to the memory available on different systems, or that when your user upgrades, your programs will do likewise? It's very frustrating to invest in 512K bytes of memory only to discover that your favorite program still behaves as if it were on a 64K system!

The solution is dynamic allocation of memory: obtaining additional memory for data *while the program is executing*. This is in contrast to the use of ordinary arrays, which must be dimensioned with constant expressions prior to execution. Once again, the C language provides no statements to handle this kind of allocation, so we will have to turn to functions from the standard library.

Let's begin with the simplest form of dynamic allocation: duplicating the contents of a string. Suppose that you want to write a function *strprint()* that is passed a string whose non-ASCII characters must be converted to question marks before the string is returned. You do not want to modify the original string that was passed, so you need to copy its contents to a new string. One approach would be to declare a new string the size of the largest possible string that might be passed. However, if the new array had *auto* storage class, a bug known as a *dangling pointer reference* would result, since the allocated storage would be freed for reuse but the address of the freed memory would still be returned to the calling function. A better alternative is to use the library function *strdup()*, which obtains new storage, equal in size to the length of the string (including the null) passed to it, *before* copying the string to the new storage:

```
/* Copy a string, convert non-ASCII characters to '?', return its address */
#include <ctype.h>

char *strprint(in_str)
register char *in_str;

    {
    register char *p_char;
    char *out_str = strdup(in_str);                        /* Duplicate in_str. */

    for (p_char = out_str; *p_char; ++p_char, ++in_str)
        *p_char = isprint(*in_str) ? *in_str : '?';
    return (out_str);
    }
```

The new memory that *strdup()* returns a pointer to is actually obtained by a call to the library function *malloc()*, and remains allocated for the life of the program, or until it is explicitly freed. Speaking of *malloc()*...

The standard library functions *malloc()* and *free()* are used to dynamically allocate and free memory. The memory allocator, *malloc()*, takes a single *unsigned int* argument: the number of bytes to be allocated. The return value is a *pointer to type char* that points to the beginning of the block of newly allocated memory. If the program requests more memory than is available, *malloc()* returns *NULL*.

The *sizeof* unary operator is often used with *malloc()*. It may be applied to any variable or to a data type in parentheses. The resulting value is the number of bytes allocated to that variable or needed to hold a value of the parenthesized type.

The following code segment uses *malloc()* and *free()* to dynamically allocate a large temporary array of *long* integers to exist for the duration of this code segment and no longer:

```
long *temp_data, *p_temp, *p_end, total = 0;

temp_data = (long *) malloc(100 * sizeof (long));

get_data(temp_data);                    /* Input 100 longs to temp_data. */
p_temp = temp_data;                     /* temp_data points to first long. */
p_end = temp_data + 100;                /* p_end points after last long. */

/* Add value of long to total and point to next long. */
while (p_temp < p_end)                  /* Loop for each long in array. */
   total += *p_temp++;
printf("Total = %ld\n", total);
free(temp_data);                        /* Release memory for temp_data. */
```

The cast operator *(long *)* before the call to *malloc()* is used to convert *malloc()*'s return value from type *pointer to type char* to *temp_data*'s type, *pointer to type long*. The value of *p_temp* (*pointer to type long*) is actually incremented by 4 in the shorthand assignment statement, because the size of a *long* is 4 bytes:

```
/* Add value of long to total and point to next long. */

   /* ... */
   total += *p_temp++;
```

The *get_data()* function may be written as if it were passed an ordinary array of 100 *longs*—it doesn't care how the memory for *temp_data* was allocated.

Linked Lists

A linked list is a variable-length chain of structures. One of the elements in each structure is a pointer to the corresponding element in the next structure. Linked lists can become very complex indeed, but you can relax: The application we're going to use here is a straightforward one that will make some applications execute faster by eliminating file inputs and outputs. What we want to do is read our inventory file into memory in the form of a linked list, so that when the order-entry function *inv_find()* wants to look up a part, it can just scan the list, instead of reading the disk.

Our *inv_find()* function performs two kinds of processing. The first time it is called, it inputs the inventory data file and builds the linked list. Every time it is called after that, it begins at the head of the list and chains along, link by link, to the link for the part it is looking for and then returns its data. Since dynamically allocated storage remains allocated until explicitly freed, the list will not be lost between calls to *inv_find()* (provided that *inv_find()*'s pointers into the list have *static* storage class, so that they don't forget where the list *is*).

Building the List

The first call to *inv_find()* has to create the linked list from the data in the inventory file. The next three diagrams show you how the memory used by the list changes as it grows from an empty list with *NULL* head and tail pointers, to a one-link and then a two-link list of inventory data:

The one-element linked list is like a one-person business, in that the link is both the head and the tail:

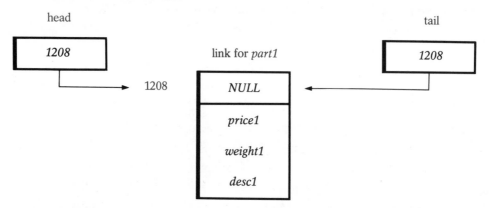

With the addition of a second link, our list finally displays all the attributes of a true linked list. Notice the first member of the link structure in the links for *part1* and *part2*. The pointer in *part1*'s link points to *part2*'s link, like a short chain:

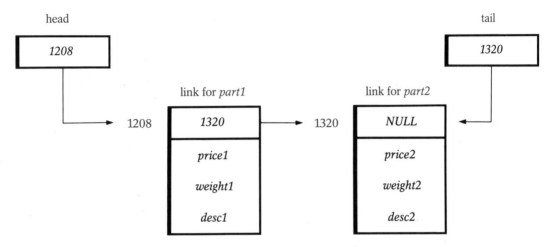

New links may be inserted anywhere in a list by using a straightforward splicing process: To insert a link between links 1 and 2, we make link 1 point to the new link and make the new link point to link 2. To remove a link from a list, we just reverse the process: To remove link 1 from our two-link list, we just make the head point to link 2 and the job is done. (You may free the storage for link 1, if you like. Otherwise, it remains allocated until the program ends.)

Searching the List

Now *inv_find()* can begin the job of searching the list. This is a looping process that begins at the head and moves down the chain, link by link, until the desired link is found or the tail is reached. In most applications, the test for whether the link sought has been found involves comparing two values. However, that is not the case in our example. Since the inventory file's data structure stores the part record's *index* in the file (see Chapter 18), rather than the part number, the program will know in

advance how many links to move down the chain: The part number is the
link number.

```c
/* SOURCE FILE:  INV_FIND.C */
/****************************************************************************/
/* inv_find() looks up part's data in inventory and returns YES if the part */
/*    is found, NO if not. Description, price, and weight are passed back.   */
/****************************************************************************/

#include <stdio.h>
#include <fcntl.h>
#include <sys\types.h>
#include <sys\stat.h>
#include <io.h>
#include <stddefs.h>
#include "ordentry.h"

struct s_inv_rec                        /* Declare structure type and define tag. */
    {
    money price;                            /* price to charge for part, in cents */
    short weight;                               /* shipping weight, in ounces */
    char desc[31];                                  /* description of part */
    };
struct s_inv_link
    {
    struct s_inv_link *p_next;                       /* next link in list pointer */
    struct s_inv_rec rec;      /* inventory record, nested structure in link */
    };
flag inv_find(part, part_desc, p_price, p_ship_wt)
char part[];                            /* part number to look up (pass in) */
char part_desc[];                           /* description of part (returned) */
money *p_price;                         /* pointer to unit price of part (returned) */
short *p_ship_wt;                       /* pointer to shipping weight (returned) */

    {
    IMPORT long atol(char[]);
    static struct s_inv_link *head = NULL, *tail = NULL;
    static long num_links = 0;
    struct s_inv_link *temp;
    static int fh_inv = 0;                              /* inventory file handle */
    long part_num = atol(part);                         /* numeric part number; */
                                                        /*    0 for first part  */
    if (!fh_inv)                            /* This is the first call, so build the */
        {                                   /*    linked list of inventory data now. */

        /* Open inventory file for binary reading. */
        if (-1 == (fh_inv = open("INVNTORY.DAT", O_RDONLY | O_BINARY)))
            perror("No file: invntory.dat"), abort();
        head = tail = temp =                        /* Initialize list pointers. */
            (struct s_inv_link *) malloc(sizeof (struct s_inv_link));
        head->p_next = NULL;                                /* no next link yet */
        while (read(fh_inv, &(temp->rec), sizeof (temp->rec))
                == sizeof (temp->rec))                      /* Loop for records. */
            {
            ++num_links;
            tail = temp;
            temp = (struct s_inv_link *) malloc(sizeof (struct s_inv_link));
            tail->p_next = temp;            /* Make previous link point to new. */
            temp->p_next = NULL;                        /* no next link from new yet */
            }
        if (num_links == 0)                             /* If no list, then no */
            head = tail = NULL;                         /*    head or tail.    */
        }
```

(continued)

```
/* Look up data for part whose number was passed in, */
/*   by moving part_num-1 links down the chain.       */
if (part_num >= num_links)
    return (NO);
for (temp = head; part_num--; temp = temp->p_next)
    ;

/* Return part data to calling function. */
strcpy(part_desc, temp->rec.desc);
*p_price = temp->rec.price;
*p_ship_wt = temp->rec.weight;
return (YES);
}


/*****************************************************************************/
/* Test driver for the inv_find() inventory-lookup function.                 */
/*    Data for invntory.dat were entered using the invmaint program from the */
/*    previous chapter.                                                      */
/*****************************************************************************/
#if defined(DBGMAIN)
#define TEST(msg, cond) if (!(cond)) fprintf(stderr, "TEST FAILED: %s\7\n", msg)

main()
    {
    short weight;
    money price;
    char desc[31];

    TEST("#1", !inv_find("99", desc, &price, &weight));
    TEST("#2", inv_find("0", desc, &price, &weight));
    TEST("#3", 0 == strcmp(desc, "DBMS"));
    TEST("#4", price == 59500L && weight == 175);
    printf("inv_find() tests complete\n");
    }
#endif
```

Linked lists may or may not have advantages over ordinary arrays, depending upon your needs. For instance, the linked list does not need to be dimensioned before compilation; an array does. And inserting and deleting new links is fast; the analogous changes to arrays are slower to implement. But access to a link requires chaining through other links, whereas array elements are accessed directly. As always, there are tradeoffs to consider.

Linked lists can become far more complex than the one we've just discussed. For instance, elements of a doubly linked list have both forward and backward pointers. And elements (known as *nodes*) in lists called *trees* may have two or more descendant elements, forming a structure like a family tree. And these are only *some* of the linked-list data structures available to C programmers!

Now let's narrow our focus one final level. In the next chapter we will discuss the lowest-level C data structure of all, the bit.

Bit-Level Operations

20

Bits are the atoms of computer memory: They are the smallest possible amount of data and are indivisible. Since the narrowest C data type is the 1-byte-wide type *char*, C programs usually access individual bits through a *pointer to type char*.

There aren't too many uses for bit-level programming in applications development, but bit-level operations are occasionally used with some standard library functions or to compress data for more efficient use of memory, so we need to spend a few minutes discussing them. First, though, let's quickly review hexadecimal and octal notation for numeric data.

Computers store data as arrays of bits that are analogous to the 1's and 0's of a binary (base 2) number, but humans often find these long strings of 1's and 0's difficult to comprehend and manage. We seem to be more comfortable with the familiar digits 0 through 9 and the letters of our alphabet, so we find octal (base 8, using 0 through 7) or hexadecimal (base 16, using 0 through 9 and A through F) notation preferable when we want to see the pattern of bits used to express the internal binary value of a variable.

Hexadecimal notation is more natural than octal for viewing binary values, since a hex digit from 0 through F translates directly into 4 bits, ranging in value from 0000 to 1111, and therefore, an 8-bit byte can easily be expressed using two hex digits. Octal works nearly as well, but an octal digit represents only 3 bits of data, so three octal digits are needed to display an 8-bit byte.

Characters whose values are not printable can be expressed in a string or character constant using either octal or hex. For instance, in Chapter 5 we saw the bell and escape characters expressed this way:

	HEX CHARACTER	OCTAL CHARACTER
BELL	'\x07'	'\007'
ESCAPE	'\x1b'	'\033'

The compiler interprets an *integer* constant with a leading 0x as hexadecimal. If only the leading 0 is present, it interprets the constant as octal.

Non-Decimal Data and Library Functions

You'll recall that the members of the family of library functions *itoa()*, *ltoa()*, and *ultoa()* convert *int, long,* and *unsigned long* values (respectively) to ASCII representation. For the third argument to all three functions, we can supply any radix from 2 through 36, giving us a great deal of flexibility for numeric conversions.

You'll also recall that the *printf()* family of formatted output functions uses format-string arguments to specify how subsequent argument data should be converted (Chapter 2). These functions can also output octal and hexadecimal data, using the following specifiers:

FORMAT SPECIFIER	ACTION
%x	Prints a *short* or *int* value in hex form.
%lx	Prints a *long* value in hex form.
%o	Prints a *short* or *int* value in octal form.
%lo	Prints a *long* value in octal form.

This next rather unusual-looking code segment shows how the hexa-decimal and octal format specifiers are used:

```
char chr;

for (chr = 'A'; chr <= 'C'; ++chr)
    printf("%c in Hex: %02x, Octal: %03o, Decimal: %03d\n",
        chr, chr, chr, chr);
```

You could use this code to print a table for the entire alphabet, if you have reason to make frequent conversions. However, the segment in our example prints only this output:

```
A in Hex: 41, Octal: 101, Decimal: 065
B in Hex: 42, Octal: 102, Decimal: 066
C in Hex: 43, Octal: 103, Decimal: 067
```

Operating a Bit

C's bitwise operators act on their operands as if they were arrays of bits, rather than single values. Although the names of the bitwise operators—*AND, OR,* and *NOT*—resemble the names of the logical operators, there is a great difference in their behavior, so we'll discuss each of them separately. They are listed in Figure 20-1, in descending order of precedence.

PRECEDENCE LEVEL	OPERATOR	ACTION	EXAMPLE
14	~	Bitwise NOT (one's complement)	~3 == 0xfffc
11	>>	Shift right	0x7f >> 2 == 0x1f
11	<<	Shift left	0x1f << 2 == 0x7c
8	&	Bitwise AND	0x8a & 0x7f == 0x0a
7	^	Bitwise (exclusive) XOR	0xff ^ 0xc3 == 0x3c
6	|	Bitwise OR	0x42 | 0x36 == 0x76

FIGURE 20-1 | *C's bitwise operators, in descending order of precedence*

Turning Bits On

The single vertical bar (|) is the bitwise *OR* operator. It pairs corresponding bits from its two operands and evaluates them, producing a single bit in that position as the result. The *OR*ing process repeats, bit by bit, until every pair has been evaluated. The binary result has 1 bits in every position where *either* operand had a 1 bit; all other bits are 0. (You can't use the bitwise *OR* on *float*s or *doubles*.)

Let's look at an example, *OR*ing the decimal integers 96 and 9. We'll express both numbers in hex and in binary, to get a better idea of what's happening:

DECIMAL	HEXADECIMAL	BINARY
96	0x60	01100000
| 9	| 0x09	| 00001001
105	0x69	01101001

Bitwise *OR* is used with certain library functions, such as *open()*, to express combinations of a number of options in a single integer value. The technique uses separate bits to hold specific options and combines them using the | operator, as in this code segment from *invmaint.c*:

```
/* Open inventory file invntory.dat for reading and writing. */
/* Create the file if it does not exist, and open it in      */
/* binary mode.                                               */
if (-1 == (fh_inv = open("INVNTORY.DAT", O_RDWR | O_CREAT | O_BINARY)))

/* ... */
```

All of these options are *#defined* in the header file *fcntl.h* (see your manual for the complete list):

> O_RDWR   0x0002
> O_CREAT   0x0100
> O_BINARY 0x8000

The program evaluates the bitwise expresssion in our example as *0x8102* and passes that value to *open()* as an integer.

Isolating Bits

The bitwise *AND* operator behaves like the bitwise *OR*, except that bits in the result are 1 only if *both* corresponding operand bits are 1.

The bitwise exclusive *OR* (*XOR*) produces a 1 bit in its result if *either one but not both* of the corresponding operand bits is 1. (In other words, 1 is the result if the operand bits are not equal.)

The unary bitwise *NOT* produces an *int* or a *long* that is the complement of its single argument: In effect, each bit's value is reversed.

The right- and left-shift operators copy the left operand and slide its bits the number of positions designated by the right operand. The result of a right shift is similar to dividing by the number in the second operand; the result of a left shift is similar to multiplying by that value. The vacated bit positions are filled with 0 bits, with one exception: In some environments right shift of a negative value will produce a negative result—that is, *1 bits* will be used to fill vacated bit positions on the left. So to ensure portable code, use the right shift only on *unsigned* data types. Since the left shift always fills with 0 bits, you needn't be concerned about portability there.

Mapping to Bits

I'd like to thank one of my former students from the Boston area for asking me how to write this little program, which I've named *bitmap.c*. In a 32-character array, there are 256 bits, which we will number 0 through 255. The initial values of the array named *bitmap* are all '\0'. The program prompts for a number from 0 through 255, turns on that bit in the bitmap, and then displays the modified bitmap in hex. The process repeats until you ask to quit:

```
/* SOURCE FILE:  BITMAP.C */
/******************************************************************/
/* The bitmap program demonstrates bit-mapping techniques. It prompts for an */
/*    integer from 0 to 255, maps it to a bit in a 32-character array called  */
/*    bitmap, and turns that bit on. The resulting bitmap is displayed in hex.*/
/******************************************************************/
#include <stdio.h>
#include <stddefs.h>
main()
    {
    static unchar bitmap[32] = {'\0'};
    short num_in, ibyte;
    unshort out_word, mask;
```

(continued)

```
    printf("Enter bit number (0-255) or q to quit:\n ");
    while (1 == scanf("%hd", &num_in))
        {
        mask = 0x80 >> (num_in % 8);              /* Select bit in byte.  */
        bitmap[num_in / 8] |= mask;               /* Turn bit on in byte. */
        for (ibyte = 0; ibyte < 32; ++ibyte)
            {
            out_word = bitmap[ibyte] & 0xff;
            printf("%02x", out_word);
            }
        putchar('\n');
        }
    putchar('\n');
    }
```

If *0, 1, 100, 255,* and *254* are input, the following output results:

```
Enter bit number (0-255) or q to quit: 0 1 100 255 254 q
800000000000000000000000000000000000000000000000000000000000000
a00000000000000000000000000000000000000000000000000000000000000
a00000000000000000000000080000000000000000000000000000000000000
a00000000000000000000000080000000000000000000000000000000000001
a00000000000000000000000080000000000000000000000000000000000003
```

Well, now you know how to use C right down to machine level. You can write clear, readable code to manage complex operations, and you can manage your files to take maximum advantage of available memory. You're ready to fly! But before you go, let me pass along some handy techniques for optimizing program performance—techniques for writing even more efficient C.

More Efficient C

21

The style rules, tips, and debugging techniques that we have looked at so far have all focused on a single goal: maximizing your efficiency as a C programmer. But there's more—the icing on the cake. Although C programs are very small and fast to begin with, there are sophisticated coding techniques and library functions that you can employ to achieve even greater performance. In this chapter, we'll look at ways to squeeze every drop of work possible out of the computer.

Performance-Tuning Philosophy

Once a program is coded, compiled, and debugged, programmers just naturally begin looking for ways to streamline it. This is good programming practice, but a word of caution:

> *Don't be bit wise and byte foolish.*

Those words express a philosophy of program optimization that has produced impressive results. I have seen so much effort wasted tuning pieces of code that are rarely executed!

However, with code that *is* executed frequently or is central to the rest of the program, don't be afraid to experiment. If you have a choice of two approaches, take the time to write both, and take measurements to see which implementation runs faster or uses less memory. Expressed more succinctly, your performance-tuning philosophy now becomes:

> *Measure before you modify.*

The little test driver you write to compare two ways of doing a job might uncover CPU power you never dreamed you had! Or perhaps you will discover that you've saved only a few milliseconds. That's why benchmarks are fun.

Performance Measurement

The close relationship between C's pointers and arrays has led programmers to write some pretty unreadable code in the name of "efficiency." For instance, let's explore the way these next two expressions obtain the same element of an array, and compare their performance:

```
array[index]
*(array + index)
```

This little program will do the job for us:

```
/* Compare array indexing using [] and using pointer access. */
#include <time.h>
#define LDIM 5000

main(ac, av)
unsigned ac;
char *av[];

    {
    long longs[LDIM], sum;                      /* Use /STACK:32768 LINK flag. */
    long beg_time, mid_time, end_time;
    long *p_long = longs, *p_long2 = longs;
    short ilong, itrial, ntrials = ((ac > 1) ? atoi(av[1]) : 1);

    time(&beg_time);                                       /* array index timing */
    for (itrial = 0; itrial < ntrials; ++itrial)
        {
        for (ilong = 0; ilong < LDIM; ++ilong)
            longs[ilong] = ilong;
        for (sum = ilong = 0; ilong < LDIM; ++ilong)
            sum += longs[ilong];
        }
    time(&mid_time);                                  /* pointer-arithmetic timing */
    for (itrial = 0; itrial < ntrials; ++itrial)
        {
        for (ilong = 0; ilong < LDIM; ++ilong)
            *(p_long + ilong) = ilong;
        for (sum = ilong = 0; ilong < LDIM; ++ilong)
            sum += *(p_long2 + ilong);
        }
    time(&end_time);
    printf("Array-Subscript Time:     %41d\n", mid_time - beg_time);
    printf("Pointer-Arithmetic Time:  %41d\n", end_time - mid_time);
    }
```

This program accepts a single optional command-line argument: the number of trials (repetitions) of the test to perform. The program uses the *time()* function from the standard library, which returns the time in seconds, so we must make enough trials to get significant results. Here are the results of a single trial:

```
Array-Subscript Time:       1
Pointer-Arithmetic Time:    0
```

As you can see, this is not sufficient to get reasonable or useful results. Now let's look at the results for 100 trials:

```
Array-Subscript Time:       49
Pointer-Arithmetic Time:    51
```

Surprised? It is true that pointers can be used to achieve faster access to array elements, but not by simply converting *array[index]* to *(array + index)*. We'll see how to use this technique properly a little later in the chapter, when we discuss pointers in registers.

CPU or Disk-Bound?

The coding techniques you use to improve the performance of a program will, of course, depend upon how that program is spending its time. To tune a program successfully, you must begin by watching and listening to your computer as it executes that program. Is the program waiting for the CPU to finish some long array operation or numeric computation? Or could those incessantly blinking busy lights on the disk be an indication that the disk is overworked?

When interactive applications run too slowly, it is rarely the speed of the CPU that is the problem. The bottleneck is almost always the disk. If you can reduce the number of disk accesses, things will speed up. The proper selection of buffered or unbuffered file access and the dynamic allocation of all available memory (Chapters 18 and 19) are the keys to reducing disk activity.

Your compiler can help, too. Once you have debugged a program and are ready to put it to use, you should recompile it using one of the compiler's optimization switches, all of which begin with */O* (uppercase letter "oh"). Microsoft's compiler allows you to select optimization for speed (*/Ot*) or program size (*/Os*). The measurements in this chapter were all made with the default optimization, which is */Os*.

Most tuning techniques are a tradeoff between program size and program speed. However, there's one technique that can improve both: *register* storage.

The register Storage Class

If you use *register* storage for frequently used *int*-sized (or smaller) variables, your functions will be both smaller and faster. In this next example, you'll see how *register* storage has more than doubled the speed of some simple calculations:

```
#define LOOPS 5000

    /* ... */
    register short ireg, ireg2;
    short iauto, iauto2;

        /* ... */
        for (ireg = ireg2 = 0; ireg < LOOPS; ++ireg)
            ireg2 += ireg * 2 - 2500;

        /* ... */
        for (iauto = iauto2 = 0; iauto < LOOPS; ++iauto)
            iauto2 += iauto * 2 - 2500;
```

The results of 300 iterations of the preceding test were:

```
Register Time:      24
Auto Time:          51
```

Macros and Functions

In Chapter 6, we discussed the fact that the improved speed a macro offers over an equivalent function may be offset by its increased memory demands: the old speed versus memory tradeoff again. Do we save *enough* time to justify the added memory? In the following macro/function comparison, what we are really measuring is the overhead of calling a function with three arguments and obtaining a return value:

```
#define AVG3(a, b, c)  (((a) + (b) + (c)) / 3)

/* ... */
long avg_3_longs(a, b, c)
long a, b, c;

    {
    return ((a + b + c) / 3);
    }
```

Fifty trials of 5000 calls each to the macro and function in this example were sufficient to demonstrate the greater speed of the macro:

```
Function Time:      79
Macro Time:         55
```

Library Awareness

The linker that comes with your C compiler will combine your object files with only those library functions that are called by the functions in your object files. That is, if your code doesn't call a particular library function, and no function that your program *does* call calls it either, then that library function will not be linked with your program. But if you *do* call a library function in even one place, then you might as well call it everywhere it's useful, because it will already be linked.

Why do I bring this up? Space again. Since most library functions are small, their size is of little concern, but there are a few functions with multiple capabilities that occupy more memory. For instance, the family of formatted input and output functions—*printf(), scanf(), fprintf(), fscanf(), sprintf()*, and *sscanf()*—are all large library functions. If you have a program that uses these functions, rewriting its calls into conversion programs could save 3000 or more bytes of memory. Let's look at an example.

The following test compares *write()*, the lowest-level output function from the standard library, and *printf()*, which ultimately calls *write()*.

For five trials, each trial outputting a line of 40 asterisks 100 times, the execution time was only slightly faster with *write()* (44 versus 46 seconds). However, look at the first lines of the link maps of the two functions:

```
Start  Stop   Length Name            Class
00000H 00AA6H 00AA7H _TEXT           CODE

Start  Stop   Length Name            Class
00000H 016E8H 016E9H _TEXT           CODE
```

A little quick arithmetic shows us that the code generated using *write()* occupied only 2727 bytes, whereas with *printf()* it occupied 5865 bytes—a difference of a hefty 3138 bytes.

Pointer Arithmetic

We've discussed several times the extremely close relationship between pointers and arrays in C. To see just *how* close, let's look at the way C adds (and subtracts) integers and pointers.

When an integer is added to or subtracted from a pointer, the integer is first multiplied (for scaling purposes) by the size of the data type the pointer was declared to point to. For instance, if you increment a *pointer to type short,* 2 is added to the pointer. However, if you decrement a *pointer to type double,* 8 is subtracted from the pointer, and if you add 3 to a *pointer to type long,* 12 is added to the pointer's value, because three *long* integers take up 12 bytes of memory. (No scaling takes place when an integer is added to a *pointer to type char* because the size of a *char* variable is 1 byte.) A pointer variable sees memory simply as a large array of values of its underlying data type:

```
static long long_array[] = {4444L, 12L};
long *p_long = &long_array[0];
```

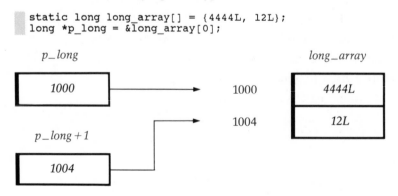

That's all pretty straightforward, but when and how would we use pointer arithmetic in our programs? Let's look at the most important application: faster array accessing.

Pointers in Registers

Pointers in registers can speed array accessing dramatically. The following code segment, excerpted from a timing program, compares various techniques for copying 40 characters from one string to another:

```
char from[41], to[41];
register char *p_from = from;                    /* pointer in a register */
register char *p_to = to;                        /* pointer in a register */

memcpy(to, from, MOVELEN);                               /* memcpy() */

/* ... */
strcpy(to, from);                                       /* strcpy() */

/* ... */
while (*p_from)                                      /* register pointer */
    *p_to++ = *p_from++;            /* Copy character and increment pointers. */
*p_to = '\0';                                     /* End the "to" string. */
```

The *while* segment in this example shows how pointers in registers can be used to copy text from the string variable *from* to the string variable *to*. The loop body statement (*p_to + + = *p_from + +;) copies the character that *p_from* points to into the location *p_to* is pointing to and then increments both pointers by 1, so that they remain in unison. These next three statements would produce the same result, but far less elegantly:

```
*p_to = *p_from;
++p_from;
++p_to;
```

When the timing program was used to measure a 40-character copy from one string to another, one character at a time, these were the results:

```
memcpy()            Time: .00036
strcpy()            Time: .00057
Register Pointer    Time: .00088
Pointer             Time: .00224
Array Index         Time: .00247
```

Obviously, the array-index copy was by far the slowest, and recoding to use pointers made almost no difference. The use of *register* storage class for the pointers made a significant difference, but surprisingly, *none* of the coding techniques was as fast as the standard library functions *strcpy()* and *memcpy()*.

Bringing It All Together

Benchmarks may be fun, but a real-world example of a string function written for speed is also helpful. Here is the *strfld()* function we developed in Chapter 18, streamlined to give maximum copying performance:

```
#define DELIM '|'

/**********************************************************************/
/* strfld() copies a field from a record string to a separate string and     */
/*    returns the starting address of the target, to_str. (A record here is a */
/*    string containing fields separated by DELIM.)                           */
/**********************************************************************/
char *strfld(from_rec, fld_num, to_str)
register char *from_rec;                     /* record string to copy field from */
short fld_num;                                       /* field number to copy */
register char *to_str;                       /* target string to copy field to */

    {
    char *p_to_str = to_str;                 /* hold initial value for return */

    /* Skip to field to copy.*/
    while (--fld_num && *from_rec != '\0')
       {
       while (*from_rec != '\0' && *from_rec != DELIM)
          ++from_rec;
       if (*from_rec == DELIM)
          ++from_rec;
       }

    /* Copy field from from_rec to to_str. */
    while (*from_rec != '\0' && *from_rec != DELIM)

       /* Copy a character to to_str and increment pointers. */
       *to_str++ = *from_rec++;
    *to_str = '\0';
    return (p_to_str);
    }
```

As a last resort, for those rare instances when C just isn't quick or compact enough...

How About Assembler?

There may come a time in your programming experience when you need the absolute maximum in efficiency. You've implemented the application in C, but the response time just isn't fast enough, or the code is very large and takes up too much disk space. These are good reasons for coding assembler subfunctions to do certain frequently needed low-level data manipulations.

The interface between assembler and C programs is clean: Data may be passed and returned with no great difficulty. In fact, the only problem with using assembler subfunctions in your applications is that your programs become less portable and more difficult to maintain.

Thanks to John Socha for the following example of the kind of assembler subroutine that can save your C applications valuable processing time. This small routine calculates the average of three numbers passed to it from the C calling function:

```
        ASSUME  CS:_TEXT
_TEXT   SEGMENT PUBLIC BYTE 'CODE'
        PUBLIC  _AVG_3_LONGS
;---------------------------------------------------------------;
; This C-callable procedure returns the average of three long   ;
;       integers as a long integer: (long1 + long2 + long3) / 3 ;
;                                                                ;
; Bugs:          The instruction IDIV divides a long by an int   ;
;                to return an int, so if the average is larger   ;
;                than 65535, you get a divide-by-zero error.     ;
; Written by John Socha.                                         ;
;---------------------------------------------------------------;
STACK_FRAME     STRUC
OLD_BP          DW      ?
RETURN_ADDR     DW      ?
LONG1           DD      ?
LONG2           DD      ?
LONG3           DD      ?
STACK_FRAME     ENDS

_AVG_3_LONGS    PROC    NEAR
        PUSH    BP
        MOV     BP,SP
        MOV     AX,Word Ptr [BP].LONG1      ;LONG1 into DX:AX pair.
        MOV     DX,Word Ptr [BP].LONG1[2]
        ADD     AX,Word Ptr [BP].LONG2      ;Add LONG2.
        ADC     DX,Word Ptr [BP].LONG2[2]
        ADD     AX,Word Ptr [BP].LONG3      ;Add LONG3.
        ADC     DX,Word Ptr [BP].LONG3[2]
        MOV     BX,3                        ;Divide total by 3.
        IDIV    BX
        CWD                                 ;Extend sign into DX.
        POP     BP
        RET
_AVG_3_LONGS    ENDP
_TEXT   ENDS
        END
```

You can use this next test driver, as I did, to verify that the assembler function really works:

```
/* Test assembler function avg_3_longs. */
main()
    {
    long avg_3_longs();

    write(1, (35L == avg_3_longs(12L, 37L, 56L)) ?
        "OK\n      " : "BUG!!!\7\n", 8);
    }
```

Well, that about winds things up. I hope you will use the techniques you've learned in this book to develop incredibly sophisticated and efficient applications, and I *know* you'll enjoy writing them. Thank-you for joining me on this journey through the world of C. And now, one parting word:

```
main()
    {
    write(1, "BYE!\7\n", 6);
    }
```

Section VII contains eight useful appendices for quick reference. Appendix A lists C's standard reserved keywords. Appendix B lists all of C's operators, with precedence and grouping. Appendix C provides a summary of preprocessor commands by type of action. Appendix D summarizes the standard library I/O functions. Appendix E presents the complete listing of Microsoft C's *stdio.h* header file. Appendix F summarizes standard C formatted I/O and conversions. Appendix G lists the ASCII codes for both printable and nonprintable characters. Appendix H provides information about the Companion Disk for VARIATIONS IN C, available from Microsoft Press.

SECTION VII

Appendix A:
Standard Keywords

These are C's standard keywords, with brief descriptions of their uses. They are reserved and may not be used as identifier names.

KEYWORD	USE	DESCRIPTION
auto	Storage class	For life of function only; the default
break	Control flow	Command to exit closest enclosing loop or block
case	Control flow	Choice in the case-like *switch* statement
char	Data type	1-byte signed integer
const	Not used	
continue	Control flow	Command to jump to start of next loop iteration
default	Control flow	Fall-through case label for *switch* statement
do	Control flow	Command to begin test at bottom of *do...while* loop
double	Data type	8-byte double-precision floating-point value
else	Control flow	Optional second half of *if* statement
enum	Data type	Enumerated list of integer-constant names
extern	Storage class	For import declarations of global variables
float	Data type	4-byte single-precision floating-point value
for	Control flow	Loop with initializer, test, and step
goto	Control flow	Anachronism and major cause of unreadable code
if	Control flow	Conditional execution of a statement
int	Data type	2- or 4-byte integer (depends upon CPU)
long	Data type	4-byte long integer

(continued)

KEYWORD	USE	DESCRIPTION
register	Storage class	For faster memory (request only)
return	Control flow	Command to jump back to caller function (after call)
short	Data type	2-byte short integer
sizeof	Operator	Number of bytes in expression or type
static	Storage class	For life of program; may be shared
struct	Data type	For combining elements of different data types
switch	Control flow	Command to choose one from any number of listed actions
typedef	Data type	For definition of a synonym data type
union	Data type	Like *struct,* but members are at same address
unsigned	Data type	Modifier in declarations; never negative
void	Data type	For function declarations and definitions
while	Control flow	Conditonal execution of statements in *while* and *do...while* loops

Appendix B:
Table of Operators

These are C's operators, in descending order of precedence. The L (for left-to-right) or R (for right-to-left) after the precedence number indicates the grouping order of the operator.

PRECEDENCE	TYPE	OPERATOR	NAME	EXAMPLE
15L	Primary	()	Parentheses	*len = (end − beg) * len;*
		[]	Subscript	*elem = array[index_val];*
		−>	Arrow	*val = struct_ptr −> membr;*
		.	Dot	*val = structure.member;*
14R	Unary	!	Logical not	*more = !done;*
		~	Bitwise NOT	*all_bits_on = ~0;*
		++	Increment	*++count;*
		−−	Decrement	*while (count_down −−)*
		−	Negative	*minus = −pos;*
		(type)	Cast	*r2 = sqrt((double) area);*
		*	Indirection	*obj = *ptr_to_type;*
		&	Address of	*ptr_to_type = &obj;*
		sizeof	Size of	*int_size = sizeof (int);* *arr_size = sizeof array;*
13L	Arithmetic	*	Multiplication	*product = first * last;*
		/	Division	*div = top / bottom;*
		%	Remainder (modules)	*is_odd = num % 2;*
12L	Arithmetic	+	Addition	*sum = prev + next;*
		−	Subtraction	*diff = current − prev;*

(continued)

PRECEDENCE	TYPE	OPERATOR	NAME	EXAMPLE
11L	Bitwise	<<	Left shift	*lsb_to_msb = val << 8;*
		>>	Right shift	*high_byte = val >> 8;*
10L	Relational	>	Greater than	*if (curr > prev)*
		>=	Greater than or equal to	*positive = (num >= 0);*
		<	Less than	*for (i = 0; i < hi; ++i)*
		<=	Less than or equal to	*for (i = 1; i <= hi; ++i)*
9L	Relational	==	Equal to	*if (cur == 5 ‖ prv == 1)*
		!=	Not equal to	*while (state != DONE)*
8L	Bitwise	&	Bitwise AND	*mst_sig_bit = chr & 0x80;*
7L	Bitwise	^	Exclusive OR (XOR)	*ms_bit_rev = chr ^ 0x80;*
6L	Bitwise	|	Bitwise OR	*low_bit_set = chr | 0x1;*
5L	Logical	&&	Logical and	*if (x > low && x < hi)*
4L	Logical	‖	Logical or	*if (c < ' ' ‖ c > '~')*
3R	Conditional	?:	Then, else	*max_ab = a > b ? a : b;*
2R	Assignment	=	Assignment	*variable = value;*
2R	Assignment	+=, /= *(see below)*	Shorthand assignment	*total += amount;* *reading /= SCALE;*
1L	Sequence	,	Comma	*++right, ++score;*

This is the complete list of assignment shorthand operators.

TYPE	OPERATOR
Arithmetic	+=, −=, *=, /=, %=
Bitwise	<<=, >>=, &=, ^=, |=

Appendix C:
Preprocessor Summary

All preprocessor commands are executed one per line. They begin with a pound sign (#), and may be continued on the following line by using a backslash (\ ). The conditional compilation commands are used to control a combination of one or more C statements and other preprocessor statements. This list groups the preprocessor commands by application.

Commands to add, replace, or remove definitions of identifiers:

COMMAND	ACTION
#define IDENTIFIER definition	All subsequent uses of the name IDENTIFIER are replaced by the definition text.
#define MACRO(x, y) (expansion statement using (x) and (y))	Replaces all subsequent uses of MACRO plus its two arguments with the expansion, with arguments substituted in it.
#undef IDENTIFIER	Removes the definition of the symbol or macro named IDENTIFIER.

Commands to insert the contents of another file:

COMMAND	ACTION
#include <pathname>	Replaces itself with the contents of the file *pathname*. The file is searched for in all the "standard" places.
#include "pathname"	Replaces itself with the contents of the file *pathname*. The file is searched for only in the current directory.

Conditional compilation of preprocessor commands or C statements:

COMMAND	ACTION
#if restricted_const_expr	Compiles lines that follow only if *restricted_const_expr* is non-zero.
#ifdef ID	Compiles lines that follow if *ID* is a defined symbol or the name of a macro.
#ifndef ID	Compiles lines that follow if *ID* is *not* defined as a symbol or the name of a macro.
#else	Ends one of the above *#if*-type commands and compiles lines that follow if the condition tested for did not hold.
#endif	Ends the closest unclosed group of lines beginning with a *#if*-type command or a *#else*.

Microsoft and ANSI extensions to conditional compilation:

COMMAND	ACTION
#if defined(ID)	Compiles lines that follow if *ID* is defined as a symbol or as the name of a macro. Is equivalent to *#ifdef ID*.
#elif restricted_const_expr	Compiles lines that follow if the condition in the *#if*-type or *#elif* command before it was zero and the condition here is non-zero. Can be chained to a single *#if*-type or *#elif* command.
#elif defined(ID2)	Like *#elif,* but tests whether *ID2* is a defined symbol or a macro name.

Appendix D:
Standard I/O Library Functions

These standard library functions perform stream-oriented input and output. The first two groups of functions output to the standard output stream, *stdout,* and input from the standard input stream, *stdin.* The rest may be used with any stream, once it has been opened using *fopen( ).*

Functions that send output to *stdout*:

COMMAND	ACTION
int putchar(c)	Outputs a character.
char puts(str)	Outputs a string, appends '\n'.
int printf(fmt, . . .)	Outputs formatted data.

Functions that obtain input from *stdin*:

COMMAND	ACTION
int getchar( )	Inputs a character and returns it as an integer. Returns *EOF* for attempts to read beyond end of data.
*char *gets(str)*	Inputs a line, replaces '\n' with '\0'. Returns *NULL* for attempts to read beyond end of data.
int scanf(fmt, . . .)	Inputs formatted data.

Functions that open or close a stream:

COMMAND	ACTION
FILE *fopen(path, mode)	Opens a stream for the file *path*, in specified mode ('*r*' for read, '*w*' for write, or '*a*' for append, with optional + for update).
int fclose(stream)	Closes a stream and flushes its buffer.

Functions that send output to a stream:

COMMAND	ACTION
int fputc(c, stream)	Outputs a character *c* to a stream.
int fputs(str, stream)	Outputs a string *str* to a stream.
int fprintf(stream, fmt, ...)	Outputs formatted data to a stream.

Functions that obtain input from a stream:

COMMAND	ACTION
int fgetc(stream)	Inputs a character from a stream.
char *fgets(str, n, stream)	Inputs at most $n-1$ characters from a stream into the string *str*.
int fscanf(stream, fmt, ...)	Inputs formatted data from a stream.

Appendix E:
Listing for stdio.h

This is the complete listing of Microsoft C's standard I/O header file, *stdio.h*. This file must be *#included* if you use the macros *getc()*, *putc()*, *getchar()*, *putchar()*, *feof()*, *ferror()*, or *fileno()*, or any of the file-oriented defined constants. If you *#define LINT_ARGS*, this header file also allows type-checking for any of the standard function parameters or return types. Notice that the commenting style is different from that used in this book. C offers considerable flexibility: Just remember that consistency is the key to readable code.

```
/*
 * stdio.h
 *
 * defines the structure used by the level 2 I/O ("standard I/O") routines
 * and some of the associated values and macros.
 *
 * (C)Copyright Microsoft Corporation 1984, 1985
 */

#define  BUFSIZ   512
#define  _NFILE   20
#define  FILE     struct _iobuf
#define  EOF      (-1)

#ifdef M_I86LM
#define  NULL     0L
#else
#define  NULL     0
#endif

extern FILE {
     char *_ptr;
     int   _cnt;
     char *_base;
     char  _flag;
     char  _file;
     } _iob[_NFILE];
```

(continued)

```
#define  stdin    (&_iob[0])
#define  stdout   (&_iob[1])
#define  stderr   (&_iob[2])
#define  stdaux   (&_iob[3])
#define  stdprn   (&_iob[4])

#define  _IOREAD    0x01
#define  _IOWRT     0x02
#define  _IONBF     0x04
#define  _IOMYBUF   0x08
#define  _IOEOF     0x10
#define  _IOERR     0x20
#define  _IOSTRG    0x40
#define  _IORW      0x80

#define  getc(f)    (--(f)->_cnt >= 0 ? 0xff & *(f)->_ptr++ : _filbuf(f))
#define  putc(c,f)  (--(f)->_cnt >= 0 ? 0xff & (*(f)->_ptr++ = (c)) : \
                 _flsbuf((c),(f)))

#define  getchar()  getc(stdin)
#define  putchar(c) putc((c),stdout)

#define  feof(f)    ((f)->_flag & _IOEOF)
#define  ferror(f)  ((f)->_flag & _IOERR)
#define  fileno(f)  ((f)->_file)

/* function declarations for those who want strong type checking
 * on arguments to library function calls
 */

#ifdef LINT_ARGS           /* arg. checking enabled */
void clearerr(FILE *);
int fclose(FILE *);
int fcloseall(void);
FILE *fdopen(int, char *);
int fflush(FILE *);
int fgetc(FILE *);
int fgetchar(void);
char *fgets(char *, int, FILE *);
int flushall(void);
FILE *fopen(char *, char *);
int fprintf(FILE *, char *, );
int fputc(int, FILE *);
int fputchar(int);
int fputs(char *, FILE *);
int fread(char *, int, int, FILE *);
FILE *freopen(char *, char *, FILE *);
int fscanf(FILE *, char *, );
int fseek(FILE *, long, int);
long ftell(FILE *);
int fwrite(char *, int, int, FILE *);
char *gets(char *);
int getw(FILE *);
int printf(char *, );
int puts(char *);
int putw(int, FILE *);
int rewind(FILE *);
int scanf(char *, );
void setbuf(FILE *, char *);
int sprintf(char *, char *, );
int sscanf(char *, char *, );
int ungetc(int, FILE *);
```

(continued)

```
#else                   /* arg. checking disabled - declare return type */

extern FILE *fopen(), *freopen(), *fdopen();
extern long ftell();
extern char *gets(), *fgets();

#endif    /* LINT_ARGS */
```

Appendix F:
Formatted I/O and Conversions

The formatted I/O functions *printf()*, *fprintf()*, *sprintf()*, *scanf()*, *fscanf()*, and *sscanf()* convert and input or output data according to the literal text and format specifiers contained in the format string.

Formatted Output or Output Conversions

All three of the output functions convert their arguments from internal binary format to an ASCII string.

FUNCTION	ACTION
printf(fmt, ...)	Sends formatted output to *stdout*.
fprintf(stream, fmt, ...)	Sends formatted output to *stream*.
sprintf(str, fmt, ...)	Converts data to specified format and returns it in string *str*.

The *fmt* argument specifies the number and types of arguments that follow it, as well as how they should be formatted for output. If the type width is too narrow to display the data, it is ignored. The format string holds literal text and zero or more format specifiers, using this syntax:

%[−][w][.p][m]t

These option symbols have the following meanings:

[−]   Left justification (default is right justification)

[*w*]   Width of field, or * to obtain width in next argument (width with leading zero gives output with leading zero)

[.*p*]   Precision (places to right of decimal point), or maximum output width if used for string output

[*m*]   modifier: *l* for *long*

t   Data type: *d* for decimal, *u* for unsigned decimal, *o* for octal, *x* for hex, *f* for floating-point decimal, *e* for floating-point scientific, *c* for character, or *s* for string

Here are some examples of the formatted output functions:

FUNCTION CALL	RESULT
printf("%09ld", x)	Outputs the *long x* as a 9-digit decimal number with leading zeros.
*printf("%*d", w, n)*	Outputs *n* as a decimal integer, right justified in a field *w* characters wide.
printf("%.2f", dbl)	Outputs double with two decimal places.
printf("%−30.25s", t)	Outputs up to 25 characters of string *t*, left justified in a field 30 characters wide.
*printf("% − *.*s", w, p, t)*	Outputs at most *p* characters of string *t*, left justified in a field *w* characters wide.

Formatted Input or Input Conversions

All of the input functions use the format passed to them to determine how to input and store data. Scalar parameters must be passed as addresses to the values.

FUNCTION	ACTION
int scanf(fmt, ...)	Inputs formatted data from *stdin*.
int fscanf(stream, fmt, ...)	Inputs formatted data from *stream*.
int sscanf(str, fmt, ...)	Converts data from string *str* to specified format.

The format specifiers for input differ slightly from those for output. With *scanf()*, formats must distinguish between *float* and *double,* and between *short* and *int.* The return value from *scanf()* is the number of successfully converted and assigned fields, or *EOF* for attempts to read beyond the end of the file. The syntax for an input format specifier is:

%*[w][m]t*

These option symbols have the following meanings:

[*w*]   Width of field

[*m*]   Modifier: *l* for *long* (%*ld*) or *double* (%*lf*), or *h* for *short*

   t   Data type: *d* for decimal, *u* for unsigned decimal, *o* for octal, *x* for hex, *f* for floating-point decimal, *e* for floating-point scientific, *c* for character, or *s* for string; *D, U, O,* or *X* for *long* decimal, octal, unsigned, or hex, respectively

Here are some examples of the formatted input functions:

FUNCTION CALL	RESULT
scanf("%hd%ld", &x, &y)	Inputs a *short* for x and a *long* for y.
scanf("%9U", &lng)	Inputs up to 9 digits, unsigned *long,* to *lng.*
scanf("%c%s", &ch, str)	Inputs first character to *ch* and next string of non-white space to *str.*

Note: The %*c* format specifier does not cause *scanf()* to skip leading spaces; instead, it inputs the next character, no matter what it is. If you want to input a single character, skipping any leading spaces, use %*1s.*

Appendix G:
Table of ASCII Codes

ASCII is a set of values that represent printable characters and characters used to control output devices such as printers and terminals. These characters can be represented using 7 bits, which means that there are 128 different ASCII characters, with decimal values from 0 through 127. The characters from 32 (space) through 126 (~) are printable; the other 33 characters are not.

Nonprinting ASCII Characters

This table lists the nonprinting characters, including the keyboard keys used to produce each character (^ means control: ^G for control-g).

DECIMAL	KEY	HEXADECIMAL	OCTAL	ESCAPE SEQUENCE	NAME
0	^@	'\x00'	'\000'		NULL
1	^A	'\x01'	'\001'		SOH
2	^B	'\x02'	'\002'		STX
3	^C	'\x03'	'\003'		ETX
4	^D	'\x04'	'\004'		EOT
5	^E	'\x05'	'\005'		ENQ
6	^F	'\x06'	'\006'		ACK

DECIMAL	KEY	HEXADECIMAL	OCTAL	ESCAPE SEQUENCE	NAME
7	^G	'\x07'	'\007'		BELL
8	^H	'x08'	'010'	'\b'	BKSPC
9	^I	'x09'	'011'	'\t'	HZTAB
10	^J	'x0a'	'012'	'\n'	NEWLN
11	^K	'x0b'	'013'	'\v'	VTAB
12	^L	'x0c'	'014'	'\f'	FF
13	^M	'x0d'	'015'	'\r'	CR

(continued)

DECIMAL	KEY	HEXADECIMAL	OCTAL	ESCAPE SEQUENCE	NAME
14	^N	'\x0e'	'\016'		SO
15	^O	'\x0f'	'\017'		SI
16	^P	'\x10'	'\020'		DLE
17	^Q	'\x11'	'\021'		DC1
18	^R	'\x12'	'\022'		DC2
19	^S	'\x13'	'\023'		DC3
20	^T	'\x14'	'\024'		DC4
21	^U	'\x15'	'\025'		NAK
22	^V	'\x16'	'\026'		SYN
23	^W	'\x17'	'\027'		ETB

DECIMAL	KEY	HEXADECIMAL	OCTAL	ESCAPE SEQUENCE	NAME
24	^X	'\x18'	'\030'		CAN
25	^Y	'\x19'	'\031'		EM
26	^Z	'\x1a'	'\032'		SUB
27	ESC	'\x1b'	'\033'		ESC
28		'\x1c'	'\034'		FS
29		'\x1d'	'\035'		GS
30		'\x1e'	'\036'		RS
31		'\x1f'	'\037'		US
127	DEL	'\x7f'	'\177'		DEL

Printable ASCII Characters

This table lists the characters that output the familiar upper-and lowercase letters of the alphabet, numeric digits, and punctuation that combine to form the set of printable ASCII characters.

DECIMAL	KEY	HEXADECIMAL	OCTAL
32		'\x20'	'\040'
33	!	'\x21'	'\041'
34	"	'\x22'	'\042'
35	#	'\x23'	'\043'
36	$	'\x24'	'\044'
37	%	'\x25'	'\045'
38	&	'\x26'	'\046'
39	'	'\x27'	'\047'
40	(	'\x28'	'\050'
41	)	'\x29'	'\051'
42	*	'\x2a'	'\052'

DECIMAL	KEY	HEXADECIMAL	OCTAL
43	+	'\x2b'	'\053'
44	,	'\x2c'	'\054'
45	–	'\x2d'	'\055'
46	.	'\x2e'	'\056'
47	/	'\x2f'	'\057'
48	0	'\x30'	'\060'
49	1	'\x31'	'\061'
50	2	'\x32'	'\062'
51	3	'\x33'	'\063'
52	4	'\x34'	'\064'
53	5	'\x35'	'\065'

(continued)

DECIMAL	KEY	HEXADECIMAL	OCTAL	DECIMAL	KEY	HEXADECIMAL	OCTAL
54	6	'\x36'	'\066'	86	V	'\x56'	'\126'
55	7	'\x37'	'\067'	87	W	'\x57'	'\127'
56	8	'\x38'	'\070'	88	X	'\x58'	'\130'
57	9	'\x39'	'\071'	89	Y	'\x59'	'\131'
58	:	'\x3a'	'\072'	90	Z	'\x5a'	'\132'
59	;	'\x3b'	'\073'	91	[	'\x5b'	'\133'
60	<	'\x3c'	'\074'	92	\	'\x5c'	'\134'
61	=	'\x3d'	'\075'	93	]	'\x5d'	'\135'
62	>	'\x3e'	'\076'	94	^	'\x5e'	'\136'
63	?	'\x3f'	'\077'	95	_	'\x5f'	'\137'
64	@	'\x40'	'\100'	96	`	'\x60'	'\140'
65	A	'\x41'	'\101'	97	a	'\x61'	'\141'
66	B	'\x42'	'\102'	98	b	'\x62'	'\142'
67	C	'\x43'	'\103'	99	c	'\x63'	'\143'
68	D	'\x44'	'\104'	100	d	'\x64'	'\144'
69	E	'\x45'	'\105'	101	e	'\x65'	'\145'
70	F	'\x46'	'\106'	102	f	'\x66'	'\146'
71	G	'\x47'	'\107'	103	g	'\x67'	'\147'
72	H	'\x48'	'\110'	104	h	'\x68'	'\150'
73	I	'\x49'	'\111'	105	i	'\x69'	'\151'
74	J	'\x4a'	'\112'	106	j	'\x6a'	'\152'
75	K	'\x4b'	'\113'	107	k	'\x6b'	'\153'
76	L	'\x4c'	'\114'	108	l	'\x6c'	'\154'
77	M	'\x4d'	'\115'	109	m	'\x6d'	'\155'
78	N	'\x4e'	'\116'	110	n	'\x6e'	'\156'
79	O	'\x4f'	'\117'	111	o	'\x6f'	'\157'
80	P	'\x50'	'\120'	112	p	'\x70'	'\160'
81	Q	'\x51'	'\121'	113	q	'\x71'	'\161'
82	R	'\x52'	'\122'	114	r	'\x72'	'\162'
83	S	'\x53'	'\123'	115	s	'\x73'	'\163'
84	T	'\x54'	'\124'	116	t	'\x74'	'\164'
85	U	'\x55'	'\125'	117	u	'\x75'	'\165'

(continued)

DECIMAL	KEY	HEXADECIMAL	OCTAL		DECIMAL	KEY	HEXADECIMAL	OCTAL
118	v	'\x76'	'\166'		123	{	'\x7b'	'\173'
119	w	'\x77'	'\167'		124	|	'\x7c'	'\174'
120	x	'\x78'	'\170'		125	}	'\x7d'	'\175'
121	y	'\x79'	'\171'		126	~	'\x7e'	'\176'
122	z	'\x7a'	'\172'					

Appendix H:
About the Companion Disk

The Companion Disk for *Variations in C* supplies you with all of the functions and header files that appear in this book, plus selected illustrative code segments that will help you become comfortable working in C. All C code is in uncompiled source form, and each program's text is stored in a separate ASCII text file, ready for you to edit and compile.

What the Disk Is For

Four kinds of C code come on the Companion Disk: an application, individual functions, header files, and code segments. Here are some ideas on how you might use each of them.

The Code Segments

The code segments have been carefully chosen for their instructive value. They provide an easy and convenient way for you to experiment with new concepts as you learn C from this book. Having the code on disk makes it simple to answer questions like: "What if that AND were changed to an OR?" or "What would happen if different input data were entered?" (Remember to recompile your source code each time you make a change.)

The Functions

The order-entry application relies heavily on the general-purpose functions from the project utility library, listed in Chapter 10. You can use these same functions (and their associated header files) as the low-level foundation for a wide variety of custom applications that you develop in the future.

The Application

The disk comes with the complete order-entry application program, as listed in Chapter 10, plus the enhanced versions of those functions that are developed further in later chapters. You can use this program directly, to take orders for your own business, or you can extend its usefulness by adding new subsystems or additional capabilities. You can also adapt the program to a different application by replacing the bodies of the *main()* function in *ordentry.c* and the middle-level functions in *ordbuild.c* with code that prompts for your own kinds of data, rather than order data. The overall program structure usually will require little, if any, modification to fit a variety of applications.

How to Use the Disk

To use the Companion Disk, you will need MS-DOS, version 2.0 or higher, and the Microsoft C compiler, version 3.0 or higher. The disk has 18 directories with the source code and header files from the individual chapters (named *ch2, ch3, . . . , ch21*). I have included only those sections of code that are more than five lines. See the *README.DOC* file on the disk for details.

Each complete function is stored in its own source file, with the same name as the function. For example, the function *prompt()* from Chapter 10 is found in directory *ch10* in the file *prompt.c*.

Illustrative code segments are stored in files named for their page number and their position among the segments listed from that page. For example, the two segments from page 22 of Chapter 2 are stored in directory *ch2* in files *page22a.c* and *page22b.c*.

Putting the Code to Work

All of the code on the disk must be compiled before it can be executed. Even the code segments will *at least* have to be preprocessed in order for you to see the effects of your experiments. When you become comfortable working with C, you might want to make the few non-compilable illustrative segments into full working programs by adding a *main()* and any necessary declarations, and then compiling your new source files (again, see *README.DOC*).

The functions in the source file *stubs.c* are just what their name implies and should be replaced with their working versions from later chapters before you compile and link the order-entry application:

STUB FUNCTION	REPLACEMENT CHAPTER
inv_find()	19
pw_find()	17
order_num()	17
logentry()	17

Instructions for Ordering

The Companion Disk is available only through Microsoft Press. To order, just complete the attached card and send it (or a sheet of paper with your name and address), with your check or money order for $12.95, plus $1.00 for postage and handling, to:

Microsoft Press
Attn: CDSK
Box 97200
10700 Northup Way
Bellevue, WA 98009

California residents please add 6.5% sales tax and Washington state residents add 8.1% sales tax. If you prefer to pay by VISA, MasterCard, or American Express, include your credit card number and its expiration date with your order. Please allow 4 weeks for delivery.

Questions About the Disk

Should you have any problems with your disk, please write to:

Microsoft Press
Attn: Sales Division
Box 97200
10700 Northup Way
Bellevue, WA 98009

If you have questions about the programs or code segments included on the Companion Disk, please write to:

Steve Schustack
968 Emerald Street, Suite A-116
San Diego, CA 92109

Index

Symbols

`!`	logical *NOT* operator 42, 307
`!=`	relational *not-equal* operator 42, 308
`"`	string constant delimiter 13
`#`	preprocessor commands, beginning of 69, 309
`%`	arithmetic *remainder* (modulo) operator 27, 307
	I/O function format specifier 19, 317–19
`%=`	arithmetic *remainder* (modulo) *assignment* operator 33, 308
`&`	bitwise *AND* operator 287, 289, 308
	unary *address-of* operator 22, 44–45, 219, 221, 307
`&&`	logical *AND* operator 42–43, 308
`&=`	bitwise *AND assignment* operator 33, 308
`'`	character constant delimiter 14, 38
`()`	with function-call argument list 59
	with function-definition parameter list 61
	grouping operator in expressions 27, 307
	in macro definitions 73
	unary *cast* operator 174, 279, 307
`*`	arithmetic *multiplication* operator 26–27, 307
	pointer declaration symbol 220
	unary *indirection* operator 223–24, 307
`*/`	comment end delimiter 9
`*=`	arithmetic *multiplication assignment* operator 33, 308
`+`	arithmetic *addition* operator 26–27, 307
	update mode for *fopen()* 254, 312
`++`	unary *increment* operator 34–35, 37, 307
`+=`	arithmetic *addition assignment* operator 33, 308
`,`	argument separator 19
	comma sequence operator 33–34, 308
	in enumeration list 163
	in initializer list 93

`–`	arithmetic *subtraction* operator 26–27, 307
	unary *minus* operator 26–27, 307
`– –`	unary *decrement* operator 27, 35, 307
`–=`	arithmetic *subtraction assignment* operator 33, 307
`–>`	structure-member *pointer* operator 247, 307
`.`	*structure-member* operator 243, 307
`/`	arithmetic *division* operator 27, 307
	UNIX directory-name delimiter 253
`/*`	comment beginning delimiter 9
`/=`	arithmetic *division assignment* operator 33, 307
`:`	after case label in *switch* statement 51–52
`;`	expression separator, *for* loop 49–51
	null statement 50
	statement terminator 45
`<`	input redirection of *stdin*, command-line 105–7, 123
	relational *less-than* operator 42, 308
`<<`	bitwise *left-shift* operator 287, 289, 308
`<<=`	bitwise *left-shift* assignment operator 33, 308
`<=`	relational *less-than-or-equal* operator 42, 308
`=`	*assignment* operator 31–33, 54, 308
`==`	relational *equal* operator 42, 54, 308
`>`	output redirection of *stdout*, command-line 12–13, 105, 107, 123, 185–86
	relational *greater-than* operator 42, 308
`>=`	relational *greater-than-or-equal* operator 42, 308
`>>`	bitwise *right-shift* operator 287, 289, 308
	output redirection of *stdout*, command-line 12–13, 105, 107, 123, 185–86
`>>=`	bitwise *right-shift assignment* operator 33, 308

Steve Schustack

After completing his Bachelor of Arts degree in Mathematics at the State University of New York at Binghamton, Steve Schustack studied computer science under Gerald Weinberg at SUNY's School of Advanced Technology. Steve has worked as a system programmer at Argonne National Laboratory and has written programs for the United States Navy. For the past four years, he has taught a series of successful seminars on professional C programming for major corporations all over the country. For more information on these seminars, Steve can be contacted at:

968 Emerald Street
Suite A-116
San Diego, CA 92109

The manuscript for this book was prepared and submitted to Microsoft Press in electronic form. Text files were processed and formatted using Microsoft Word.

Cover design by Ted Mader and Associates.
Interior text design by Ken Sánchez.
The high-resolution screen displays were created on the IBM PC and printed on the Hewlett-Packard LaserJet.

Text composition by Microsoft Press in Rotation and Rotation Italic with display in Futura Medium Condensed, using the CCI composition system and the Mergenthaler Linotron 202 digital phototypesetter.

Cover printed on 12 pt. Carolina by Philips Offset Company, Inc., Mamaroneck, New York. Text stock 60 lb. Glatfelter Offset, supplied by Unisource. Book printed and bound by Fairfield Graphics, Fairfield, Pennsylvania.

Other Titles from Microsoft Press

THE IBM ENVIRONMENT

Running MS-DOS   The Microsoft Guide to Getting the Most Out of the
Standard Operating System for the IBM PC and 50 Other Personal Computers,
Van Wolverton, ISBN 0-914845-07-1, $19.95

The Peter Norton Programmer's Guide to the IBM PC   Peter Norton,,
ISBN 0-914845-46-2, $19.95

Managing Your Business with Multiplan   How to Use Microsoft's
Award-Winning Electronic Spreadsheet on Your IBM PC, Ruth K. Witkin,
ISBN 0-914845-06-3, $17.95

Getting Started with Microsoft WORD   A Step-by-Step Guide to Word
Processing, Janet Rampa, ISBN 0-914845-13-6, $16.95,

Word Processing Power with Microsoft Word   Professional Writing on
Your IBM PC, Peter Rinearson, ISBN 0-914845-05-5, $16.95

Exploring the IBM PCjr Home Computer   Peter Norton,
ISBN 0-914845-02-0, $18.25

Discovering the IBM PCjr Home Computer   Peter Norton,
ISBN 0-914845-01-2, $15.95

GENERAL

Online   A Guide to America's Leading Information Services, Steve Lambert,
ISBN 0-914845-35-7, $19.95

Silicon Valley Guide to Financial Success in Software   Daniel Remer, Paul Remer,
and Robert Dunaway, ISBN 0-914845-09-8, $19.95

Out of the Inner Circle   A Hacker's Guide to Computer Security,
"The Cracker" (Bill Landreth), ISBN 0-914845-36-5, $9.95 softcover,
ISBN 0-914845-45-4, $19.95 hardcover

A Much, Much Better World   Eldon Dedini, ISBN 0-914845-50-0, $6.95

Learning Commodore 64 Logo Together   An Activity Book for Creative Parents,
Teachers, and Kids, Kenneth P. Goldberg, ISBN 0-914845-24-1, $14.95

AVAILABLE WHEREVER FINE BOOKS ARE SOLD

or write: Marketing Department
Microsoft Press
10700 Northup Way
Box 97200
Bellevue, WA 98009